THE TRADERS

INSIDE CANADA'S STOCK MARKETS

Alexander Ross

Collins Toronto

First published 1984 by
Collins Publishers
100 Lesmill Road, Don Mills, Ontario

Canadian Cataloguing in Publication Data

Ross, Alexander, 1935–
   The traders : inside Canada's stock markets

Includes index.
ISBN 0-00-217381-6

1. Brokers — Canada. 2. Money market — Canada.
3. Stock-exchange — Canada.   I. Title.

HG5152.R67   1984   332.6'2'0971   C84-099220-3

Printed and bound in Canada by John Deyell Company

The Traders

Also by Alexander Ross:

The Risk Takers
The Booming Fifties
The Toronto Guidebook

For Minette

CONTENTS

Acknowledgments

For a work like this one, involving scores of interviews, the chief debt an author owes is to his subjects. I'm no exception. The book literally could not have been written without the co-operation of all kinds of people in the securities industry. I'm especially grateful for time and insights to Peter and Ralph Brown, Norman Short, Bob Bellamy, Murray Pezim, Morton Shulman, David Allan, Don Ezra, Ian McAvity, Murray Sinclair, Andy Sarlos and stock exchange officials in Vancouver, Toronto and Montreal for their patient instruction in the mysteries of the market. The board of directors of McLeod Young Weir also deserve special thanks for their decision to allow me and film-maker Peter Raymont unrestricted access to their innermost deliberations.

My agent, Nancy Colbert, and Nick Harris and Michael Worek at Collins also get my warmest thanks for their patience and constant encouragement. But the biggest debt of gratitude goes to my wife Minette, who endured a long period of cohabitation with an increasingly obsessed author.

Also, special thanks to: Nick Steed, Molline Green, Ron Hume, Wallace Wood, Peggy Wente, Michael de Pencier, Mike Macbeth, Geri Savits-Fine, Jackie Carlos, Bob Fulford, Marq de Villiers, Michael Bliss and Peter Newman. Some of these people may not even be aware of the contributions they made to the production of this book. But I am.

Introduction

This book is a reporter's enquiry into the workings of one of the most powerful, least-understood subcultures in the country: the Canadian capital markets and the people and institutions that run them. More than two million Canadians have money in the stock market, thousands more play the bond and commodity markets and millions more are indirect investors, whether they know it or not, through their participation in various pension plans.* The way those markets work has a direct impact on everyone's pocketbook, including yours.

Let's first dispose of the question I can already hear you asking: Will this book show me how to make money in the stock market? Maybe, but not necessarily. I emphatically am not holding myself out as an expert on How to Get Rich. Like most of us, I've never parlayed a $300 stake into a Georgian mansion, three Mercedes, a Caribbean villa and a seven-figure personal portfolio. But because this is virtually the first full-length descriptive account of Canada's capital markets and the people who make them run, the book might help to demystify those markets, and thus help you achieve your own investment goals. In these pages you will meet some of Canada's shrewdest, most successful investors. Any insight into how these people think and the rules by which they play, no matter how tenuous and incomplete, can't hurt.

Maybe you didn't even know that you're *supposed* to have investment goals. Perhaps, like so many people who play the market occasionally, you operate on the straightforward principle that what you'd really like is a nice little stock that will double by next week. If this book succeeds in disabusing you of that widely held but infantile notion, it will already have saved you several hundred dollars, or even more if you're especially foolish. As Benjamin Graham, the father of securities analysis, once observed, the first thing you must know about winning in the market is how not to lose. I hope this book will help you to avoid losing.

It is a *descriptive* book. That means I'm more concerned with conveying a feeling for how the machine works than with making judgments about its social utility. God knows, there's been

---

* In 1979, some 989,560 Canadians declared dividend income on their personal tax returns, and 273,910 reported either gains or losses on shares. About 14.6 million Canadians filed tax returns that year.

enough moralizing on that subject over the past century or so. We fear what we don't understand, so it's natural that many people should mistrust the workings of a mechanism that is so mysterious, so seemingly wasteful, so purely dedicated to self-interest, so prone to occasional unexplained convulsions which seem to trigger world-wide depressions.

I once knew the son of a university President, a young idealist who hadn't figured out what to do with his life. As a sort of experiment, he went to work for a brokerage house. He lasted exactly one week, then quit. "They told me that what runs the market is fear and greed," he later explained. "Can you imagine? *Fear* and *greed*? I don't want to spend my life dealing with those emotions." But that is exactly what stockbrokers deal with, day in and day out. So what? What's to deplore? Fear and greed, after all, are only unflattering names for pessimism and optimism. They're part of the great theatre of life, so we might as well enjoy the spectacle.

Another equally common reaction is to deplore the wastefulness of a system which squanders so much talent, energy and money on the apparently straightforward business of transferring assets from savers to producers. Can't there be a more efficient way of financing business than through the unseemly cacophony of a stock exchange? Can't these things be *planned*? Doesn't the Soviet Union mange to find and mine a lot of gold without the assistance of a tribe of stock promoters?

To the tidy-minded, the answer is obvious. But I am personally dismayed by tidy-minded solutions to human problems, whether they're perpetrated by large corporations, by urban planners, or by commissars. Those who set out to quell the chaos and disorder of the human condition often end up erecting hideous New Towns, creaking bureaucracies, National Energy Programs, government liquor stores or planned subdivisions.

All such planned environments presuppose the existence of some central authority which purports to know what's good for the rest of us. Most of these places feel as if they were designed not for people, but for some officially formulated abstraction of what people are supposed to want and need. Communities designed from on high are usually ghastly places. But cities or neighborhoods which spring from the disorderly contention of hundreds of diverse elements and interests – good old fear and greed again – are usually vital and exciting, because they're never *finished*; they're in a constant state of becoming. No central authority, no matter how benevolent its intentions, can engineer this quality of urban aliveness. The best that planners can do is to impose a few guidelines aimed at avoiding total breakdown, and then stand aside to let things happen as they will.

The same could be said of the stock market. What I'm attempting to describe in this book is a diverse network of people, institutions and subcultures that is magnificently wasteful, and which fulfils many of the same functions as successful cities; this diversity is a central part of the dynamic, innovative process by which new work is created.*

I confess to a tremendous sense of wonder about this whole process. Think of it. Tens of thousands of people getting up every morning, reacting to the morning's news, interpreting the complex signals from within their own businesses and their own stomachs, weighing their fears for the future against their own ever-welling optimism; and somehow, every instant of every trading day, it all comes together in a set of numbers that float across those electronic screens in the brokers' offices. There's something so adorably *human* about it – a great thrumming dance of shifting emotions and self-interested calculation. In the face of a phenomenon so infinitely complex, so very much like life itself, one can only gape in delight.

Most of my reservations about the market are related to the fact that there isn't *enough* of it. The stock market is a magnificent vehicle for connecting people with savings to entrepreneurs who need money to conduct experiments aimed at creating new kinds of work. But it isn't as pervasive a phenomenen as it should be. Why? Because business itself isn't as pervasive in this country as it should be.

Consider the structure of corporate Canada: There are about 750,000 incorporated businesses. About 700,000 of them have annual sales of less than $2 million – we're mostly talking here about variety stores, dress shops, Chinese restaurants, and men trying to make a living with a backhoe or a dumptruck. Another 21,000 companies have annual sales of between $2 million and $20 million. There are only about 2,000 "big" businesses with annual sales of more than $20 million. Needless to say, many of the largest companies are foreign-owned, and many of them won't sell shares to Canadian investors. (General Motors Canada is a sadly typical example.) What we have, in other words, is a woefully lopsided structure. On the bottom, hundreds of thousands of inherently small businesses, with very marginal prospects for future growth; on the top, a small number of quite large companies. The largest firms tend to prosper not through

---

* I'm indebted to Jane Jacobs, the brilliant urbanologist, for this notion about the creative chaos of cities.

innovation, but by swallowing smaller companies. This lopsidedness also has a geographical dimension. Entire cities, entire regions, are almost wholly dependent on government or a few large extractive industries to generate employment. The entire province of Saskatchewan, for instance, after generations of democratic socialism, has fewer corporations than the city of Mississauga, Ontario.

What's conspicuously absent here is a healthy layer of innovative, medium-sized companies with genuine growth prospects. In isolated pockets of the country, we've already seen such efflorescences. Before the National Energy Program ended it all, there was an astonishingly innovative oilfield-servicing industry flourishing in Alberta. Dozens of small and not-so-small companies were developing new techniques for finding, lifting and transporting oil and natural gas, and selling their technology all over the world. In the environs of Ottawa, the ultimate company town, entrepreneurial dropouts from IBM, Northern Telecom and the National Research Council have created the beginnings of a Canadian computer industry. But such instances only demonstrate the rarity of such entrepreneurial surges.

The Canadian financial community, especially the banks and the investment houses, could play a key role in the creation of more such industries. They've been only moderately successful at doing so. As far back as 1968, economists such as Geoffrey Conway were pointing out, in a study commissioned by the Toronto Stock Exchange, that there was a shortage of suitable equity vehicles. Canadians were willing to risk their money, but there simply weren't enough Canadian stocks to supply the depth and diversity that investors require.

Too few stocks means too few companies. The real trouble with this country is that there just isn't enough business in Canada. Government must bear its share of the blame for this state of affairs, but the real villain is business itself: excessively concentrated, insufficiently competitive, insufficiently innovative. Why do you suppose, for instance, that in a country with so many trees, we import so much Scandinavian furniture?

You can quarrel with the way our surplus capital is deployed, but the stock market is nevertheless a marvellously efficient mechanism for deploying it. It works, and it works pretty honestly. Even so severe a critic as Ed Waitzer, the activist securities lawyer who used to be a vice-president of the TSE, cites the exchange as a uniquely successful example of self-regulation. Even the Vancouver Stock Exchange, the wildest and woolliest in the country, is better regulated than it used to be; an English financier once told me he believes that investors get a squarer deal in Vancouver than they do in London.

Furthermore, the stock market needn't be nearly as risky as most Canadians imagine it to be. During the inflationary 1970s, millions of Canadians saw a substantial part of their savings evaporate as the dollar's purchasing power shrank. Savings accounts, Canada Savings Bonds and life-insurance policies – those impregnably secure investments in which several generations of Canadians so touchingly placed their faith – turned out to be cruel traps for elderly people who'd dutifully worked and saved all their lives. The stock market, that legendary sinkhole of uncertainty, looked awfully good by comparison.

Between 1972 and 1981, for instance, the average rate of return on the TSE's 300 Index was 11.7 per cent, compared to an average inflation rate of 9 per cent. Between 1977 and 1981, the average TSE return was 19.4 per cent – far better than the 9.7 per cent average inflation rate during the same period. If you'd been playing the market during those periods with only average success, in other words, you'd have stayed ahead of inflation, and perhaps done better than if you'd put your money in the bank. The picture looks even better when you consider the tax breaks now available to Canadian investors. If you're in the 30 per cent tax bracket, for instance – and most taxpayers are – you'd have to earn 16.5 per cent on a bank account to get the same after-tax return as you'd receive from an 11 per cent dividend.

Even people who are aware of this are deterred from investing by a visceral mistrust of Bay Street and all it represents. The very busy-ness of the stock market frightens them, as opposed to the reassuring dullness of trust companies and banks. They have a profound faith in the probity of institutions which *physically* take your money away from you and stick it in a huge metal vault. There's something terribly Canadian about this attitude, but it's not supported by reality. For instance, it's been the trust companies, not the brokerage houses, that have been the major arena for financial scandals in the past 20 years or so. Hundreds of people, including a number of sweet little white-haired old ladies, have lost every nickel of their savings through the defalcation of various Canadian trust companies. Tens of thousands more would have been cleaned out if the federal government hadn't stepped in with deposit insurance. There hasn't been a Canadian bank failure since 1923, but there have been some spectacular near-misses, including the Unity Bank and the Bank of Western Canada. The securities industry, by contrast, has operated a national contingency fund since

1969 which protects investors from loss through the failure of a brokerage house. "I've never met anyone who remembers a legitimate client who'd lost money because of a member firm failure," says Diane Urquart, the TSE's chief economist. "Even before modern capital rules and the current contingency fund, the members passed the hat to protect the public."

Investing in the stock market needn't be horrendously risky. Moreover, you can choose the degree of risk that feels appropriate, all the way from preferred shares that pay guaranteed dividends to the flakiest of junior mining or industrial stocks. The truth is that the world has grown immeasurably richer in the twentieth century, and the world's stock markets, by and large, have reflected this increasing capacity to generate wealth. Since 1923, there have been 39 years in which the market rose over the previous year, and only 22 years when it fell. Even during the most desperate years of the great Depression, even ordinary people who had money to invest could have made a profit. In 1933, for instance, the market rose by 34.1 per cent over the previous year.

Most of the horrors that people associate with stock-market collapses are caused not by investing itself, but by *borrowing* to invest. Leverage is a wonderful thing when the market is going up, but it can exact a savage toll on the way down. If you buy $1,000 worth of stock, and if it zooms to $1,500, you've made 50 per cent on your money. But if you buy the same stock on 50 per cent margin – that is, if you borrow half the money from the bank or, more typically, from your broker – and it hits $1,500, you've doubled your money. The arithmetic of this proposition can become maddeningly seductive in the later stages of a bull market, when everyone is buying and everything is going up. But suppose the market breaks, and your $1,500 stock falls to $900. You've now lost 20 per cent of your $500 investment and you're getting phone calls from your banker or broker, urging you in forceful terms to come up with another $100. If you can't come up with it, your broker will sell enough stock to make up the difference, thus driving down the price even further. Multiply that simple example by a factor of many thousands, and you can see that leverage acts on the market the way cannabis acts on the psyche; it makes the highs higher, the lows lower.

In the 1920s, people bought stock on 20 per cent margin or even less. Today, as brokers virtuously remind themselves, the minimum margin for most stocks is 50 per cent, thus providing a built-in cushion against market gyrations. What they *don't* remind themselves of, and what they'd prefer not to think about, is the emergence of the options and futures markets, which allow investors to play on margins of as little as one per cent – put up a penny, gamble a dollar. The profits can be enormous – although it's estimated that about 90 per cent of the players are losers – but the potential losses are truly horrendous. This potential has been vastly magnified in recent years. The futures and options markets used to be mainly the preserve of professional traders – chocolate companies hedging their investments in cocoa, for instance. Today, as stock exchanges across North America compete to offer sexier, more attractive "vehicles" to investors bored with trading plain old stocks and bonds, the options and futures markets are being played by tens of thousands of smaller, and much less experienced, investors.

Many Bay Street authorities think a 1929-style crash is no longer possible. I don't believe them. Through most of the postwar era, Western capitalism has financed the market's growth, and cushioned the social impact of its periodic declines, through a constant increase in private and government debt. Much of our prosperity is borrowed, not earned. Does anyone believe, for instance, that the U.S. government can ever repay a *trillion-dollar* national debt? Historically, societies have dealt with unmanageable levels of debt by abolishing it through a process of periodic currency collapse. Having bought the goodies with borrowed money, society in effect wipes the financial slate clean and starts over. I see no evidence that our financial system has acquired immunity from a fever that has been recurring since before the days of the Medicis.

When I began this book, I thought I was dealing with a relatively settled phenomenon: the investment industry and how it works. By the time I'd finished, the industry was in the process of the greatest shakeup in half a century. The winds of deregulation were whistling down Bay Street, threatening to blow away any firm that tried to pretend it was business as usual. The largest firms, which hadn't changed their underwriting methods for 60 years, were being rudely challenged by an upstart firm, Daly Gordon Securities, which almost single-handedly was forcing the entire industry to play by a new and tougher set of rules. The banks were beginning to muscle in on the business. Large pools of capital, such as Power Corp. and Edper Investments Ltd., were positioning themselves to become financial "supermarkets" as soon as the rules changed. The biggest firms were seeking foreign partners and more capital. They could see that the only long-term survivors would be the firms with international connections, firms with as much of a presence in London or New York or Zurich as in Toronto. No one knew how it would all turn out. Everyone I talked to assured me that *they* were going to survive, but they weren't so sure about the firm down the street.

So this is an album of an industry, not the offical portrait collection. It contains selections on history, mechanics, technique – and snapshots of the traders themselves – the people who get up every morning and try to outguess the market. But no matter what structural convulsions overtake the industry, the traders won't change. The dance of fear and greed and human ambition is timeless, endlessly renewing itself. This is Bay Street's music, and I hope it never stops.

1

The Bay Street Village

Money may be only a commodity, like soybeans or pork bellies. But in the glass and marble skyscrapers that constitute the Bay Street village, money is an essence you can almost breathe. You can smell it in the vast reception areas of the big corporate law firms, designed to overawe their clients with oriental tapestries and circular staircases. You can sense it in the neurotic clamor around a hundred circular trading desks, crammed with computer consoles, where young, shirtsleeved traders (there are very few old ones) bark into telephones and exchange billions of dollars' worth of stocks, bonds, currencies and commodities every day. You can savor it in the top-floor dining rooms of the great banks and the largest investment dealers, where important corporate clients are entertained at lunch in surroundings that sometimes resemble Georgian country houses.* And you can witness the almost savage urgency of money on the squash courts and rooftop jogging track of the Cambridge Club, where some of Bay Street's leading citizens come daily to whip their bodies into a state of competitive readiness.

---

* The companies involved would never consent to it, but a published collection of photographs of Bay Street's secret corporate pleasure-domes would make *Architectural Digest* look tacky. The Royal Bank's Toronto dining room, and its adjoining drawing room, are so grand that even newly appointed bank directors feel intimidated. McLeod Young Weir has two magnificent dining rooms, one big and one small, an antique-strewn drawing-room and a French maîtresse de cuisine named Josephine. At the Toronto Dominion Bank's dining room, the lemon wedges accompanying the fish course used to be wrapped in cheesecloth, to avert the unseemly possibility of accidental squirts in the eye or of a seed landing on the trout. But to Montreal goes the distinction of the nation's highest working fireplace; it warms the Place Ville Marie head office of the Royal Bank of Canada.

A Landscape of the Mind

At ground level, Bay Street is unimpressive. Like the fabled intersection of Hollywood and Vine, it looks a little tacky to be freighted with so much mythology. What you see, sandwiched between the office towers, are coffee shops, variety stores selling shampoo and digital watches, a storefront law office, a couple of computer stores – a fairly standard downtown streetscape, perhaps a little blowsier than most.

Bay Street; it's still a landscape of the mind. In the 1930s, Prairie farmers hissed those words like a curse as the sheriff's men moved in to chase them off their mortgaged acres. Radio Moscow, in its short-wave broadcasts to North America, has used those words as a shorthand description of the forces of entrenched privilege. Generations of young men, endowed with straight, even teeth, respectable tennis backhands and a languid recognition of the need to make as much money as Daddy did, have "gone to work on the Street" as though they were pledging a particularly congenial fraternity. Plenty of ferret-faced young punks have gone to work on Bay Street too, usually beginning as board-markers on the floor of the stock exchange and sometimes ending up owning racing stables and islands in Georgian Bay. Some come to the Street to preserve capital, others to amass it, others simply to study it.

But because Bay Street is so obsessed with money, it is the focus of the culture's ambivalence about money and what money represents. Puritan hostility is one aspect of this ambivalence; money is fecal, money defiles, money corrupts. But money also creates, and there are many minds on Bay Street which regard the stuff simply as a medium of growth; money is the yeast which transforms human dreams into mines and shopping centres and cities. But most of all, Bay Street is a place of envy and ambition, the locus of the delusion that money can liberate you, strengthen you, transform your life, somehow make you complete.

There is something special about Bay Street ambition. The street is the centre of an industry, as surely as Detroit or Pittsburgh; but the fact that Bay Street's only raw material is money produces a species of ambition that is purer, more urgent than the sort of upward-thrusting scheming you'd find in an advertising agency or the Parliamentary back benches. There is something endearingly trustworthy about Bay Street ambition: so many people, operating in so many separate disciplines, focused so unswervingly on a single goal – to make more money than they made yesterday, and if possible, to make more money than anybody else.

Fool's Gold

Naked ambition, naked greed, are more assumed than discussed on Bay Street. But there is a novel, published pseudonymously in 1974 by a stockbroker named Christopher Ondaatje, which offers a rare glimpse into the speculator's desperate psyche. Ondaatje, one of the founding partners of Loewen, Ondaatje, McCutcheon & Co. Ltd., is one of Bay Street's more established figures, a multimillionaire broker, a publisher and art dealer. The Ondaatjes are one of Sri Lanka's oldest families, whose family tree is thick with judges, physicians, capitalists and plantation owners. But an alcoholic father had reduced the family to penury, and Ondaatje saw the stock market as a means of regaining the wealth and assurance he regarded as his birthright.

Ondaatje's novel, *Fool's Gold*, is a portrait of a sexual schemer, a coldly methodical social climber, a penniless speculator driven to madness and near-suicide by a terrifying quest for wealth: "I was driven as relentlessly as any upstart from the slums," says Ondaatje's fictional hero. "I had tasted the golden fruit once, and nothing would keep me from making it my own again! That was how I came to put too much value on money. Experience had taught me nothing that would allow me to see it in perspective, or resist the fascination that wealth exerts on those who crave it above all else."

Ondaatje's novel (published under the pseudonym of Simon Marawille) tells how, in the late 1960s, his protagonist parlayed a few thousand dollars of borrowed funds into a fortune of $1.3 million by pyramiding his holdings of a fast-moving stock called Velcro; and how he lost it all in 1969 by borrowing $800,000 to bet on three other speculative stocks: Neonex International, OSF Industries and Revenue Properties. "Every day," he writes, "I would work out exactly what my holdings were worth. I became more and more obsessed with the mounting numbers. By mid-May . . . my whole identity had become inextricably entangled with the seven-digit figure that I calculated daily as soon as the markets closed." But then the market fell out of bed. By July, our hero's holdings were worth less than $1 million, and he still owed the bank $800,000. His fortune was rapidly dwindling to the vanishing point, and so was his self-esteem: "The recession brought a new fear: personal bankruptcy, the irrecoverable loss of the entire Velcro windfall. And that would mean self-obliteration. The money was part of my being. The money was I; and I was the money."

His stocks fell further, the banks began pressing him, and the character in Ondaatje's novel experienced the special horrors reserved for speculators who define themselves by their bank balance. When the balance is seven digits, they feel omnipotent. When the balance is zero, they become human zeros, literally non-persons, robbed of all identity: "All that afternoon and through most of the night I wandered about the downtown areas, moving, walking, trying to get away from the fear . . . Next morning the fear was worse. It had become a pain, a searing pain. There was a roaring in my ears. I had to struggle to keep my mind on the reality outside me, to persuade myself that I, my body, my bones, blood, limbs – were still a part of the palpable world. I had begun to feel as if I had no real existence. I was a ghost, a shadow, a nothing." In the novel, Ondaatje's hero breaks down completely, tries to throw himself beneath a subway car, but is rescued by Bay Street friends who cover his margin call and nurse him back to psychic and financial health.*

The trauma Ondaatje describes is not unique. The phenomenon of a trader's identity being erased along with his portfolio is so familiar that psychiatry should have given it a name by now. As 'Adam Smith' observed in his 1968 stock-market classic, *The Money Game*: "If you don't know who you are, the stock market is an expensive place to find out." The weak may never recover from the anguish of losing everything; but for the strong, getting wiped out is a by-station on the road to wealth and maturity. Ondaatje is now a multimillionaire and has more than regained the social cachet his father squandered; there was a minor traffic jam on King Street one noon-hour in the summer of 1983, when Prince Andrew dropped in for an intimate little lunch at the Loewen, Ondaatje boardroom.**

A Successful Seduction

Bay Street has few illusions about what money can do for you. Most of us imagine that owning a million dollars would change

---

* Ondaatje stresses, however, that *Fools Gold* was not autobiographical; the author did not, for instance, lose his shirt in go-go stocks in the late 1960s.

** What's the connection? Ondaatje's son and Prince Andrew were once classmates at Ontario's Lakefield College.

our lives. But Bay Street shuffles so many billions of dollars every day that the numbers often become abstractions, devoid of emotional content. In fact, at the upper reaches of achieved ambition, Bay Street has surprisingly little interest in what money can buy. There are people on Bay Street, more than a few of them, who earn – or, more precisely, collect – better than a million dollars a year. They tend to live in large but unostentatious homes, drive cars that no one notices and spend their summer weekends in cottages that are almost perversely primitive.* For them, accumulation is no longer a primary goal. The game itself is the reward. For some men of a certain age, outguessing the market confers psychic rewards that constitute an alternative to sexuality. Dr. Morton Shulman, by his own speculative efforts, has accumulated a fortune worth between $30 million and $50 million, and he sees certain similarities between Mammon and Eros: "It's the same high," he says. "When I was very young, all I could think about was beautiful women and the joys and delights that come with them. As you get older, your vision broadens somewhat and there are other things you wish to acquire. In fact, you don't have much energy for women. But if you short the Mexican peso because you think it's going to collapse, and if you're right and the peso *does* collapse – well, the high you get is comparable to that of a successful seduction."

The Electronic Village

The quasi-sexual adventuring of which Dr. Shulman speaks takes places in an arena that has the physical dimensions, and many of the characteristics, of a nineteenth-century village. This village occupies an area of about 20 square blocks, and has a daytime population of about 80,000. Its inhabitants work in close proximity to one another, often in large, noisy, fluorescent-lit rooms that resemble newspaper offices. The office towers are packed so close together that two brokers talking to each other on the telephone can sometimes look out their windows and *see* each other.

In 1980, when the Toronto Stock Exchange was outgrowing its old headquarters on Bay Street and looking for a new home,

---

* One of the few exceptions to the custom of automotive understatement is Bell Gouinlock's Bob Canning, who arrives at work each morning in a black, chauffeured Rolls. Since Canning is confined to a wheelchair, the car is equipped with a power-driven ramp that raises or lowers the chair between street level and floor level.

5

Bob Canning, president of Bell Gouinlock Ltd. and a member of the TSE's building committee, was delegated to look for a site. He picked up the phone to discuss the problem with Albert Reichmann, one of the founders of Olympia & York Developments Limited. The two men are colleagues and corporate neighbors; Canning's office is on the tenth floor of the Reichmann-owned First Canadian Place complex, and Reichmann's is on the thirty-second. Albert Reichmann came downstairs to discuss the problem in person. As they gazed out Canning's window, they realized that an area behind a new tower on the west side of the site would be perfect for the purpose. That was the beginning of a complex, $10-million property swap that took two years to negotiate. The agreement spelling out the deal is three inches thick and 600 pages long. But this immensely sophisticated transaction began with two men gazing out a window, like a couple of small-town shopkeepers, and noticing what was happening next door.

If Bay Street is a village, it closely resembles the electronic village that Marshall McLuhan envisaged. Its streets tend to be vertical instead of horizontal, its currency is electronic information and its town hall is the trading floor of the stock exchange. In an arena the size of a large department store's main floor, some 800 traders and TSE staffers mill around like cattle in a pen, bawling buy and sell orders at one another. The instant when two floor traders jot down the details of a completed trade on their order pads is the culmination of a process as complex and unpredictable as the movement of ocean waves or the dance of molecules. All the interconnected electronic ganglia of Bay Street, all its players – the traders, the brokers, the analysts, the retail customers, the pension-fund managers – all the fears and dreams of all the people who play the market – everything is factored into that single transaction, and the next one, and the next one, and the next one, and the one after that.

Million-Dollar Salesmen

Bay Street is a tube through which money flows, and the wealth of Bay Street is only the residue which sticks to the inner surface. Still, in a good year it can add up to a lot of residue. "I've seen guys with cheques for $100,000 sitting on the corner of their desks," says one former Wood Gundy salesman, "and that was their quarterly income-tax payments." Great floor traders like Don Bainbridge of Daly Gordon Securities are rumored to earn more than a million dollars in their good years. Retail salesmen who earn $300,000 to $400,000 during bull markets certainly aren't common, but neither are they utterly exceptional. Investment counsellors, in return for their insights on what to buy and what to sell, usually charge their clients a percentage of the value of their portfolios, generally ranging between one and two per cent. If you're a six-person firm managing a billion dollars of other people's money, the revenues can be fabulous and the expenses fairly negligible. In Vancouver, in the good years, million-dollar salesmen (or salesmen who *say* they're making a million a year) are almost as common as Mercedes 300SLs. Even junior floor traders, barely out of their teens, are driven almost berserk by the money that rolls in during a hot market. "These guys have been in the market six months, and it's as if the money is pouring into their pockets," says Marc Foreman, a veteran floor trader who now directs trading operations for the Vancouver Stock Exchange. "If you were 22, just out of school, how would you like to find yourself with $10,000 or $15,000 at the end of the month? So you go out and make a down payment on a Corvette. Living high and living fast; there are a lot of them who do it."

A certain amount of mythology surrounds the question of Bay Street's personal incomes; to demystify the subject, 31 Bay Street securities firms in 1981 commissioned a management consulting company to find out who makes how much. The study has never been made public, but the results – if certain leaked figures are to be believed – indicate that salaries in the brokerage business are handsome, though not huge.

But paycheques aren't really the issue. The real money on Bay Street is made not through salaries, but through sales commissions and, for the inner circle of partners, from profit-sharing. McLeod Young Weir's top retail salesman in 1983, for instance, was Jacques Maurice of the Montreal office; he earned $1.2 million. The year before, the 70-odd member firms of the Investment Dealers Association of Canada, according to Statistics Canada figures, netted about $33 million on revenues of $445 million. The industry employed just under 17,000 people that year. Within that group there was an elite corps of senior executives, probably numbering fewer than 1,000 people, who were shareholders in their firms, and were thus entitled to a piece of those profits in addition to their salaries, their sales commissions and whatever money they made in the market. The IDA firms distributed about 12 per cent of that year's profits to their owners; which indicates that in 1982, 1,000 or so people, as an added fillip on top of everything else, split about $4 million.

And 1982 was not a great year. In the boom year of 1983, even without profit-sharing, the four top salesmen at Midland Doherty Limited earned between $200,000 and $250,000 each. Statistics like these are the origin of the ancient Bay Street joke about the small investor who lunched with his broker at the Royal Canadian Yacht Club. The broker showed his client around the place, proudly identifying each yacht and its owner. At the end of the tour, the client said: "I've seen the brokers' yachts and I've seen the bankers' yachts – but where are the *customers'* yachts?"*

Beyond Toronto: Village Neighborhoods

Since "Bay Street" is more a state of mind than a place, it extends far beyond the confines of Toronto. Montreal's St. James Street is largely an extension of the Bay Street Village – although the Montreal Exchange is doing its best to change that state of affairs – and Vancouver complements it. In fact, Toronto and Vancouver represent the yin and yang of the Canadian securities business: investment versus speculation; sober fiduciary responsibility – or at least the carefully maintained appearance of it – versus the hair-raising ups and downs of a market that bounces like a yo-yo according to the latest drill-core rumor; the buttoned-down professionalism of a Bay Street mandarin such as Tony Fell, of Dominion Securities Pitfield Ltd., versus the almost oriental flamboyance of a Peter Brown.

But there are also striking similarities among the three financial communities. Their clubs, their gathering-places, their shared lingo, their folklore, mark them as separate neighborhoods of a single village. In Toronto, the young traders gather each afternoon at Sammy's Exchange in the basement concourse at First Canadian Place, to swap stories about the day's triumphs and disasters. In Vancouver, the favored after-hours spots tend to be luxury restaurants with discos attached, like Viva's or Pelican Bay on Granville Island. Two branches of the Hy's Restaurant chain, on Richmond Street in Toronto and on Hornby Street in

---

* The old joke may need some updating. Two media personalities, author Peter C. Newman and Southam Inc. president Gordon Fisher, both own larger yachts at the RCYC than does Robert Korthals, president of the Toronto Dominion Bank.

8

Vancouver, are treated almost like company cafeterias by the "shooters" of their respective cities.* But big, boozy lunches are passé, and the popularity of health and athletic clubs is a growing phenomenon.

The Neighborhood Doctor

In Toronto, the elite place to sweat is the Cambridge Club, 90 per cent owned by Jim Bentley, a squash and tennis pro, and 10 per cent by Dr. Jim Paupst, a general practitioner. Dr. Paupst, with an office in the Toronto Dominion Centre, qualifies as Bay Street's neighborhood doctor. Most of his patients work within a few hundred yards of his office – either horizontally or vertically – and most of them are senior financial and media executives. After 16 years in the same location, he's become the Dr. Spock of executive stress. He claims he can tell how the market is doing on any given day simply by taking the blood pressure of a few of his patients. When the stress gets too tough, some of these patients suffer from imaginary heart attacks. "I was seeing three times as many of those cases when the market slumped in 1981 and 1982," he says. "I call it executive coronary. When the stress is great enough, your body has to make a statement. But it's funny how it makes it. The pain will be around the left nipple area, which is where most people *think* the heart pain should be, instead of behind the breastbone. Invariably there's left arm involvement, because everybody knows you're supposed to have pains in your arm when you're having a heart attack."

But as the recession deepened in 1982, Dr. Paupst noticed a peculiar, spontaneous adjustment among the inhabitants of the Bay Street Village. "They started developing a sense of tranquillity, of patience. I'm talking about that incurable disease, hope. One guy who works for Burns Fry expressed it to me in a really beautiful way. He told me: 'Even the gods cannot unscramble eggs.' Resignation! It's amazing! It makes my practice easier."

The Clubs

The Cambridge Club, to which many of Dr. Paupst's patients belong, is a serviceable symbol of the new forces at work in

---

* Hy Aisenstat, the owner, has so many stock-market players among his clientele that in 1969 he took the restaurant chain public at $5 per share. Seven years later he bought the shares back for $5.50, and Hy's once again became a private company.

the industry. The old Bay Street used to clinch its bond issues and underwriting deals over three martinis and a cholesterol-laden lunch at one of the right clubs: the Toronto, the National, the York, the Ontario or the Albany. The new Bay Street runs five miles before breakfast on the Cambridge's rooftop jogging track, plays a fierce game of squash on one of the Cambridge's six courts, and talks business over a Cambridge Club lunch of cottage-cheese salad and B-29s (a wholesome drink consisting of beef broth, Clamato juice and Beefeaters gin, which Dr. Paupst invented). The old Bay Street was clubby and assured, went to all the right schools and tended to share the available business according to the gentlemanly assumption that, so long as up-starts were excluded, there would always be plenty of business to go around. The new Bay Street is hotly competitive and much less gentlemanly – so much so that some senior brokers, such as Peter Eby, vice-chairman of Burns Fry Ltd., won't take po-tential clients to the Toronto Club; it merely tips off competitors who might be sitting at the next table.

Eby is one of the Cambridge's founding members. He and 21 other Toronto honchos, most of them from Bay Street, each loaned the founding partners $15,000 in 1972. Most of the re-mainder of the start-up capital was raised by Jack Lawrence, a founding member and dedicated marathon runner who is pres-ident of Burns Fry Ltd. Lawrence personally guaranteed half of a $405,000 bank loan in return for a 25 per cent share in the company which owns the club. Once the Cambridge was op-erating in the black, Lawrence sold his shares to Bentley, who in turn sold a piece to Dr. Paupst. Within four years of its founding, the 22 original backers were repaid their $15,000 plus interest. They also received a testimonial banquet, and if they resign or when they die, one of their sons will automatically be enrolled as life member.*

The Cambridge has fewer than 1,000 members, but they in-clude much of Bay Street's younger blood. There are three Eatons (John Craig, Thor and George), and until Edward dropped out, there were two Bronfmans. There are also two bank pres-idents (Robert Korthals of the Toronto Dominion and Bill Bradford

---

* Among the 22 founders are Ron Gunn, a Burns Fry vice-president; Alan Marchment, a black belt in karate who is president of Guaranty Trust Co. of Canada; Donald C. (Ben) Webster, president of Helix Investments Ltd.; and entrepreneur Murray Sinclair, a former partner in Guardian Capital Group Ltd.

of the Bank of Montreal), one bank chairman (the TD's Dick Thomson), one former finance minister (Donald MacDonald), any number of brokers and promoters and, for exotic contrast, Gordon Lightfoot and Pierre Berton. The financial gossiping and whispered deal-making around the lunch tables, and in the upstairs bar overlooking the squash courts, remind Dr. Paupst "of the Empire Hotel in Timmins, back in the days of the Texas Gulf Sulphur strike. You can't see the tables for the smoke."

The Cambridge is only one of several institutions which lend continuity to the neighborhood. Another is the Ticker Club, an exclusive luncheon club which has met in various clubs and hotels around Bay Street almost every second Friday (except for the summer months) since 1929. It was founded by Floyd Chalmers, then editor of *The Financial Post*, and its membership is still limited to 30 active members, most of them in the investment business, plus a few associate members. The speakers have included finance ministers, economists, brokers, corporation presidents and other luminaries, but their words are almost never reported in the press. Once a year the club stages an annual forecast dinner, usually at the Toronto Club, at which various financial experts issue their predictions for the stock market and the economy. An optimistic broker named Ed Kernaghan startled this gathering when, at the 1946 dinner, he predicted that the Dow-Jones Industrial Average which was then slumbering below 200, would achieve a level of 500 by 1956. The Dow did exactly that and so, at the 1957 meeting, Kernaghan, as a tribute to his prescience, was presented with a silver dollar on a red ribbon.

"When I placed the ribbon around Eddie's head," recalls the Ticker Club's 1956-57 president, Jack Rhind, "there was a great cheer from everyone in the dining room, as they sprang to their feet with an uproarious ovation. Then Eddie said he would like to make a further forecast. A hushed silence fell on the room as Eddie said, 'My friends, we have only seen the beginning. We shall all live to see the Dow Jones reach 1,000.'

"I will never forget the moment of deathly silence that followed this wild statement," says Rhind. "Perhaps it lasted only a fraction of a second, for it was quickly followed by a mixed uproar of foot-stamping, catcalls and booing, the like of which I'm sure had never before been witnessed within the staid walls of the Toronto Club.

"Our idol had fallen with a crash. Some demanded I take the medal back. With some difficulty I brought the meeting under control and reminded members that we were honoring Mr.

Kernaghan for his past clairvoyance, and that it was just possible that some day the Dow Jones average might reach 1,000." It did, in 1965.

Bay Street even has its own exclusive investment club, the Canyon Beauport Club, whose 15 shareholder-members include some of the nation's canniest investors. The club, which is now incorporated as a private company, was founded around 1960 by Trevor Eyton, then a rising young corporate lawyer, now president of Brascan Ltd., the $3.3-billion conglomerate controlled by the Edper branch of the Bronfman clan. Among its members are Norman Short, president of Guardian Capital Group Ltd., which manages more than $1 billion worth of investment funds; Ross Kennedy, a partner in Eyton's old law firm, Tory Tory Des Laurier & Binnington; Warren Grover, a partner in another Establishment law firm, Blake Cassels & Graydon; George Bonar, sales and marketing vice-president of Falconbridge Ltd.; Ilmar Martens, a globe-trotting consultant who's paid for his encylopedic knowledge of nickel; Charles Loewen, Chris Ondaatje and Fred McCutcheon, co-founders of the investment firm that bears their three names; David Lewis, president of the Continental Bank of Canada; broadcasting entrepreneur Allan Slaight; cable TV tycoon Geoff Conway; investment counsellor Tony Griffiths; and Julian Porter, lawyer and chairman of the Toronto Transit Commission. Bruce McLaughlin, the controversial land developer who practically invented the Toronto bedroom suburb of Mississauga, was another of the club's founders, but later resigned. Fred McCutcheon, a former chairman of the Toronto Stock Exchange, runs the bulk of the club's investment portfolio.

McCutcheon won't tell outsiders what it's worth, but anyone wishing to join the Canyon Beauport Club these days would have to put up at least $30,000. In 1975, each member's stake in the club was worth about $2,500. Until the mid-1970s, members chipped in $50 or less a month, and the club's investments were mainly in stocks and real estate. Then, after a three-year hiatus, it was re-formed, with Short and Ondaatje running the stock portfolio, and McCutcheon trading commodities, often with brilliant results. "You can always ask Freddie if he's short the Mexican peso," says one member, "and he always is."

Status Symbols

Flirtations with the arts are commonplace in the Bay Street village. Andrew Willman, vice-president of the Toronto investment firm called McConnell & Co. Ltd., is also president of the Frederic Chopin Society of Canada, many of whose members are affluent brokers, or simply affluent. Willman is a Polish-born émigré who affects a gold-headed cane, kisses ladies' hands, smokes Brazilian cigars which he imports from London and, with his mittel-European accent and lordly manner, bears a disturbing resemblance to Béla Lugosi. The Society stages concerts and exhibitions on the romantic period, and gives financial assistance to promising young pianists. About six times a year, Willman hosts black-tie private concerts at his penthouse apartment. But the most notable event is the Society's annual concert at Casa Loma or the Ontario Club, at which Willman, with his flair for the theatrical, does his best to duplicate the vanished civilities of the Austro-Hungarian Empire: evening dress and ball gowns, little glasses of sherry served on silver trays, and an evening of polonaises and mazurkas performed by promising local pianists or distinguished visiting musicians.

But the village's deepest cultural interest is reserved for the kind of art which shows a decent prospect for capital appreciation. When the Vancouver Stock Exchange vacated its old premises on Howe Street in 1981, John Woods, a vice-president of Canarim Investment Corp., commissioned a painting by Toronto artist Gordon Halloran of the VSE's old floor, crowded with recognizable likenesses of its better-known floor traders. Woods then sold a limited edition of 40 prints of the painting at $500 each. The prints became an instant status symbol on Howe Street, and even before the old building closed, they were changing hands at $1,000; to a stockbroker, that's art appreciation. (In 1983, Woods commissioned a similar Halloran print to mark the move by the Toronto Stock Exchange to *its* new headquarters, and sold them for $500 each. "It gave us a lot of satisfaction to make those bastards in Toronto pay *us* for a picture of their own exchange," says one Canarim official.)

Another status symbol, on both Bay and Howe Streets, is a lissome, husky-voiced art dealer named Lonti Ebers. In 1982-83 Ebers bought more than $1 million worth of art for a list of blue-chip clients that included Brascan's Trevor Eyton, Argus Corp's. Conrad Black, investment counsellor Andy Sarlos and Sam Belzberg of Vancouver-based First City Financial Corp. Ebers takes a resolutely capitalist approach to her work. When she hung out her shingle as an art consultant in 1979, she persuaded 10 of Bay Street's shrewdest investors each to buy a $1,000 preferred share in her fledgling company. Those backers included Eyton, Belzberg and Chuck Loewen; Phil Holtby, president of Midland Doherty Ltd.; Elaine Beutel, the wife of

Austin Beutel of Beutel-Goodman Ltd., one of Bay Street's top investment-counselling firms; Hal Jackman, chairman of E-L Financial Corp., an influential financier and Tory bagman; and David Allan, a vice-president and director of Walwyn Inc. The resultant share issue was the smallest ever approved by the Ontario Securities Commission, but it gave Ebers the working capital she needed to launch the business. Her clients, some of whom are also her shareholders, pay her between 15 per cent and 20 per cent of the purchase price of any art objects she buys on their behalf. "What they pay me they can recoup in discounts," she says. "But I'm not a discount operation. I buy the best works. Most of these guys don't have the time to buy art. But they know how to delegate."

Enough Bay Street shooters have delegated their aesthetic chores to Lonti Ebers to enable her to pay off her 10 original shareholders with interest and, as she points out, to generate a healthy 71 per cent return on equity. For Trevor Eyton of Brascan, she tossed out almost every painting the company owned – "It was the kind of stuff you'd buy off the back of a truck," she says – and replaced them with small Inuit sculptures of ivory and whalebone. For Conrad Black, she bought nineteenth century Dutch and French paintings of the Barbizon school, because they blended nicely with the cornices and panelling on the ground floor of the company's famous little building, an 1853 architectural gem built to resemble the Temple of Minerva, which once served as Toronto's seventh post office. Upstairs at Argus, however, Ebers has hung contemporary Canadians such as Riopelle, Borduas and Cullen, and persuaded Black to exhibit his own purchases – mostly scenes of eighteenth-century naval battles, with all guns blazing – at home. For Andy Sarlos, she selected paintings by Jean-Paul Riopelle (an untitled 1954 work which cost $50,000), Milton Avery, Alexander Archipenko, Maurice Vlaminck and A.Y. Jackson. That was in 1980, when Sarlos was one of the most successful traders on Bay Street. But when the bottom fell out of the stock market in 1981, Ebers helped the hard-pressed Sarlos sell some of those same paintings. "Andy bought at the top of the market," she says, "and sold at about a 10 per cent loss. Considering that the art market was down between 20 per cent and 40 per cent he didn't do badly."

For the Toronto Stock Exchange, she staged a competition for the art to adorn the entrance to the trading floor, and selected a large relief sculpture with a bull-and-bear motif by General Idea, a three-man consortium of Toronto artists, and a bas-relief by a fashionable New York realist named Robert

14

Longo. Longo's piece depicts a group of business people who seem to be marching resolutely out of the wall toward the viewer. The businessman on the extreme right of this grouping happens to be black, which alarmed some TSE members, who would have preferred the representative of a more distinctively Canadian ethnic group – Chinese say, or Ukrainian. Ebers was adamant, and the black capitalist stayed: "I couldn't go back to Longo and tell him to turn the guy into an Inuit, could I? At least he's carrying a briefcase, not a ghetto-blaster."*

Ebers owes much of her success to the small-town quality of the Canadian financial community. At the upper echelons, most of the high-rollers in Toronto and Vancouver know one another; and the news of Ebers and the aesthetic services she offers has been passed by word of mouth from one end of the country to the other, like a hot stock tip. "There's no question that my being female has been an asset," she says. "For most of my clients, their whole business day is one man after another. So I'm a bit of a change. And in this market, your name becomes an item." Like next week's quarterly earnings report, like the gossip at the Cambridge Club, Ebers has become part of the oral tradition of the Bay Street Village.

---

* In more than two years of researching this book, the only black I encountered in the securities industry was a young man I saw on the old TSE floor after trading hours. He was sweeping discarded trading slips into large piles and stuffing them into green plastic garbage bags.

2
The Rules
of The Game

To understand exactly what's going on in the Bay Street village, you must understand that most people and most companies, despite vivid impressions to the contrary, spend less than they earn. One way or another, the difference gets invested. What Bay Street is really doing, in an intricate variety of ways, is transferring money from people or organizations who have saved it, to people and companies and governments who want to spend it. The institutions which perform this function, including goverments, banks, trust companies, pension-fund and investment dealers, deploy the money they collect in a variety of ways. The Canada Pension Plan, for instance, to which almost every wage-earner in the country contributes – whether they know it or not – had $21.5 billion in the kitty in 1982; all of it was loaned to provincial governments at rates slightly lower than those charged by the banks. The banks themselves are sitting on about $170 billion in customers' deposits. In 1983 they'd loaned about $115 billion to corporations and to individuals; held about $32 billion in mortgages; and loaned billions of dollars more to governments, in the form of municipal, provincial or federal bonds and treasury bills. The trust and loan companies attracted another $54.9 billion in deposits, and most of this was reinvested in stocks and mortgages. Private pension plans held another $60 billion worth of other people's savings. All of this money gets reinvested. It's either loaned out to individuals, companies or governments, or it's used to buy shares in one or more of the thousands of companies whose stock is traded on Canadian or foreign stock exchanges.

The Bond Market

Governments, you will not be surprised to learn, are the largest consumers of other people's savings. In mid-1983, Canadian companies, financial institutions and individuals held $534 billion worth of bonds or short-term notes issued by Ottawa, by municipalities, or by the provinces or their money-hungry corporate creatures, such as Ontario Hydro or Hydro Quebec. Directly or indirectly, all those bonds and notes represent money loaned by people to their governments. Bay Street is intimately involved in this process. Both the banks and the investment houses profit handsomely by selling new issues of government bonds to their clients. In 1983 alone, the government borrowed $11.6 billion from its own citizens by selling CSBs, plus another $14.8 billion in the form of treasury bills and Canadian bonds, which are sold almost exclusively to financial institutions.* The federal Department of Finance and the Securities Department of the Bank of Canada allocate sales of government bonds among the various banks and investment houses, and its officials are subject to continual sales pitches by large Bay Street investment firms which want larger allocations, or by smaller firms seeking a berth on the gravy train.

Large corporations also issue bonds to finance expansion; they're bought by financial institutions and individuals looking for a safe, guaranteed return on their money. In 1983, Canadian corporations, including banks, utilities and manufacturers, borrowed $3.1 billion in this manner. Bay Street investment houses act as sales agents in these transactions. They advise the companies on the best time to issue the bonds and suggest the most advantageous price. The investment houses then buy the company's bonds and resell them – usually to pension funds – at a slight markup. Once these new bond issues are launched on the market, the investment houses buy and sell them daily, trying to make a small profit on each transaction and, in the process, ensuring that their customers can always sell their bonds if they need to.

The bond market constitutes a separate Bay Street subculture. In the early days of the century, most of Canada's development, from street railways to municipal sewer systems to railroads to pulp and paper mills, was financed through long-term bond issues. The largest investment houses, such as Wood Gundy Ltd., Dominion Securities-Pitfield Ltd. and Burns Fry Ltd., are

---

* Treasury bills and Government of Canada bonds fluctuate in value every day, according to the latest rumors of where interest rates are headed. If they're headed up, the price of bonds goes down, and vice versa. Canada Savings Bonds, by contrast, don't trade and their value doesn't fluctuate. They can be sold only to individuals, not companies or institutions; and, unlike conventional bonds, you can cash them in any time, instead of waiting for the maturity date.

most heavily involved in the bond business of issuing and trading bonds.

Selling Shares

But there is another way for companies to raise money. Instead of borrowing it through a bond issue or a bank loan, they can raise it by selling shares. A share is simply a piece of paper which states that you own a certain percentage of the capital stock of a given company.

Most companies, when they're getting started, have very few shareholders – typically the cousins, aunts, parents and friends of whoever started the company. But as a company grows, it needs more money. Some firms raise it by asking the original shareholders to kick in more cash. Some lucky companies make so much money that they can finance expansion from their own profits. But thousands of companies choose to raise additional capital by "going public" – that is, by selling their shares on the open market. To do this, they must persuade an investment dealer that their company has a track record of several years of reliable profits, or that it's got such a great idea or such a great product that people will want to buy its shares in the expectation of profits later on.

The process of bringing those shares to market is called underwriting. The investment house which underwrites a public share issue usually commits itself to selling a certain number of shares to its customers. (Some issues, however, are underwritten on a "best efforts" basis, which means the underwriter promises only to sell as many shares as possible.) The company whose shares are being underwritten gets the proceeds of the stock issue, minus the underwriter's commission.

Going public can, and often does, create instant millionaires – but not necessarily among the people who buy the shares. The founders of a company, at a time when it's only a gleam in the entrepreneur's eye, usually award themselves thousands of shares in return for their small initial investment. At the beginning, those shares are worth pennies or less. In fact, they're usually worth nothing at all, because there's no market for them. But if the company is successful enough to be taken public, you and I may be happy to pay several dollars for those same shares. And once those shares are trading on the market, they may go up even further. Sometimes, in the case of a Xerox or an IBM, the multipliers can be fantastic. That's the basis of most of the great twentieth-century fortunes. But for the stockbrokers who help create those fortunes by bringing the shares to market, it's like being a eunuch in a harem. "Wall Street never makes the real money," a partner in an investment firm once complained to 'Adam Smith.' "You see somebody build up a little firm, you sell some stock to the public for him, and you know that now he has $50 million in that stock. But you can work your whole life on Wall Street, and be very successful, and end up with a lousy four or five million dollars."

Where the Money Is

It is, alas, all true. There are scores of entrepreneurs, running companies most Canadians have never heard of, whose share-holdings make them far richer than almost any stockbroker. Vern Lyons, president of Calgary-based Ocelot Industries Ltd., in mid-1981 owned about 6.4 million shares of the company he founded. At the height of the oil boom in 1981, Ocelot shares traded as high as $69, and Lyons, on paper, was therefore worth upward of $440 million.* (But in 1983, after the bottom dropped out of the oil and gas boom, Ocelot shares traded as low as $5, which dragged the unfortunate Lyons down to the $32-million neighborhood.) Gordon Lang, president of a Toronto-based packager of household products called CCL Industries Ltd., owns 36 per cent of his company's 8,345,713 issued shares. In mid-1984 those shares were trading in the $17 range, which meant that Lang's stake, on paper, was worth more than $50 million.

It is therefore credulous to suppose that Bay Street is where the money is. A disproportionate share of this country's pro-ductive assets are owned either by foreign corporations or by families such as the Richardsons, Irvings, Bronfmans, Westons, Websters, McConnells, Blacks, Belzbergs and Reichmans. Bay Street and its battalions of brokers, lawyers and accountants function as handmaidens to these and other fortunes. They shelter wealth by trying to ensure that the richer one gets, the less tax one pays. They reshuffle wealth by stage-managing mergers which are often merely exchanges of assets from one rich man's son to another. And they help create wealth by deploying idle cash from the people who earned it to people who think they can make it grow by reinvesting it.

---

* In practical terms, though, he was worth a whole lot less, because the price of his shares would have dropped if he'd tried to sell them all at once.

Bad Years, Great Years

It's often a very profitable business. But Bay Street has bad years as well as great ones, and even the mighty have been known to suffer when their commissions dry up. Although the number of firms doing business in Canada has remained relatively constant since the 1970s, there is a constant churning of members, as weak or failing firms merge with stronger ones, and new firms are started. Since 1964, more than 300 investment firms have either gone broke, gone out of business or merged with another firm. In fact, there isn't a single major firm in the country, except Wood Gundy Ltd., which isn't the product of at least one merger; and even Wood Gundy, in the 1930s, avoided a face-saving merger only through the mercy of its bankers. In 1981, A.E. Ames, in a last-ditch attempt to avoid bankruptcy, merged with Dominion Securities; the following year the venerable Montreal firm of Greenshields Inc., which was losing about $600,000 a month, merged with James Richardson & Sons Ltd.; in 1983 R.A. Daly & Co. Ltd. merged with Gordon Securities Ltd. to create a powerful new presence in the underwriting business; in 1984, as the winds of deregulation blew through Bay Street, Dominion Securities Ames Ltd. swallowed Pitfield Mackay Ross Ltd. to form Dominion Securities Pitfield; and a small, Montreal-based firm named Jones Heward & Co. Ltd. was bought by Burns Fry Ltd.

Rising to the Top

Many mergers stem from amateur management. The trouble seems to be that people who are good at trading stocks aren't necessarily good at running companies. But because of Bay Street's unique degree of management ownership, it's the successful traders, not the plodding but effective managerial types, who tend to rise to the top. If you're a good trader or a good salesman, you can earn enough money to buy a piece of the firm; then, as a shareholder, your position becomes stronger and stronger as older employee-shareholders retire. In the end, you may wind up as president, without having the foggiest notion of how to control costs, forecast revenues or motivate people.

That's why, until the 1970s at least, some Canadian investment houses were managed by people who would have been out of their depth running laundromats. Too many brokers have ignored one of the basic rules of business: Hoard your

20

profits for the bad times, instead of spending them on Krieghoffs and Ferraris. "The investment industry is strange," says Peter Brown, president of Vancouver's Canarim Investment Corp. "When they get a great year, all the partners are at the trough, they expand their offices, they withdraw 100 per cent of the dough. Then they have one bad year – and we know, by the way, that for the past century every fourth year in this business seems to be a clanger – and all of a sudden they've run out of capital and they're firing people, closing branches, laying off research guys, stripping down salesmen's services, cutting salaries, destroying the attitudes of their people. These guys advise companies to save some of their earnings for a rainy day, but they don't do it themselves."*

Instead, they try to play their firms like accordions, hiring people in good years and firing them during the inevitable downturns. In 1979, a slow year, about 14,000 people worked in the securities industry. As the energy boom gained strength in 1980, the workforce swelled to nearly 18,000. During the recession year which began late in 1981, employment fell below 17,000. By 1983, with the market rebounding, employment rose above 19,000. By the time you read this, the market may have dropped again and several hundred former stockbrokers will be back peddling real estate, running windsurfing franchises or collecting pogey. It's all part of Bay Street's endearingly small-town quality; in spite of the industry's sophistication and skill at predicting market cycles, the grasshoppers vastly outnumber the ants.

A Cosy Sort of Place

There is even something aw-shucks about the stock exchanges themselves. The public tends to view them either as fountainheads of probity and wisdom, or as bearpits of chicanery and greed. But from the inside they tend to be cosy and amiably slow-moving – the kind of places where employees intermarry, sons and nephews drift into the business and secretaries stage bridal showers in the boardroom. Marc Foreman, Director of Trading Operations for the Vancouver Stock Exchange, came into the business because he had an uncle who ran the VSE's clearing department. Foreman also met his wife there; she now runs the VSE's depository, where share certificates are stored

---

* In mid-1984, during a slow market, Brown put scores of Canarim employees on a four-day week, even though the firm was still profitable.

in a vault, instead of being ferried back and forth around Howe Street by messengers, with a computer keeping minute-to-minute track of who owns them.

Stock exchanges are essentially small, high-technology businesses, owned by the brokers themselves,* which run the daily auction of stocks and options, sell electronic services to their members and, with varying degrees of severity, attempt to regulate them. The Toronto Stock Exchange, which handles about 80 per cent of the nation's total trading value, is Canada's largest exchange and, in terms of the market value of its trading, the fifth-largest in the world. The Montreal, Calgary and Vancouver exchanges split the remaining 20 per cent of the business. There's also an exchange in Winnipeg, but it's a negligible factor in the national picture. The value of trading on the Calgary-based Alberta Stock Exchange is about one-tenth that of Vancouver, and the Winnipeg Stock Exchange is smaller still. In fact, it doesn't even have a trading floor; its members trade stocks by phoning one another. Edmonton also had an exchange without a trading floor, but scarcely anyone noticed when it folded in 1958.

Owning a Seat

Owning a seat on a stock exchange is more a matter of business convenience than of prestige. All the large investment houses own seats, of course, since you can't make trades unless you're a member. But many smaller firms don't own exchange seats; they subcontract – or "jitney" – their trading to a member firm instead. Some small investment counsel-firms, whose real business is selling advice to pension funds, own stock-exchange seats as a convenience. They execute the trades they recommend to their clients, and are paid in the form of brokerage commissions rather than in the form of monthly retainers. There are even a few individuals who own seats on the TSE, including Fred McCutcheon, a former TSE chairman who operates his

---

* Sometimes those brokers complain about what the TSE is costing them. Early in 1984, the TSE's members forced the exchange to lay off staff, and grumbled publicly about the lavishness of TSE President Pearce Bunting's vast, wood-panelled suite of offices. One broker, who toured the suite when it was under construction, was appalled to find that a wine cabinet had been included among Bunting's corporate amenities. The offending cabinet was ripped out. "We don't advertise," Bunting explains, "so we establish our image through visibility."

own one-man investment counselling business, Arachnae Securities Ltd., out of an office at Buttonville Airport.

At the end of 1981, there were 126 seats on the TSE, owned by 80 member firms. To become a member, a firm must own a seat, must satisfy the TSE's board of governors of its experience and expertise, must have enough capital to meet the TSE's current requirements, must be approved by other member firms, and its principals must pass a qualifying examination. Ownership of a seat permits a member firm to place as many as 10 traders on the floor – a maximum of 5 trading shares and no more than 5 trading options. The price of those seats is an accurate barometer of the market itself. Just before the Great Crash of 1929, TSE seats changed hands for as much as $200,000. The low point came in 1940-1941, when seats sold for as little as $12,000. Even today, the fluctuations in seat prices can be greater than those of the market itself. In 1980-1981, for instance, TSE seats changed hands for as little as $40,000 and as much as $166,000.

Getting a Listing

The stocks that trade on the TSE are scrutinized almost as carefully as are the firms that trade them. Before a firm can sell its shares to the public, it must convince an investment dealer that its future is sufficiently rosy to give the shares at least a fighting chance of attracting buyers. That usually means a track record of several years of consistently profitable operation. Once convinced, the investment firm underwrites an issue of the company's shares. Before this happens, however, the proposed issue must also be scrutinized by the watchdogs of the Ontario Securities Commission, who comb through the company's prospectus (a booklet describing the company's operations, its financial condition, its future prospects and the details of the share offering) to ensure that it fully discloses everything an investor needs to know. Once the company's share issue has passed those hurdles and has been sold to the brokers' clients, the shares enter the "secondary market" – that is, they can be freely bought and sold by the public.

But hundreds of stocks, usually those of smaller companies, trade freely without being listed on any stock exchange. They're known as "over-the-counter" stocks, and they're bought and sold over the telephone, through brokers operating on behalf of clients. Some companies trade for months or years on the OTC market before applying for an exchange listing. Other companies never bother to apply. But when a company reaches a certain plateau of size and stability, with hundreds or thousands of shareholders, it usually makes sense to get listed on a stock exchange; it confers prestige and, through the stock quotations that are printed daily in the newspapers, keeps the company's name constantly before the investing public.

Applying for a listing involves another set of regulatory hurdles: scrutiny by the TSE's listing committee, further probing by the OSC. The entire process of steering a share issue through the underwriter, the OSC and the TSE can take several months and swallow several hundred thousand dollars in printing bills and lawyers' and accountants' fees.

Not surprisingly, most TSE-listed stocks are those of senior, established corporations. In Vancouver, which prides itself on its specialized role as a "venture-capital exchange," the listing process is faster, cheaper, less heavily regulated and far more suitable for resource and industrial companies in the early stages of their development. The VSE has often been criticized as a haven for fast-buck promoters selling moose-pasture mining stocks. But even the VSE's severest critics admit that in a resource-rich country like Canada, there has to be *some* streamlined method of raising money for fledgling resource and high-technology companies. These are inherently long-shot ventures. Most of them will fail, and most investors will lose their money. But in the process – or so the argument goes – a few fabulous winners will emerge. It may be a wasteful process, and it may be riddled with hype and even outright fraud. But most of Canada's resource wealth has been created this way; the whole appeal of the penny-stock game is based on the undeniable proposition that today's moose pasture just might turn out to be tomorrow's Noranda.

Regulatory Procedures

Both the TSE and the Montreal Exchange have weathered stock-fraud scandals which led to the installation of regulatory procedures that protect investors, but which make it damnably difficult for young companies to raise risk capital. In recent years, both exchanges and both provincial governments have recognized the problem, and have simplified their rules accordingly. In Toronto, listing procedures were streamlined in 1982 to permit companies with as little as $350,000 worth of working capital (including the amount raised in the underwriting) to secure a TSE listing. In Montreal, Exchange Presi-

24

dent Pierre Lortie has not only streamlined his exchange's listing procedures; he has even set up a new department to seek listings, and to guide them through the regulatory maze. He also talked the Quebec government into subsidizing part of the costs of going public. In 1983, some 18 young Quebec companies applied for listings on the Montreal Exchange. "That's more new listings than we've had in the last decade," says Lortie.

The eastern exchanges are both uncomfortably aware of the money that Vancouver sometimes coins through its more permissive approach to regulation. One senses that they'd love to have a piece of all that Vancouver action – but not at the cost of sullying their images. Says TSE President Pearce Bunting: "I'd love to see a mining situation [on the TSE] that goes from being just a drill hole to a billion dollars. But if the price you have to pay is potentially destroying the confidence of $150 billion worth of listed securities – well, we're not interested." Bunting wants the business, but he wants clean hands even more.

Bunting is an appropriate spokesman for the industry he represents: genial and assured, well-tailored, not terribly aggressive. He has a shiny, open face, an obliging manner and owns three blue suits. He's worked on Bay Street nearly all his life, and his closest brush with poverty came in the mid 1940s, when his father, a mining broker, experienced some business reverses. "I can still remember my father driving me down to the bottom of Navy Street in Oakville, beside the river, stopping the car and saying, 'I have to tell you that I just haven't been able to earn enough money this year; I'm going to have to take you out of Appleby College.'"

But the market must have taken an unexpected upturn, since Bunting was never taken out of Appleby. He was graduated in Commerce from McGill in 1952, and spent three years working for McLeod Young Weir in Montreal and Toronto before joining his father's now-prosperous firm, Alfred Bunting & Co. Ltd. During his 20 years with the firm his father founded, Bunting *fils* saw it transformed, like Bay Street itself, from a racy mining emporium into a sleekly professional manager of large private fortunes and one of Bay Street's most highly regarded institutional boutiques. "The firm went from mining in the 1930s to the carriage trade in the 1960s," he says. "Our clients had gotten rich."

When Bunting speaks with distaste of Vancouver's free-wheeling mining market, he sounds a bit wistful – almost as if he were referring to his own origins. "I could never be what my father was, and he could never have done what I did," says

Bunting. "He was a person who really loved people. He lived on contacts, and information derived from those contacts. I realized I could never be that kind of broker. I always tried to be the opposite, in a sense. I tried to be a professional broker who did a first-class professional job. In dealing with my retail clients, I wasn't interested in individual hot-tip relationships. I was only interested in an account that I could handle from a portfolio point of view, and handle the whole thing – or at least know at all times what was going on." The dichotomy between Howe Street and Bay Street has seldom been better expressed.

3
Market Psychology: When to Buy When to Sell

He sounded baffled and wounded, as if his wife had walked out on him without warning. He'd bought several hundred thousand dollars' worth of a certain company's stock, because he's a prosperous and well-informed consultant who had worked on some technical aspects of the underwriting deal himself. Because he was so close to the financing, because he'd worked with some higher-ups in the company, he *knew* that the stock, issued at $10, would soon double. But it didn't. Within a few months it dropped as low as $2.87, and my friend was looking at a loss twice the size of his own mortgage.

Thank God he hadn't borrowed to buy the stock! But just the same, it hurt. He didn't blame his friends at the company, some of whom had suffered more than he had. In that baffled, wounded way of his, he blamed the market itself. He'd always dealt honorably with his colleagues and his clients. How could the market have betrayed him like this? He sprawled on the down-filled sofa in his Rosedale mansion, a glass of Scotch in his hand, and kept saying: "Dammit, I don't *understand* it!"

The market sometimes eats its children, and best of all it enjoys devouring the innocent. As it moves through its fairly predictable cycles, first seducing and then engorging financial virgins, the market requires constant supplies of fresh meat. It's true that a reasonably astute small investor, if he's not too greedy, can often do very well on the stock market. Like the economy it so faithfully reflects, the market's overall tendency is to grow; and simply by hanging in and doing your best to play the peaks against the troughs, you can often participate in that growth. Unlike the commodities and futures markets, where every gain is matched precisely by someone else's loss, it's sometimes possible in a booming stock market for almost everybody to win – at least for a while. But no pie can expand indefinitely; so the market's growth is dependent, to some extent, on the contributions of the world's losers – people like my friend, the consultant.

Many critics of the securities industry regard this regularized rape of the innocents as its most immoral feature. I'm not so sure, because the only way losers can become winners is by losing. Only then – but even then, not always – will they confront the network of illusion and expectation which helped them to lose. "It doesn't concern me in the least that unsophisticated people regularly blow their brains out on the Vancouver Stock Exchange," says an analyst whom I happen to admire. "That's how people learn to grow up."

The Small Investor – or odd-lot trader, as he is sometimes called – carries a heavy load of mythology on his drooping shoulders. It is for his benefit, we are told, that the stock market exists. His savings, when channelled through the medium of a relentlessly efficient stock market, are magically redirected to animate the sinews of industrial growth. The fruits of the nation's enterprise are thus disseminated widely throughout the population. If only they could be disseminated even more widely, we are assured by the market's apologists, then we would witness the dawning of a new era of People's Capitalism. How could serious inequality exist in a nation where almost everyone, through the magic of share ownership, owns a small but productive piece of the public wealth?

Bay Street has comforted itself for generations with this uplifting notion. It is a myth, of course. But it is a very durable myth, because it contains the seeds of a powerful truth. As an ideal, it is infinitely preferable to the mythology of social democracy, which supposes that an army of selfless politicians and all-seeing bureaucrats can perform the same distributive function. But it is a myth nevertheless, because the major levers of wealth in this country are still controlled by the chartered banks, which scarcely need to answer to anybody; by foreign corporations, which seldom offer Canadians a chance to buy a piece of their Canadian subsidiaries; by governments, of which the less said the better; and by a few very wealthy private players, often the sons of wealthy fathers, who swap assets among themselves like Regency bucks at the baccarat tables.

These large and generally secretive pools of capital often bypass the stock market entirely. And of the public trading in blue-chip stocks that does occur, a high proportion – between 50 and 70 per cent – is conducted by large financial institutions, such as pension and mutual funds. In this battle of the giants, the Little Guy has two choices: he can offer up his greed, and be trampled; or, like the African birds that live off the backs of rhinoceroses, he can find his own tiny niche in the market's scheme of things, and survive.

Becoming a Market Player

But how does one execute this magical transition from victim to victor? The answer is, largely through education. And the best way to educate yourself – perhaps the only way – is through a process of aversion therapy. Reading books about how to beat the stock market is like learning how to make love by reading *Penthouse* magazine. There is absolutely no substitute for experience, because the market is not the same for everybody. In order to succeed at the game, you must discover your own individual relationship to it. You must learn to understand your own personal quotient of fear and greed. Once you've been hurt a few times, you begin to understand that the game can be won only through an accretion of small triumphs which outweigh your small failures. You learn to hedge your bets by selecting an assortment of stocks that reflect an entire spectrum of possible outcomes. And, if you are very wise, you may even learn how to listen to what The Crowd is saying, and then do the exact opposite. As a market player, what you are trying to achieve is a specialized form of maturity.

As one of the canniest and best-respected stock salesmen in the industry, Al Pearlstein has become an expert in teaching people to grow up. "Only 10 or 15 per cent of my clients ever listen to me," he says, "and it's a continual challenge to improve on that percentage. I'm just a high-priced schoolteacher." Pearlstein himself never plays the market; but after more than three decades in the business, nearly all of it in Toronto with Pitfield Mackay Ross Ltd. (merged in 1984 to become Dominion Securities Pitfield Ltd.), he's seen seven or eight market cycles come and go, he's read and absorbed the writings of all the masters, and he can usually size up a new client's personal ratio of fear and greed the moment he walks in the door. Pearlstein sits at one of several dozen small desks in the large office bullpen; and what he mostly does all day is talk on the telephone. He has the air of a vaudeville booking agent who went legit after he discovered Sophie Tucker. The man is a philosopher.

Market Cycles

Pearlstein always gives his new clients a list of six books to read. "I have a standing offer to buy lunch for any of my clients who read all six books. I tell them it's basically five years' experience. But I don't buy many lunches."* He believes the market moves in a cycle lasting roughly nine years, with several smaller cycles occurring within this period. The big cycle is the capital-goods cycle. At its height, industry spends billions to renew or modernize plant and equipment. The smaller cycles are "inventory cycles." At their peaks, industry spends heavily to buy raw materials such as, say, copper. This causes a boom in copper stocks until inventories are loaded and the price of copper and other raw materials has been driven too high; then prices collapse and a new inventory cycle begins. When an inventory cycle and a capital-goods cycle coincide, as they usually have every nine years or so since 1880, you get a major bull market. Perlstein believes this process is as regular and predictable as the phases of the moon.

Equally predictable is the behavior of the market's ingenues. "You get a hot market, see," says Pearlstein, "and the investor wants some action. So he hears about this piece of crap at a dollar. He hears it's going to $5, but he says, 'Naw, those guys are liars – I don't trust them. I won't wait for the stock to go to $5 – I'll sell at $2.' It's the greed that gets him. The carnival operators, the promoters, are feeding him all these rumors. He sees some article in a business magazine, he hears rumors at the golf club; this president and that brother-in-law and the guy at the drill hole and all this crap.

"So the pooch buys at $1. He wants to make a quick score. But of course he doesn't buy what he can afford. Instead of buying 500 shares, he buys 5,000. It goes to $1.10 or $1.15, and

---

* Pearlstein's reading list, which he recommends reading in the following order, consists of *The Intelligent Investor*, by Benjamin Graham, the granddaddy of securities analysis; *The Battle for Investment Survival*, by Gerald Loeb; *My Own Story*, the autobiography of Bernard Baruch; *Extraordinary Popular Delusions and the Madness of Crowds*, by Charles Mackay; *The Money Game*, by "Adam Smith," George J.W. Goodman's classic 1967 enquiry into Wall Street's go-go years; and *The Stock Promotion Business*, by Ivan Shaffer, published by McClelland & Stewart, an exposé by a former financial PR man of how the penny-stock game was played in Toronto in the 1950s.

all of a sudden – bingo! New York goes down, the drill misses, there's a lawsuit, somebody's shorting the stock – there's always some story to explain why the stock fell out of bed. What's really happening is the promoter is unloading. He's pitching paper to the pooches.

"That's what happens. That's the psychology. It's always happening, it's always the same. The same type of thing does on with bigger stocks, too, not just penny stocks. It's always the same old story: Some guys have got control blocks of shares, and they're trying to sell stock. The name of the game is to sell stock. The big guys can always buy it back. But there are only certain periods when they can get a bunch of fish to sell to."

Those periods, of course, are when the market is hot. That's what a hot market is, by definition: a time when everybody wants to buy. That's when scores of companies decide to go public for the first time, or to issue more stock if they're already public; they know there are plenty of people out there wanting to buy. "Because I have a large clientele," says Pearlstein, "I'm almost my own Gallup poll. When I get clients calling me, telling me to buy, I know it's time to sell. When I get a whole bunch of clients telling me to sell, I know it's time to buy. It's ironic, but that's the way the world goes."

Even though these buyers or sellers are otherwise sensible widows and dentists and consultants, and even though they're not gathered together in some stadium or town square, they are subject to the same laws of crowd psychology that rule the average lynch mob. As the German poet Schiller once observed: "Anyone taken as an individual is tolerably sensible and reasonable; as a member of a crowd, he at once becomes a blockhead." A mob's consensus, once arrived at, is difficult to resist. Maurice Strong, now chairman of the Canada Development Investment Corporation, still remembers a buying panic in the 1950s, when he was a young analyst with Richardson Securities. "There was an actual lineup at the broker's office of people waiting to buy," he says. "I remember talking to one man at the end of the line who'd come to sell. By the time he got to the head of the line, he'd become a buyer too."

Everyone on Bay Street is aware of these realities, and many have read and disgested the two nineteenth-century classics of mob psychology: Gustave Le Bon's *Psychologie des Foules* (translated as *The Crowd*) and Charles Mackay's *Extraordinary Popular Delusions and the Madness of Crowds*. Le Bon, who concluded that a crowd of individuals behaves as unpredictably and erratically as a woman, is no longer fashionable. Mackay's vastly more entertaining work is a survey of mass delusions through-

31

out history, including witchhunts, the Crusades, alchemy, end-of-the-world cults and curious attitudes toward facial hair, including Peter the Great's tax on beards. But it is Mackay's chapters on two of history's most disastrous stock promotions, the South Sea Bubble and John Law's Mississippi scheme of 1719-20, and his account of the Dutch tulip-bulb mania of the 1630s, which have fascinated and instructed several generations of financial men.*

When tulips were introduced to Europe from Turkey around 1550, they quickly became a rich man's status symbol, a passion which was soon adopted by the middle classes. By 1636, tulip-mania was so well advanced that tulip exchanges had been established throughout Holland. If you've ever been tempted to invest a few thousand dollars in the stock market because everyone else seems to be making money, Mackay's account of what happened in Holland more than three centuries ago may be enough to save you from grievous loss:

> Symptoms of gambling now became, for the first time, apparent. The stock-jobbers, ever on the alert for a new speculation, dealt largely in tulips, making use of all the means they so well knew how to employ to cause fluctuations in prices. At first, as in all these gambling mania, confidence was at its height, and everybody gained. The tulip-jobbers speculated in the rise and fall of the tulip stocks, and made large profits by buying when prices fell, and selling out when they rose. Many individuals grew suddenly rich. A golden bait hung temptingly out before the people, and one after the other, they rushed to the tulip-marts, like flies around a honey-pot. Everyone imagined that the passion for tulips would last forever, and that the wealthy from every part of the world would send to Holland, and pay whatever price was asked of them. The riches of Europe would be concentrated on the shores of the Zuyder Zee, and poverty banished from the favoured clime of Holland. Nobles, citizens, farmers, mechanics, seamen, footmen, maid-servants, even chimney-sweeps and old clotheswomen, dabbled in

---

* Bernard Baruch, the legendary Wall Street speculator, once told an interviewer that Mackay's book had saved him millions of dollars. In a foreword to a 1932 reissue of *Extraordinary Popular Delusions*, Baruch wrote: "Without due recognition of crowd-thinking (which often seems crowd-madness) our theories of economics leave much to be desired. It is a force wholly impalpable – perhaps little amenable to analysis and less to guidance – and yet, knowledge of it is necessary to right judgments on passing events."

tulips. People of all grades converted their property into cash, and invested it in flowers. Houses and lands were offered for sale at ruinously low prices, or assigned in payment of bargains made at the tulip-mart. Foreigners became smitten with the same frenzy, and money poured into Holland from all directions. The prices of the necessaries of life rose again by degrees; houses and lands, horses and carriages, luxuries of every sort, rose in value with them, and for some months Holland seemed the very antechamber of Plutus.

The tulip market collapsed, naturally, and the effects were eerily reminiscent of the 1929 crash, or of what happened in Calgary after the oil boom collapsed in 1981-82:

Defaulters were announced day after day in all the towns of Holland. Hundreds who, a few months previously, had begun to doubt that there was such a thing as poverty in the land, suddenly found themselves the possessors of a few bulbs, which nobody would buy, even though they offered them at one-quarter of the sums they had paid for them. The cry of distress resounded everywhere, and each man accused his neighbour. The few who had contrived to enrich themselves hid their wealth from the knowledge of their fellow-citizens, and invested it in the English or other funds. Many who, for a brief season, had emerged from the humbler walks of life, were cast back into their original obscurity. Substantial merchants were reduced almost to beggary, and many a representative of a noble line saw the fortunes of his house ruined beyond redemption.

The tulip-bulb madness still slumbers in the heart of every would-be small investor, and it only takes a hot market to awaken it. Most stockbrokers know that much about the Little Guy. But that's about all they do know. Despite its professions of concern for his welfare, the truth is that the industry cannot afford to spend much time with the small investor. He generates small commissions, and commissions are what the industry lives on.

Until very recently, in fact, the industry hadn't troubled to find out much about who these small investors actually are. Most industries that make their living from the public, from department stores to swimwear manufacturers, routinely spend large sums to find out what their retail customers want. The securities industry, by and large, has never bothered. Survey firms such as Toronto's Brendan Wood, Tutsch and Partners are paid handsomely by various investment firms to conduct minutely detailed interviews of institutional customers, the people who buy 100,000 shares at a time on behalf of pension funds, or who spend millions of dollars in underwriting fees. But with the possible exception of Midland Doherty Ltd., which specializes in retail sales, most firms display a distinct lack of curiosity about who their small customers are, and what they might want. Pitfield Mackay Ross, for instance, was the first Canadian securities firm to advertise on television. But the firm's president, Ward Pitfield, when we questioned him, didn't know how many retail accounts his firm had, and didn't seem to regard the question as particularly relevant.

Virtually the only serious market-research study ever conducted was commissioned in 1983 by the Toronto Stock Exchange. Designed by a Toronto market-research firm called The Creative Research Group and conducted by Canadian Gallup Poll Ltd., the TSE's Canadian Share Ownership Survey queried about 1,200 adult Canadians about their attitudes to, and involvement in, the stock market.

Two Million Shareholders

The survey's most striking finding was that slightly more than two million Canadians own shares directly. (People who own shares through pension or mutual funds own their shares indirectly.) This represents about 11 per cent of the adult population. In the United States, according to the New York Stock Exchange, the corresponding figure is 22.8 per cent. Canadians, in other words, invest in the stock market only half as much as Americans do. In fact, the Canadian participation rate is even lower, since about 340,000 of those two million Canadians are shareholders in the B.C. Resources Investment Corp., popularly known as BRICK, a company created by the B.C. government, which gave free BRICK shares to every resident of the province.

According to the TSE study, nearly seven out of ten adult Canadians invest in *something*. Nearly half the respondents, for instance, own non-term insurance policies. Slightly more than one-third own Canada Savings Bonds. Some 20 per cent have invested part of their savings in the safest imaginable vehicle: term deposits or guaranteed investment certificates. Even more Canadians, some 26 per cent, invest in tangible assets such as gold coins or bullion, antiques or stamps. About 15 per cent are real-estate investors; that is, they own property in addition to their principal residences. But only 11 per cent own shares.

Their portfolios, on the average, are not large. Half the shareholders own less than $5,000 in stocks; about 23 per cent own less than $25,000. For two-thirds of the stockholders, shares constitute less than one-fifth of their total assets. Only 11 per cent of these shareholders had 40 per cent or more of their investments in stocks.

Canadian stockholders, as you might expect, tend to be older than the general population, but the survey also revealed a surprisingly high incidence of share ownership among younger people. About one-quarter of Canadian shareholders are 55 and older – but the same proportion is between 25 and 35. Nearly half of all shareholders live in Ontario; 18 per cent live in B.C., 16 per cent in Quebec and 13 per cent in Alberta. Only 6 per cent of Canadian shareholders live in Manitoba, Saskatchewan and the four Atlantic provinces. On a per-capita basis, B.C. is the most stock-market-conscious province, with a 31 per cent shareholding level (or 14 per cent if you exclude BRICK shareholders). Alberta comes next on a per-capita basis, Ontario third. Sixty-two per cent of shareholders are male, 38 per cent female.

Midland Doherty Limited, with 160,000 retail accounts, has also sampled 300 of its own customers and came up with figures that tend to support and supplement the TSE study. According to Paulette Filion, the firm's marketing specialist, the average Midland Doherty client is in his or her 40s, earns between $40,000 and $50,000 per year, has been playing the market for more than ten years, and tends to grow more conservative in making investment choices as he or she grows older and more experienced. In Ontario, where two-income families are especially common, about half the firm's clients are women. In Quebec, there is a surprising upsurge of share ownership among younger people. "In French Canada," says Filion, "people who get into the market tend to be university graduates. The older people still keep their money with the caisses populaires. If they buy stocks, it will be through the bank."

What must one make of these figures? Perhaps the most striking – and saddest – finding is that a large number of Canadians are either frightened of the stock market, or don't understand it. In the TSE study, some 22 per cent of the respondents who don't own shares said they didn't understand the market; another 23 per cent of non-shareholders were concerned by the risk.

Terrified of Risk

The picture that emerges from these studies is of a nation of financial milquetoasts. We save at twice the rate of Americans, and we invest in the stock market only half as much. Yet it can be demonstrated that the stock market, historically, is a relatively safe place to put at least some of your money; and that the returns for prudent investors are better than those available from bank accounts or insurance policies. In fact, the record of the past 20 years or so demonstrates that people who put their money in the bank actually lost some of it through the erosive effects of inflation; and people who used life-insurance as a savings vehicle lost even more. Are we truly so terrified of risk, so blindly obsessed by security, as these figures suggest?

"The banks have done a marvellous marketing job," says Paulette Filion of Midland Doherty. "They've been so effective that people believe them." How do Canadians view their banks? Says Filion, playing the role of a typical Canadian, as revealed by her surveys: "The banks are motherhood. Sure, they try to rip me off when I try to borrow money and all that and, yes, they make unreasonable profits – but I trust them. They're like my parents. I don't like everything my parents do, but I know they're there and I know it's safe."

The Presidential Theory

If small investors hope to earn better than bank interest in the stock market, they must think constantly in terms of its cycles. Almost everyone agrees that the market does indeed run in cycles. But, as you might expect, there is endless disagreement over *which* cycles are operative at any given moment, and at which stage.

Perhaps the most widely accepted cyclical theory is the Presidential Theory. Its leading Canadian proponent is technical analyst Ian McAvity, whose charts demonstrate that the market usually rises in the two years preceding a U.S. presidential election (it happened in 25 years out of 30 between 1924 and 1984) and usually falls in the two years following an election (it's happened 16 years out of 30 since 1924). There is a plausible reason to explain it: Incumbent U.S. administrations always try to stimulate the economy before an election by pumping up the money supply, facing the unfortunate consequences once – they hope – they've been re-elected. McAvity always gets a big hand when, as a star performer at investment seminars, he

projects his presidential charts on a screen, then turns trium-
phantly to the audience and says: "All you analysts can go
home now. What else do you need to know about the market?"

The Frontiers of Flakiness

Al Pearlstein's belief in a nine-year capital goods cycle, accompanied by shorter inventory cycles, also enjoys wide currency among analysts. From there on, out to the frontiers of
flakiness, there is less and less consensus on which cycles really
matter. Some chartists believe commodities and interest rates
rise and fall in cycles lasting about five and one-half years. Real-
estate cycles, according to Dr. Al Owen, editor of an Alabama-
based investor newsletter called *Newsletter Digest*, are supposed
to last precisely eighteen-and-one-third years, which means the
next housing boom is due to happen around the year 2,000.

Mechanical formulae like these may be comforting for some
investors. But in the end they're only paint-by-numbers con-
cepts, and they're inadequate substitutes for the Real Thing,
which is a rare sort of investment wisdom that is easier to
recognize than to describe. The real thing? Some people have
it, that's all. They weren't born with it. They earned it because
they know themselves, and because they love the market and
its fickle ways. "The only goddam thing I ever learned down
here," growled a 75-year-old sage who'd built a billion-dollar
empire, "was to trust my own instincts."

For the wisest, most experienced traders, the market is a
natural, elemental force. It is astonishing how often they choose
metaphors borrowed from the savage world to describe it. "The
market is a funny beast," they will tell you. A lifetime of trading
has taught them to think of the market as a single impersonal
entity, like the ocean. "It's *running* today," they say, on days
when the volume is up and the shouting and hand-waving on
the exchange floor have reached a new level of intensity.

And then there are the days and weeks and months when
nothing happens: when the market, after a prolonged plunge,
remains becalmed. It is amazing, at times like these, how often
images of death come welling up from the bottom of the mind
and surface into speech. The market is "dead in the water."
Individual investors have "blown their brains out." Once, during a down market, I spent a morning beside a stock salesman's
desk, listening to him commiserate on the telephone with various clients who'd "blown their brains out" on particular stocks.
For months he'd been guiding them upward through a rising

market. Now he spent his days explaining to the same clients that the tens of thousands of dollars they'd lost were not going to be recovered in the foreseeable future. The phone kept ringing and the salesmen kept dispensing reassurance: "Well, at the moment there's a good possibility of a summer rally . . . Well, you won't lose anything if you don't sell. They'll all turn around eventually . . . Sure, Sam, New York's down 13 points today, but it'll bottom out sooner or later . . ."

Salesmen call this process hand-holding. I asked the man how it felt, holding his clients' hands all day. He was silent for a moment, then said, almost to himself: "Working in a funeral parlour would be a terrible thing, wouldn't it? All those people crying all the time . . ."

The market isn't just numbers on a screen, you see. It's a mirror in which a society instantly glimpses its own collective perception of the future. The ingredients of that collective perception are more magical than rational. They can range from a Vancouver dentist's response to something he overheard that morning on an elevator to the measured calculation of a pension-fund manager who makes million-dollar investment decisions every week of his life. But underlying all these perceptions, regardless of the level of sophistication, is a common notion: The trader thinks he's spotted something that the market itself hasn't yet recognized. The dentist thinks he knows something the market hasn't heard yet. The fund manager, scanning his charts and reviewing the latest research reports he's received from importuning institutional salesmen, detects an anomaly which soon – but not yet – will be smoothed out by the market. Every trader is trying to outsmart every other trader.

Russ Morrison, one of Bay Street's shrewdest investment-fund managers, has toyed with this notion in a series of scholarly articles which appeared in *The Financial Analysts Journal*. "Two conditions are necessary for a worthwhile speculation," he writes. "First, one must have an idea of how others view the security in question. Second, one must disagree with their view." The fundamental trick, in other words, is to discover a consensus – and then to bet against it. The more people who agree on a proposition, the likelier it is that they're wrong. That's what impelled Joe Kennedy, the millionaire father of a future U.S. president, to dump all his stocks in 1929, when he heard the elevator boys talking knowledgably about the market. That's why most technical analysts carefully monitor the trading behavior of small investors and large institutions. They believe, and have been proved correct many times, that when too great a consensus develops, it's time to do precisely the opposite. "I'm a very simple man," says Stephen Jarislowsky, a Montreal investment counsellor whose annual income, it is rumored, can be measured in the millions. "When everybody wants to sell me stock, I buy it from them. When they want to buy, I sell."

The seasoned stock-market player inhabits a world of risk and illusion and the madness of crowds, and the experience often produces a peculiar, weary sort of wisdom. Some of the best stock-market players even remind you of sailors – or, more precisely yachtsmen. You see them milling around a trading post on the stock exchange floor, or watching the quotations on the electronic monitors in their offices; and they scan those ever-changing numbers the way a yachtsman measures with a glance the wind and waves and tide. There is a kind of crinkly, half-humourous quality to that glance – an unspoken acknowledgment that the market, like the sea, cannot be controlled or understood. It can only be ridden in the direction it's going.

4
The Floor Traders

There are plenty of jobs on Bay Street where success is won through contacts, charm, economic expertise or the ability to massage retail customers or underwriting clients. These jobs are usually held by people with undergraduate degrees or MBAs, or by people whose fathers knew George Drew. But floor traders inhabit a world of primitive purity: almost nothing else matters but their ability to trade shrewdly; and an exact record of how well or how badly they've done is tallied by their employers' computers at the end of every trading day. Their job, in effect, is to outguess and outsmart their fellow floor traders.

That's what gives the floor of any stock exchange its peculiar creative tension. Most floor traders are kids from the wrong side of the tracks who have accidentally stumbled into a job that pays more money than most of them ever dreamed existed. Street smarts, that visceral instinct for grabbing the slightest edge in any transaction, is not merely a desirable qualification for the job. With hundreds of transactions occurring every minute, street smarts are a condition of survival. The floor is a highly organized piranha tank, and those who flourish within its confines have already developed the appropriate jungle instincts. But they are oddly gentle fish. Although they routinely devour their fellows, they do so in a peculiarly co-operative and affectionate way.

It is an intense, enclosed world, and the rewards for survival within it can be very great. According to a salary survey commissioned by 31 member firms of the Toronto Stock Exchange, many floor traders routinely earn as much as airline pilots; and the best ones, in a good year, can earn more than the president of a large Canadian corporation. The survey showed, for instance, that the median income for 57 registered options traders was $52,100 in 1980, and that the highest-paid options trader that year earned $327,400. Registered equity traders, the people who make markets in the 1,350 stock issues listed on the TSE, earned a median income of about $53,000; the highest-paid man in this category earned $455,900 in 1980. I asked several floor traders about these figures. Their reaction was that they were probably understated. Most floor traders believe that in good years, a few of their colleagues carry home more than $1 million.

In recent years, two new elements have been introduced to the floor which threaten to change it beyond recognition: computers and women. But for the rest of the 1980s at least, the floor will remain overwhelmingly human and overwhelmingly male. It still revels in its status as the bloody arena of capitalism; and the floor traders are still its gladiators. They are a separate, special tribe, and the way they work has changed very little since the first stock exchanges emerged in Florence and Amsterdam more than three centuries ago.

Today, in places as diverse as Zurich, Tokyo, New York, Paris, Vancouver, Kuwait or Singapore, wherever in the world individuals are allowed to own productive assets, you will find organized stock exchanges. What's truly remarkable is how alike they all are; a roomful of grown men milling around like cattle in a large pen, continually waving their arms and shouting at one another. To the participants, it is an ordered choreography, a stylized warfare, with rules as clear-cut as those of Parliament or chess. But to the uninitiated outsider, it looks like chaos.

It is a process that must seem profoundly alien to anyone accustomed to centralized control: a *two-way* auction. At an auction of, say, antique furniture, it is only the would-be buyers who compete, bidding up the price to the seller's maximum advantage. But on the floor of any stock exchange, sellers compete as well as buyers. Would-be buyers try to pay as little as possible for a block of shares, would-be sellers compete to get the best price. The concept is so elegantly simple that it sometimes eludes people. Imagine, then, an antique action in which hundreds of potential purchasers are waiting in their seats in the usual manner, ready to bid. But they are not facing the traditional lone auctioneer, whose only function is to exhort those would-be buyers to pay more. Instead, the buyers are facing a crowd of *hundreds* of auctioneers, each willing to undercut the other by a fraction in order to make a sale. Now, imagine further that the role of buyer and seller can be instantly interchanged; the lady who bid for a Georgian settee five minutes ago is now shouting at the top of her voice, trying to flog an Art Deco wall sconce. Finally, imagine that all these buyers and sellers, instead of furniture, are trading pieces of paper representing part-ownership of a company, or (in the case of futures and options) are trading the right to acquire such ownership at a later date. Imagine all that, and you can understand precisely what is happening on any trading floor, anywhere.

41

Betting Against the Market

The floor is a metaphor, a pure and perfect expression of the market system in action. As such, it is an affront to the bureaucratic mind. No central authority governs the behavior of the prices established within its confines. They are forged instead in an arena where, at least in theory, each player is allotted powers that are precisely equal. Each player, moreover, is an instrument of the vast, mysterious world beyond the floor. Each order to buy or sell that he executes is an instantaneous expression of the world's hopes, fears and fantasies. The floor really is a barometer that continually monitors the emotional temperature of the culture

Theoretically, anyway. In practice, there are all kinds of fiddles and human machinations diluting the perfection of the theoretical model. Some exchanges permit more manipulative behavior than do others. But to a suprisingly large extent, the three major Canadian stock exchanges, in Toronto, Montreal and Vancouver, really do function as impartial two-way auctions. The efficiency of those markets can be roughly measured by the degree of "liquidity" – that is, by the smoothness of the price fluctuations, and the extent to which sellers can find buyers and vice-versa. Ideally, each trade should take place at a price very close to the one preceding it. On most exchanges, including the TSE, liquidity is promoted by allowing some traders (officially known in Toronto as "registered traders" and unofficially as "pros") to buy and sell stocks on behalf of their firms. In return for this privilege, they're obligated to "make a market" in specific stocks – that is, to buy when there are no other takers, or sell when no one else wants to sell, at least 70% of the time. This rule assures that outside investors will be able to sell their shares, even in a sharply declining market, at something close to the previous price. The traders, needless to say, are not being altruistic. They make far more money betting against the market trend than by betting with it.

Tracking the Market

Pro traders became part of the TSE's official structure in 1962, when the rules were rewritten to accommodate them. Traders had always bought and sold for their own and their firms' accounts, of course. But under the new rules, only specially designated traders could trade on behalf of their firms, and without paying commission. Non-pro traders are required to time-stamp their own personal orders as soon as they're received, to ensure that they're executed as swiftly as possible (although they can hang on to clients' orders as long as they want, hoping to execute a trade at a more favorable price). But pro traders are exempt from this time-stamping requirement. They can hang on to orders for hours on end, waiting for the most strategic moment to buy or sell.

In Toronto and Montreal there's an additional guarantee of liquidity: a file of orders to buy or sell stocks at prices just slightly above, or slightly below, the official bid and ask prices listed on the exchange board. On the TSE's new floor, the computer system arranges these competing bids and offerings in order of price and size, so that at any given moment there is always a "queue" of purchasers ready to buy for slightly less, and of sellers willing to part with their stock for slightly more, than the current trading price.

In Vancouver there is no queue of waiting buyers and sellers. As a result, VSE-listed stocks often plunge precipitously, because there is no mechanism in place to cushion their descent. Many owners of VSE-listed stocks have had the rude experience of trying to sell a stock when it was trading at, say, $5.75 and later discovering that the trade wasn't completed until the price had dropped to $4.25. "Vancouver? Oh, God, it's a zoo," says George Chisholm, who's been a TSE floor trader since the 1940s. "Just awful! Just dreadful! It used to be so bad in Vancouver that you couldn't guarantee that a client's order will be filled. There was no protection. But the system's now improved somewhat."

How much of an edge do pro traders have over ordinary customers? Does their proximity give the pro traders an unfair advantage? Do the activities of the pros really add to the market's liquidity? And if so, at what cost to the investing public?

The answers are hard to come by. No one knows what pro trading costs the Canadian public, because neither the TSE nor the Ontario Securities Commission keeps track of the profits earned by pro traders as a group. The question was last studied in 1965, as part of a royal commission enquiry into the Windfall Oil and Mines trading scandal. The commission's conclusion was that pro traders' profits were not excessive. Or, as Don Bainbridge of Daly-Gordon Securities puts it: "We earn a hell of a lot less than it would cost the public, in terms of an inefficient market, if we weren't there."

Does access to the "off-market" file give the TSE's pros an edge in trying to outguess the market? Perhaps not, since instant access to the same file is available to anyone with an electronic quote monitor. But simply being on the floor day after day, tracking the market minute by minute, still constitutes a formidable advantage. Floor traders, by definition, are closer to the market than anyone else, so their chances of making profitable trades are unquestionably better than those of, amateur investors. Besides, even pro traders aren't infallible. The salary statistics quoted earlier look fairly impressive; but it must be remembered that 1980 was an extraordinarily good year in the market. In 1978, 1979 or 1981, most traders probably earned substantially less. The survey's finding that half the pro traders earned less than $53,000, even in a terrific year like 1980, may suggest that, if anything, the public is buying its liquidity fairly cheaply.

Intricacies like these are hard to imagine as you gaze out over the TSE's new trading floor, all 30,000 square feet of it. The floor is jammed with traders and lined with small booths, in which harassed-looking young people scribble on bits of paper and bark into one of the 1,800 telephones. Their job is to take down orders that are phoned in from the firm's office, and pass them to the traders on the floor. In the old exchange building, traders were summoned by shouts and hand signals. Now they carry pocket-sized pagers which the phone clerks use to alert the traders when they've got an order. If the phone from the brokerage office rings twice without being answered, the call is automatically routed through to the pager in the floor trader's pocket – which, to cut down on the floor's decibel level, *vibrates* instead of beeps. The pagers even have tiny, 10-digit display screens like a pocket calculator's, so that coded orders to buy or sell specific stocks can be relayed automatically. The TSE must have more electronics per square foot of floor space than anywhere else on earth, outside of a NASA facility or an American political convention. Everywhere you look there are television-style computer terminals, more than 500 of them. There are banks of them on the eight huge electronic trading posts, five for stocks and three for options, each roughly the size and shape of a small tugboat. There are more screens surrounding the futures pits – two small declivities, the size of childrens' wading pools, into which the futures traders step when they want to consummate a trade. There are other screens at the trading posts which display the status of the "off-market" buy and sell orders on any stock. To read them, the trader simply touches the screen.

Finally, in a special area along the northwest corner, there are further banks of terminals which are used for computer-assisted trading (known by its acronym CATS), a system which threatens to make all those shouting men in their colored blazers about as relevant as blacksmiths. The CATS terminals don't even need to be adjacent to the trading floor; the only reason they're there is as a courtesy to the smaller brokerage firms, which don't have CATS terminals in their offices. But most of the larger firms do, which means that CATS traders sitting in offices at opposite ends of Bay Street can punch bids and offers into their terminals, and have them matched and recorded electronically, without the intervention of human hand or voice. More than 800 of the TSE's 1,350 listed issues are traded this way. Some people in the securities business think all stocks could be traded by CATS. Who needs people running around shouting at one another on the floor? "The future of the stock market," says Andy Kniewasser, a dedicated technocrat who is president of the Investment Dealers Association of Canada, "is a bunch of people with MBAs wearing suits and sitting at computer terminals in nice, clean rooms. You don't need all those crowds, all that cigar smoke."

King of the Jungle

Don Bainbridge's eyes narrow when he hears that kind of talk. He starts looking mean and contemptuous, like the leader of a street gang whose turf is being challenged by a troop of boy scouts. The words come out like bullets: "I believe I have more trading knowledge than Andy Kniewasser – indeed, as much as anyone on Bay Street. And I'm telling you, you cannot trade exclusively with machines, because you can't negotiate. You can't go with the ebb and flow of the market."

Bainbridge is King of the Jungle and knows it; the smartest, shrewdest, richest, toughest, best-respected floor trader on the largest stock exchange in the country. As such, he represents both the past and future of the floor. He's old enough to have witnessed the fabled wickedness of the 1950s. And he was instrumental, in the early 1980s, in persuading the TSE's governors to build a new trading floor three times the size of the old one – a resounding affirmation, one would think, of the eyeball-to-eyeball theory of trading.

Bainbridge is president of Daly-Gordon Securities, the most feared firm in the business. A high school dropout, he started in 1946 as a clerk in the stock transfer department at Montreal Trust, where ancient messengers shuffled in and out all day, picking up and delivering stock certificates. Within a few months, he was acting as unofficial bookie for every messenger on the

Street. In the 1947 World Series between the Dodgers and the Yankees, he made more than $500 taking their bets. When he was 18 he left Montreal Trust and became a messenger and mail boy for R.A. Daly, then a small bond house with about 20 employees. Then, at 19, he won $1,500 "in a poker game in a hotel room with a bunch of Greeks," and decided to strike out in business on his own. He spent a year of 18-hour days as part-owner of an electrical contracting business. At the end of the year he discovered that the firm owed its suppliers $10,000 and was owed $11,000 by other people. Bainbridge was determined never to be poor again; and he already knew of a better way to make a living. In November 1950, he returned to Daly as a phone clerk on the TSE floor. His principal duty was to fetch orange juice every morning for one of the firm's floor traders and, as soon as the liquor store opened at 10 a.m., to rush out and fetch a fresh bottle of vodka. On July 23, 1951 – Bainbridge remembers the date because it was the day after his twenty-first birthday – he stepped onto the floor as a trader for the first time. Since then, in the ensuing 30-odd years, he's missed the opening siren no more than two or three times. The floor is his life, and all he needs to know of life.

Bainbridge spends most of his day standing near Post Six on the TSE's vast trading floor, where the stocks in which he specializes, including Inco, Cominco and Falconbridge, are traded. His firm has 20 people on the floor – 13 pro traders, three equity traders, two options traders and two clerks – and Bainbridge, standing at his post watching the numbers, orchestrates their efforts with glances, imperceptible nods and whispered conversations, like a masterful head waiter. Every few minutes or so he makes a trade of his own, which usually nets him some small sum – $200 or $500, say. Over the course of a year it all adds up.

"If any pro trader wished they had anyone's talents, it would be Don Bainbridge's," says an admiring colleague. "He's all business. If you can get 10 seconds of his attention during the course of a day you're doing very well. He'll walk over to one of his young men, and say, 'Jesus, you've got 20,000 CP – what are you going to do? Then another of his guys will come over to Don's post and tell him something about options – he keeps track of what everyone's doing, plus his own positions, plus he's got his arbitrage, plus he's got his own staff. He's got so much going at all times – plus his family plus his wife, plus everything. The fact that he manages it all so successfully is the mark of amazing abilities."

"When I first came to the floor," says Bainbridge, "trading

was regarded as a cost for the firm. I saw it as a profit centre." Soon after he became a trader he talked his boss, R.A. Daly, into giving him $2,500 to play with. By exploiting small, minute-to-minute trading opportunities, he started making money for the firm and for himself. In those days, says Bainbridge, "they literally had no goddam rules. You could do whatever you wanted on the floor." Traders routinely made their own trades first, and *then* executed their clients' buy orders at higher prices – a practice which is strictly forbidden on today's TSE. They also could, and did, manipulate the market in a stock, churning up volume to create the illusion of activity. Bainbridge remembers with awe one master he observed in his youth: "The guy was like a goddam artist. He could *paint* that tape. He'd have a handful of order tickets in his hand, and he'd use them to make the stock do whatever he wanted. Unbelievable!"

Other floor traders look up to Bainbridge because he was just another kid off the streets, like most of them, and ended up owning the firm that hired him. He and George Chisholm, of Hector M. Chisholm & Co. Ltd., are the only TSE floor traders who are also presidents of their own firms. But Chisholm is not a rags-to-riches exemplar, because he inherited the firm from his father. Bainbridge and several colleagues were given a chance to buy the firm in 1960 by R.A. Daly, who was planning to retire. Until Daly merged with Gordon Securities in 1983, Bainbridge owned 31 per cent of the company, which had grown from about 20 employees in 1960 to about 150 in 1983.

Even in a slow year, Bainbridge's trading skills would be enough to assure him a six-figure income. But at Daly he was also entitled to 31 per cent of the firm's net profits. In a good year, that added up to a nice, round sum. Once, at a party, a very prosperous trader said to Bainbridge: "C'mon, Bainie – how much did you make last year? A million? I did, you know!" Bainbridge looked at him, sipped his drink and asked: "Before or after tax?" The consensus is that, since the merger with Gordon, he's probably doing even better.

Bainbridge has probably done more than any other trader to establish professional standards for his craft. He's been a dominant member for years of the TSE's Floor Procedures Committee, and of the committee which planned the introduction to the floor of computer-assisted trading. He's also served on the TSE's Board of Governors, where he acted as a spokesman for the floor traders. As far back as 1962, he helped draft the rules which officially established pro trading on the TSE, and he's had a major say in most of the reforms affecting the floor ever since.

Bainbridge has done all this, moreover, without a shred of higher education – an ornament which, for a floor trader, can be a serious impediment. "It's one of the few businesses where a formal education isn't really an advantage," says Carl Christie, a pro trader for Davidson Partners Limited who's been on the floor since 1960. "I had a friend who was a commerce and finance graduate of the University of Toronto, a brilliant young man, who found himself trading unlisted stocks in one of the brokerage houses. He was one of those methodical types and, as a result, when quick decisions were required, especially on the penny stocks, he wanted to stop and analyze them. He wasn't that successful. He finally went into sales, where he could analyze things and do a little research, and now he's doing fine."

Even a trader as established as George Chisholm recognizes the dangers of a university education. Chisholm is one of the very few members of a FOOF (Fine Old Ontario Family) to be found on the floor. He is a sociological anomaly. Seeing him on the floor, with his understated, English-tailored suits, his military moustache and his dignified bearing, is like encountering Vincent Massey at a bowling banquet. But Chisholm is perpetuating a Bay Street tradition. As a teenager, his grandfather went to work for the Bay Street Oslers in the 1890s. His father, Hector M. Chisholm, also skipped university to take a job on Bay Street in 1919. His duties included polishing the brass plate which read "F.H. Deacon & Co." at the firm's entrance. Hector Chisholm bought a seat on the old Standard Mining Exchange in 1925, traded on the floor until 1932, made a lot of money and, in the process, gave his son the sort of education that isn't available at university. In the 1930s, the father used to trade arbitrage between London and Toronto – that is, exploit the small price differences which sometimes exist momentarily between the same stock trading on two different exchanges. One of George Chisholm's earliest educational experiences was listening to his father, who kept a telephone under his bed, lying there at four in the morning, buying and selling stocks via a long-distance connection to London. One of the maxims his father taught him was: "Bulls make money and bears make money, but pigs never make money."

With a background like that, university would have been redundant for George Chisholm. He joined his father's firm as soon as he got out of the Royal Canadian Air Force in 1946. "You're either a trader or you aren't," he says. "You watch some of the kids on the floor, you can pretty well tell within a week the ones who are going to be good and the ones who won't make it. There's a rhythm to trading. If you don't have it, you can't be trained. Some of the best traders down here have a grade-eight education."

A lot of the time, in fact, many traders act as if they were still in grade school. Like hockey referees, psychiatrists and air traffic controllers, they face long periods of intense concentration, and the penalties for inattention can be costly. On January 4, 1983, for instance, Carl Christie lost $52,000 in four hours of trading, because he shorted 30,000 shares of Sherritt-Gordon Mines just as the stock was beginning to climb. "It's just one of those things," he explains. "You have to be attentive 60 minutes an hour for six hours, and I wasn't. I let my guard down." (He made it all back and then some by the end of the month, however.)

The tension takes its toll on minds and bodies. Alcoholism is a fairly routine occupational hazard. Stress is a constant. Says Don Walker, a veteran floor trader: "I get severe chest pains and they get so bad I end up in hospital. They keep me in because they think it's my heart, but it isn't my heart. They tell me it's anxiety. This has happened every three years or so for the past nine years. I guess it's just the body's way of saying, 'That's enough, slow down.' So now I take lots of holidays and try not to get too uptight. And I don't trade stocks any more. I trade options. I find it less frantic, because there's no yelling."

One trader told me about a colleague who, troubled by sleeplessness and a nameless anxiety, consulted a psychiatrist. At the initial session, the therapist listened to the man's complaints for half an hour, then asked him what he did for a living. "I'm a floor trader at the Toronto Stock Exchange," said the patient. The psychiatrist angrily summoned his receptionist and told her, "Dammit, I *told* you not to send me any more floor traders. I've had three of them as patients, and there's nothing you can do for these guys."

It's not surprising that the traders relieve the tension of their jobs with an unending series of parties and pranks. What they do for fun is as revealing as what they do for money, and a lot of the fun happens on the floor itself. The mere appearance of a buxom woman in the visitors' gallery has more than once triggered pandemonium on the floor. A well-known stripper named Chesty Morgan, for instance, once made an appearance in the visitors' gallery as a publicity stunt. Even though she was fully clothed, the very sight of her was enough to evoke a huge roar from the crowd below. But when, cooing and writhing, she pressed her melon-sized breasts* against the window of the gallery, the baying and hooting from the floor reached a crescendo that has never been exceeded, not even on the biggest trading day in TSE history, September 17, 1982, when nearly 20 million shares – worth $727,516,833 – changed hands. Lesser personalities have been known to evoke similar responses. Whenever Raoul Engel**, the former business reporter for Global Television Network, appeared in the gallery with a film crew, the traders would set up an unearthly baying:

RAOUOOOOOOOOOOOOOOOOL!
RAOUOOOOOOOOOOOOOOOOL!
RAOUOOOOOOOOOOOOOOOOL!

Marc Lalonde, then federal Minister of Energy, was greeted in the gallery one morning by the floor traders yelling in unison: "Jump! Jump! Jump!" When Joe Granville, the famous market analyst and proprietor of the *Granville Letter*, was being interviewed by a film crew from the gallery, a knot of floor traders tried to distract him by throwing balls of paper and – in a gesture made famous by Pierre Elliott Trudeau – tugging their ties upwards above their heads, their faces hideously contorted, miming men being hanged.

It's the same on every North American exchange. "People in the observation booth liken this place to the Stanley Park Zoo," says one experienced floor trader in Vancouver. "There are paper airplanes flying around and people goosing each other, and the spectators can't understand why there's such an aura of irresponsibility in a place that's dealing with millions of dollars of the public's money. Well, it's a release. Should we be screaming and crying and breaking down on the floor? Or is laughing and joking and sliding down banisters a better way?"

In search of better ways to avoid nervous collapse, the pranksters seem to get more inventive every year. Carl Christie, the TSE's self-appointed emcee and court jester, has been dreaming up practical jokes to enliven the market's quiet periods for most of his trading career. He started small: turning a trader's new hat into an aquarium by filling it with goldfish, or swiping a colleague's new shoe and converting it into a flower-pot. Later, undaunted by a $200 fine that the floor gov-

---

* In her publicity material, Miss Morgan lists her measurements – in inches, not centimetres – as 73-26-36.

** Engel graduated from covering the stock market to playing it. In 1982 he inherited several million dollars, quit the TV business and moved to the Bahamas, where he spends his mornings talking long-distance to his brokers and his afternoons on his yacht.

ernors levied after an incident involving two strawberry custards, he graduated to organizing parades around the floor, complete with funny hats, penny whistles and a bass drum. Christie's dream is to make Don Bainbridge lose his legendary cool. He used to organize a line of traders to march past Bainbridge's post, stomping their feet in unison as hard as they could. Bainbridge, always in deep concentration, seldom even noticed. Desperate, Christie later scrounged a motorized bicycle and crash helmet, brought the moped up the freight elevator to the trading floor and circled around Bainbridge's post, racing the moped's motor and beeping its little horn. Bainbridge was reading a newspaper at the time, and didn't even bother to look up.

Traditions endure on the floor, and old traders don't always fade away. One trader, for years after his retirement, used to return to the old TSE floor several days a week, take up a position in a seat beside a trading post, and doze all day. Another trader, Harry Abbey, started as a phone clerk on the old Standard Stock and Mining Exchange in 1928, just before The Crash; fifty-four years later, at the age of 81, he was still working full-time for Walywyn Inc. as a floor trader. "It keeps my mind more active," he explains, "than if I stayed home gardening." Abbey was there when they closed down the Standard exchange in 1934. To mark the occasion, the traders staged a huge party on the floor. "Someone let in some pigeons, and they fluttered around inside the big dome over the floor. Then one of the traders went next door to a gun shop and got a shotgun and shot the pigeons. You can't imagine the noise! A couple of members practically fainted."

A Very High Pressure Job

You are entitled to conclude, on the basis of the foregoing evidence, that floor traders are not the sort of fellows who sit around in fern bars, eating quiche. It's a miracle that women survive there, but they do. "It's a very high-pressure job," says one female CATS trader, "and to have the added pressure of being female makes it much harder." One woman trader – she's no longer on the floor – was presented by her male colleagues with a box of roses with a double-ended dildo packed inside. Other women on the floor are patted, goosed, leered at, patronized and, after a rough period of initiation, occasionally respected. "It helps to dress very dowdy when you're down there," says my informant. "Eventually I managed to gain some

51

respect – although, for most of those guys, you could be the Queen Mother and they wouldn't care. But at least I established that I wasn't going to put up with any of their bullshit. I wasn't going to run off the floor crying, or anything like that. At the beginning, they'd really put you through the wringer. One man had me completely mortified. He kept asking me if I was kinky and things like that. I'd tell him, 'If you're a pervert, why don't you go home and be a pervert by yourself?' Down there on the floor they're like a bunch of little boys let loose. They're in their own little world – and they regulate their own little world. So it doesn't matter what they do."

In 1984 there were 9 women floor traders in Toronto, 10 in Montreal and 2 in Vancouver. Only a few years earlier there were none in any of the cities. By the end of the decade there could be enough women traders to undermine the macho swagger that is the very stuff and substance of the floor's mystique. Many of these women traders, one suspects, will not be engaged in belly-to-belly confrontations in the milling throngs beside the trading posts. Instead of shouting all day until they're hoarse, they'll be sitting at computer terminals in broker's offices, insulated from the floor's sweat and profanity – and trading just as savagely as their floor-bound counterparts.

Among Friends

That's why there was a certain elegiac quality to the "roast" that was held in honor of Don Bainbridge on April 18, 1983. The ostensible purpose of the $100-a-plate banquet at Toronto's Royal York Hotel was to raise money for Carl Christie's favorite charity, St. Aidan's Boys' Club. But the real purpose was to have a lot of laughs, preferably at Don Bainbridge's expense, and to affirm the male bonds that are so much a part of the floor's social dynamic. Under the tough-guy code which floor traders observe, men are not allowed publicly to express affection or regard for one another – except in the form of outrageous insults. You could tell, from the ferociousness of the insults, how highly his colleagues regard Don Bainbridge.

First Carl Christie formally presented him with a baseball cap emblazoned with the word, "shithead" and, on its peak, an alarmingly realistic mound of plastic dog-poop. That, along with the matchbooks at every place-setting that read "Bullshit – Don Bainbridge," more or less set the tone for the evening. As a tribute to Bainbridge's legendary wealth, he was presented with a leather wallet the size of a tabloid newspaper. "We knew it was Bainie's," said Christie, "because inside it we found the foreclosure papers on three orphanages." Then came the tributes, in the form of one-liners which could have been coined by Don Rickles: "Don bought a pocket calculator because he couldn't count to 21 unless he was naked." "When Don was born, his mother looked at the afterbirth and said, 'Thank God – twins!' " "I knew Don $4 million and four wives ago." Christie, the emcee, even brought in an actress who faced the roomful of men from the podium and announced that she was Bainbridge's oh-so-friendly secretary. "Aren't you awfully young to be secretary of such a big firm?" asked Christie. "Well, there's nothing *big* and *firm* about Bainie," the darling girl replied. "In fact, it's so cute I call it Odd Lot." Roars from the floor.

There was a marvellous, unrehearsed moment when Bainbridge finally rose to speak. The entire roomful of several hundred well-wishers spontaneously rose with him – and started heading out the door. But they returned to their seats to hear Bainbridge hurl insults at everyone who'd insulted him. "Carl, I keep telling you," Bainbridge shouted in conclusion, "the TSE is not a betting emporium. It's a legitimate vehicle for investment and liquidity." Puffing on after-dinner cigars, the crowd roared and applauded, as if that were the funniest sally of all. Don Bainbridge, high-school dropout, former mail clerk, president of the toughest firm on the street, King of the Floor, was among friends.

5
The
Toronto Stock
Exchange

When the Toronto Stock Exchange proudly unveiled its new building on March 20, 1937, the 76-foot frieze by Charles Comfort over the entrance created its own instant folklore. Using a heroic style somewhere between Early Stalinist and Late Art Deco, Comfort depicted a parade-like grouping of economic arche-types: sturdy miners, oaken-hearted construction workers, ear-nest lumberjacks and, near the right end of this lineup, a figure in top hat and tails, obviously intended to represent a banker or broker. This person, it was widely noted when the frieze was unveiled, seemed to have his hand firmly implanted in the neighboring worker's pocket.

But the jokes about that light-fingered broker were the only negative note in the obsequies surrounding the TSE's move to its latest and grandest home. The country was still stumbling through the depths of the worst depression in its history. Job-less men in cloth caps clung like hungry insects to the freight trains that rolled across a nation whose very landscape, in the barrens of the prairie dust bowl, seemed to reflect the desper-ation of the times. But on Bay Street, the fresh granite and Indiana limestone of the TSE's $750,000 monument stood out like a beacon in a rainstorm. Inside, all was progress and breath-less modernity. It was Canada's first completely air-conditioned building. The 8,000-square-foot trading floor had indirect light-ing, a 40-foot ceiling, nine trading posts and the latest in elec-tronic marvels: an automatic stock quotation system which posted the bid and ask prices of each stock on the face of the six-sided trading posts, and allowed brokers to get these prices simply by dialing the stock's numerical symbol (International Nickel, for instance, was 111) on special telephones installed in their offices. From Comfort's eight heroic murals overlooking the trading floor to the Georgian-style boardroom, panelled in white

54

oak, the entire building was designed as a symbolic assertion of Toronto's growing power as a financial centre.

In any developing country there tends to be a dichotomy between New Money and Old Money, between the strivers and the established, between the sources of current prosperity and the new industries and technologies that are striving to displace them. That division has always been reflected in the operation, and the premises, of the country's stock exchanges.

The stocks of established companies, by and large, tend to be traded by established people. The stocks of companies which are little more than a gleam in the eye of their promoters tended to be traded by – well, by the disestablished. Throughout the history of Canada's capital markets, you continually encounter this creative tension between the old and new. The trading of blue-chip stocks and bonds, an eminently respectable activity, is what gives the market its momentum and continuity. But it is the trading of the stocks of younger, less established companies which gives the market its dominant flavor and generates most of the excitement. The history of Canada's stock markets consists of successive waves of speculative excitement, each wave generated by some external economic development, such as the discovery of a new mining camp or the introduction of some new technology. But concurrent with those speculative waves, the quiet turnover in established stocks continues, year in and year out.

New Money, Old Money

In 1937, Toronto represented New Money and Montreal's St. James Street was Old Money personified. Since the beginning of the fur trade, Montreal had been Canada's financial centre as well as its largest city. Until 1914, most of the money to finance Canada's development had come into Montreal from British investors, in the form of bonds and debentures – money from abroad, loaned for 20- , 30- and even 50-year terms at the prevailing interest rates of five or six per cent. The road and sewer systems of frontier cities, the electric street railways that replaced horse-drawn omnibuses, the railroads that spanned the continent, the pulp and paper mills and hydro-electric developments dotting the forest wilderness, the entire infrastructure of a modern industrial state – most of these projects were conceived and financed through Montreal. The city's financial power was still symbolized, in 1937, by the towering presence of Sir Herbert Samuel Holt, the hard-boiled, hot-tempered financier (he'd been known to throw reporters bodily down stairs) who had helped put together the Canadian Pacific Railway, had financed dozens of utilities across the country and, at 81, still dominated the Canadian financial landscape as chairman of the Royal Bank of Canada. In 1928, he was said to exercise authority over $3 billion worth of assets, which was about 10 times the amount of currency then in circulation.

In 1937, Montreal's stock exchange reflected the established character of the proud commercial barons who lived in the mansions of Westmount and Redpath Crescent. It had received its first listing fee in 1870 (the members spent the funds on champagne), was incorporated in 1874, and was still the largest stock exchange in the country, with most of its trading in the shares of large, established companies such as the CPR and the banks.

The TSE, by contrast, was the embodiment of New Money – with all the aggressiveness, ostentation, uncertainty and chicanery that the term implies. For more than a century, from the founding of the city's first, short-lived stock exchange to 1964, when the latest in a long series of stock scandals forced a crackdown by regulatory authorities, much of Toronto's financial history had been sleazy in the extreme.

That first exchange was launched in 1854 (after an initial meeting to organize a brokers' association on July 26, 1852) by a group of Toronto merchants who wanted a local centre for mercantile transactions, mainly for the shipping and grain trades. It opened for business in 1856 in a new building at Wellington and Berczy Streets, on land swapped for shares by Charles Berczy, Toronto's postmaster. The building, designed by architect Charles Grand, was as imposing as the hopes of its founders: three stories, 31 offices, each with its own private wash basin, a public reading room, a "refreshment saloon," a barber shop in the basement and a trading hall in the oval-shaped central rotunda, beneath a graceful dome. But the meetings of the exchange, the forerunner of today's daily trading sessions, were not well attended. The brokers mainly traded farm commodities and cattle – and, on occasion, handled a few stocks. The exchange venture eventually failed and the building was sold to the Imperial Bank of Canada.

The exchange was reorganized in 1861 as a casual assemblage of brokers who staged sporadic trading sessions in a variety of locations. The stirrings of Canada's infant mining industry prompted the establishment in 1867 of another, entirely separate exchange, the Toronto Stock and Mining Exchange. By

1869, after the collapse of the gold boom and the failure of three banks, both exchanges were defunct.

But the game began again in the 1870s, with a new boom in the shares of banks and building societies, and the introduction of margin trading. In 1871, 14 members of the Toronto Stock Exchange Association reactivated the dormant exchange by chipping in $250 each for membership fees. In 1878 the revived organization received a provincial charter and, by the end of the decade, was holding regular trading sessions and issuing official price quotations. In 1881, a boom year in which some brokers paid as much as $4,000 for a seat on the exchange, the TSE leased permanent quarters and hired its first full-time employee, one Lyndhurst Ogden. That was the year the stock ticker was introduced to Toronto. For the first time, Toronto brokers could receive up-to-the-minute quotations from New York. Five years later, with the completion of the first transatlantic cable, European investors began trading Canadian stocks.

Or rather, they thought they were. The 1890s were the heyday of "bucket shops," brokerage houses which accepted money from clients to buy shares or commodities – and then didn't buy them. If the price of the stock or commodity the client *thought* he'd bought went up, the client would receive his profit when he sold. But if the stock or commodity went down, the client was out of luck. If the broker didn't skip town, you could sue him. But even if you succeeded in getting a judgment against him, you probably couldn't collect, because there would be no assets left to seize.

The shares of banks, mortgage companies and building societies were the staples of the exchange in its early years, because land and real estate were still the prime forms of wealth. In 1865, for instance, the listings in Toronto were for eight banks, two gas companies, three insurance companies, three building societies, plus listings for government and county debentures. But by the turn of the century the transition from an agrarian to an industrial economy was beginning to be reflected in the stock markets. In 1895, there were 10 "miscellaneous" listings on the TSE – street railways, iron and steel foundries and the like. By 1901 there were 36 of these industrial listings.

The Ground Breeds Millionaires

The other source of new wealth was mining. The completion of the CPR in 1885 had opened the resources of the west to the markets of the east, and in the 1890s it sparked a brief mining boom centred around claims in Rossland, B.C. Like most such booms, it consisted of a few promising properties surrounded by a blizzard of worthless paper, and quickly fizzled. Then, one day in the summer of 1903, two laborers named Ernest Darragh and James McKinley were sent into the bush near Cobalt Lake, 700 miles north of Toronto, to chop down trees for railroad ties for the Temiskaming and Northern Ontario Railway. They noticed some strangely colored rocks on the beach. "We immediately got down to business, picking up the loose pieces of rock," McKinley later recalled. "In washing some of the gravel in the lake, there were flakes or leaves of a bright metal which we could bend. I immediately thought of the advice of the old forty-niner and placed a piece between my teeth, and I succeeded in marking it very easily." The ore they'd discovered was later assayed at four thousand ounces of silver to the ton. That was the beginning of a mining boom which, in the excitement it created and the wealth it generated, rivalled the Klondike gold rush of 1897.

It was a peculiarly democratic boom, since the ore was so rich, and so close to the surface, that any man with a strong back, a pick and shovel and a wheelbarrow could plausibly dream of getting rich. Treasure-seekers flocked by the thousands to the area. The hills around Cobalt Lake became crisscrossed with the trenches they dug. By 1906, established mining firms were blasting away the topsoil with high-pressure jets of water to expose the ore beneath. Later, Cobalt and Kerr Lakes themselves were drained to get at the ore on the bottom. An English financier named R.J. Barrett visited the area in 1906 and reported, perhaps for the benefit of prospective investors back home: "At Cobalt it seems almost impossible to exaggerate; the riches were so palpably there. Any urchin in the street could unerringly take the stranger to half a dozen mines and point to wonders which fairly beggar description." Then came hydro-electric projects, concentrators, refineries and several mines which produced silver for generations. "Here the ground breeds millionaires," wrote the *Cobalt Nugget* in 1909. "One bumps into them everywhere. Yet only a year or two ago many of them were but laborers . . . the region has been turning out the millionaires almost as fast as the nuggets." As the mines probed deeper and deeper underground, the region turned out widows even faster. In 1913, the Ontario Bureau of Mines boasted that *only* one miner, on the average, was killed to produce each $170,000 of ore.

Most of the fortunes, of course, were made – and lost – on Bay Street. The Toronto and Montreal exchanges disdained most mining stocks (only two were listed on the TSE in 1898), but that didn't prevent promoters by the score from peddling dreams in the form of stock certificates. The Cobalt boom generated immense excitement, and it wasn't restricted to Canada; at one point, mounted policemen were called out on Wall Street to control the crowds of speculators. In Toronto, two rival mining exchanges had been formed in the 1890s in the wake of the Rossland and Klondike booms; they merged in 1899 to become the Standard Stock and Mining Exchange.

The Cobalt boom and the discoveries that followed it near the future cities of Timmins, Sudbury and Kirkland Lake made the SSME the most important mining exchange in the world – and, quite possibly, the most crooked. Junior mining issues, then as now, reflected more hope than reality. Promoters formed hundreds of companies by buying mining claims – often quite dubious ones – from prospectors, then issuing shares in these companies by the millions. Through rumor, planted publicity and shameless market manipulation, they tried to drive up the price of their stocks. Once they'd succeeded, they would sell – leaving the promoter with a fortune and the speculators with large quantities of engraved wallpaper. "It is high time," one newspaper editorialized at the height of the Rossland boom, "that some warning was given to investors of the futility of supplying money to dig holes in the ground in the hope that Canada may at some time produce a few odd ounces of precious metals. In this paper we decry the use of inveigling home and foreign money for this fallacy."

It wasn't all blue sky, however. The mines were too rich for that. Of the 36 issues listed on the SSME during the Cobalt boom, 24 paid dividends totalling $6 million in a single year. And while the Cobalt boom was still soaring, the excitement was sustained by gold discoveries in the Porcupine area in 1909, which created the Hollinger, Dome and McIntyre Mines, and by further discoveries near Kirkland Lake, which created the Lake Shore, Wright-Hargreaves and Sylvanite Mines.

When war was declared in 1914, the exchanges shut down until the spring of 1915. When they reopened, there was nothing much to do – other than sell war bonds – for those brokers who hadn't enlisted. But this turned out to be a better business than anyone in the financial community had expected. In 1917 alone, patriotic Canadians invested $546,136,300 in Victory Loans, plus another $170 million in various war bond issues. Most of the bond buyers had never before in their lives bought a security. One little old lady, it was said, turned up at the bank demanding to *pay* the interest on her Victory Bond.

The New Prosperity

The million-plus Canadians who bought war bonds proved to be an attentive audience for the flashy vaudeville show that the world's stock markets staged in the late 1920s. It was a period of giddy, almost infantile speculation, but underlying it was the bedrock of solid economic growth. The decade began with a burst of inflation and overheated prosperity, followed in 1921 by an abrupt bust. Then came recovery and renewed growth as the roller-coaster of speculation gained speed. It was an easy time to be an optimist, because the evidence of mass prosperity was everywhere: Pierce-Arrows and Stutzes for the wealthy, modest Fords and Chevs for everyone else; wind-up phonographs in middle-class living rooms; huge wooden radio sets; amazing new electrical appliances that toasted bread, washed clothes, cleaned carpets, even ironed shirts. The cities themselves seemed to manifest the thrusting prowess of this new industrial age: the Bank of Commerce Tower on Toronto's King Street, at 784 feet, four and one-half inches, the tallest building in the British Empire; the Empire's largest hotel, Toronto's Royal York – these buildings were more than 1920s landmarks. They were monuments to, and physical manifestations of, the New Prosperity. The automobile took command of an expanding highway system (there were a million cars on Canadian roads by 1929), exports boomed, mines and paper mills sprang up in the northern wilderness, prairie grain elevators groaned with surplus wheat. The harvest in 1928 was an all-time record: more than 544 million bushels.

There had never been such glorious times on Bay and St. James streets. Speculation in land and in commodities had been a feature of the railroad age and the agricultural boom that settled the Canadian west. But now, in a period characterized by rapid industrial and resource development, the prime speculative medium was common stocks. The Standard Stock and Mining Exchange spent the last half of the decade in a state of perpetual frenzy, propelled by a succession of major mineral discoveries in northern Ontario and Quebec, plus the discovery of oil in Alberta's Turner Valley. From all over the world, funds poured in from speculators eager to double their money overnight. The value of shares traded on the SSME climbed from $6 million in 1920 to more than $710 million in 1929.

On Toronto's senior exchange, the TSE, speculation was scarcely less restrained. The 1920s was the decade when common stocks replaced bonds as the public's favorite investment medium. A new vehicle called the investment trust heated up the market, accelerating its rise until the crash, and then hastening its fall. Investment trusts were companies whose only assets were the shares of other companies. The theory was that, like the mutual funds which enjoyed a vogue in the 1960s, they would allow small investors to own a small piece of a large variety of companies, thus reducing the risk. The financiers who floated these vehicles competed in dreaming up the most reassuringly sturdy names, names that fairly thundered with Anglo-Celtic prudence: Dominion Scottish Investment Trust; Dominion and Anglo Investment Corporation; The Debenture and Securities Corporation of Canada; Pacific Atlantic Investment Trust; and so on. In fact, many of these sturdy-looking vehicles were fundamentally risky. Most trusts traded for slightly more than the per-share value of their underlying assets. Most trusts borrowed heavily to buy shares. In a rising market, that leverage meant fabulous profits. But leverage is a double-edged sword; and when the market fell, the decline of the investment trusts was correspondingly steep.

Individual investors played the same risky game, borrowing money from their brokers to buy stock. The demand for borrowed funds was so great that, by 1929, interest rates on margin accounts had risen to 15 per cent. In the United States, during the summer before the crash, brokers were lending $400 million a month to their customers. By the end of the summer, more than $7 billion in borrowed funds was supporting a market which had risen 110 points (from 339 to 449 on the *New York Times* index) in five months. Many brokers would allow clients to trade on as little as 20 per cent margin; you could buy $1,000 worth of stock, in other words, by putting up $200. If the price of those stocks rose by 20 per cent, you almost doubled your money, even after paying interest charges and brokerage fees. It was the same joyful, inflationary arithmetic which prompted thousands of Canadians to gamble with their homes in the 1970s, and win big – for a while.

When it came, the Great Crash didn't *feel* like a shipwreck to most of its Canadian victims. They experienced it as a series of nasty shocks, but there had been nasty shocks in the market many times before. Most professionals on Bay Street saw it, initially at least, only as a severe but salutary correction of an overheated market. Even as the shocks continued, one after another – Black Thursday, Black Tuesday and all the other black days in between – there was still plenty of evidence to suggest that the downward plunge was a transient phenomenon, that the successive waves of panic sellers would soon be replaced by legions of shrewd bargain-hunters, that the upward trend would soon reassert itself. But the reversal never arrived.

Black Tuesday

The stock market is a marvellous barometer of people's emotions, because their hopes and fears can be translated instantly into action, and those actions into fluctuating prices. On Wednesday, October 23, 1929, the market's collective consciousness finally concluded that prices had gone high enough. In New York, in Montreal, in Toronto, in Vancouver, on the grain exchange in Winnipeg, the sell orders came flooding in. The volume of trades was high enough to become front-page news. But Wednesday was nothing compared to Black Thursday.

That was the famous day when Richard Whitney, an official of the New York Stock Exchange and a doyen of the American financial Establishment, tried to stem the selling panic by striding onto the NYSE's trading floor and, in a gesture aimed at restoring public confidence, buying $20 million worth of blue-chip stocks on behalf of a consortium of U.S. investment banks. The Montreal Stock Exchange traded a record-breaking 400,000 shares that day, and in Toronto the ticker recording the day's frantic transactions was running behind by noon. But Whitney's bold gesture in New York did succeed in creating a pause in the downward plunge. Friday's and Saturday's trading was inconclusive. Some blue-chip stocks even staged a slight comeback. The high priests of finance, who always dispense reassurance in times of crisis, sounded almost smug. "Considering everything that has happened in the New York market," said Charles Abbs of A.E. Ames & Co., "I think we may conservatively say that the Toronto market did not give a bad account of itself."

By this time, brokers across North America had sold out the accounts of tens of thousands of margined investors. Their dreams of effortless wealth had vanished in an afternoon, and many found themselves with a burden of debt it would take them a lifetime to repay. But those were the little fish, the Johnny-come-latelies, the unfortunates who are always the first to be sacrificed in a market collapse. By Monday, October 28, the conflagration had begun to consume all but the very wealthiest investors. The trading volume that day was only about two-thirds of Black Thursday's, but the losses were even more severe. The *New York Times* industrial index dropped 49 points.

All over the world there were traffic jams in the financial districts as the lords of the new industrial age arrived by taxi and chauffeured limousine at their brokers' offices to meet their margin calls. Across North America, broken men returned to houses they could no longer afford and told their wives: "We're ruined."

Tuesday, October 29, was the worst day of all. Brokers had been phoning their clients all through the previous night, demanding further cash to shore up sagging margin positions. But the sell orders accumulated all night, and Tuesday morning on the world's exchanges was a disaster unlike anything before or since. International Nickel dropped nine points overnight. Eight million shares changed hands on the NYSE by noon, and it was only after a secret meeting that the governors decided to stay open for trading through the afternoon. In Montreal, in Toronto, in Vancouver, people gathered in brokers' offices and on the floor of the exchanges, watching in sick fascination as the numbers chalked on the blackboards by sweating clerks plunged steadily downward. The stock tickers were hours late, and it was several days before investors in smaller centres were aware of the full extent of the calamity. One TSE member, more prescient than most, told a reporter at the end of Black Tuesday: "It's more than a stock market panic. It's a world tragedy." Bay Street itself was a litany of small tragedies. J. Harold Crang, who set up his own brokerage house on Bay Street in 1929, later recalled: "The suicide thing was *not* a myth. I personally knew 14 men who took their own lives after the Crash, and at least six of them were from Toronto. Some of them took poison or pills. Some shot themselves. Most just shut the garage doors and turned on the motor of their car. Most of them made sure their insurance policies were big enough to take care of their wives."

Bay Street's Hangover

The party was over. For Bay Street, the hangover came three years later, when 27 stockbrokers, including several millionaires, were arrested and imprisoned, partly as a result of an exposé launched in November 1929 by Floyd Chalmers, then editor of *The Financial Post*. Chalmers' series, oddly enough, named no names. But between November and the following January, Chalmers detailed the many ways in which crooked brokers fleeced their customers. One of the most popular methods was a sophisticated variation of the old bucket shop. What the crooked brokers were doing, Chalmers revealed, was to use only part of their customers' money to buy stock. They'd use the rest to take short positions in the same stock – in effect, betting against their own customers. Since the broker was often in a position to influence if not control the stock's price, and since the customer was usually heavily margined and therefore not in a position to demand delivery of the stock, the system was virtually risk-free for the broker.

These revelations were somewhat belated. Toronto mining brokers, after all, had been running bucket shops on Bay Street for generations. But Canadians were newly bruised and angered by the Great Crash and eager to find scapegoats. The *Post* series triggered a nation-wide outcry and government investigations in British Columbia, Alberta and Manitoba. In January, the police pounced. I.W.C. (Ike) Solloway and his partner Harvey Mills, proprietors of Solloway, Mills and Co., Canada's largest mining brokerage house, were arrested in Vancouver and Toronto and tried in Calgary on four counts of conspiracy. Solloway was fined $225,000 and sentenced to four months in jail; Mills was fined $25,000 and sentenced to one month. Both served additional time because they couldn't raise the money to pay their fines. Later in January, police arrested another nine brokers in Toronto, including the proprietors of Stobie Forlong & Co., one of the largest SSME firms.*

That scandal was the end of the Standard Stock and Mining Exchange, but it wasn't the end of mining speculation in Toronto. The SSME lingered on until 1934, when it merged with the TSE. There was a solid revival in the gold-mining market between 1932 and 1934, triggered by President Roosevelt's decision to embargo gold exports and, in 1934, to peg the price of gold at $35 per ounce. That policy was a godsend for Canadian gold mines. The stocks of established producers such as Dome, Hollinger and Wright-Hargreaves shot upward – Hollinger, for example, soaring from $4.25 to $21.25 between 1932 and 1934. Other marginal mines which had closed for lack of marketable ore in the 1920s reopened across the country, and some traders made a lot of money. O'Brien Gold Mines, for instance, soared from 34 cents to $14 in 1936. Pickle Crow Gold Mines, in the space of a few years, moved from 50 cents to $9.20.

But for the next 15 years on Bay Street, through the slow upward crawl of the Depression years and the war bond sales-

---

* I'm indebted to Douge Featherling's *Gold Diggers of 1929* for many of the details of the Great Crash in Canada

manship of World War II, Bay Street was a backwater. George J.W. Goodman, the New York financial writer whose pseudonym is "Adam Smith," beautifully captured the flavor of this hiatus period in the words of an old broker who recalled how it was on Wall Street in 1937: "Sometimes the tape would stand absolutely still for 20 minutes. There was no air conditioning and all the windows were open, and on a summer day you could walk the length of Wall Street and hear nothing but the rattle of backgammon dice through the open windows above."

The somnolence of Canada's financial markets was not broken until February 13, 1947, the day that drillers for Imperial Oil Ltd. struck oil at Leduc, outside Edmonton. A belching roar of flame and a plume of dense black smoke signalled the discovery of the largest oil and gas field in Canadian history. It was the beginning of a string of discoveries which established Western Canada as one of the world's major petroleum-producing regions: Wizard Lake in 1951; Acheson, Bonnie Glen and Westerose the following year; Mobil's discovery of the Pembina field the year after that; Home Oil's Swan Hills discovery in 1957. By 1953, only six years after Leduc, Alberta was producing more oil and gas in a single year than Turner Valley had produced in all the years since its discovery in 1914. Those discoveries also triggered a pipeline boom. Entrepreneur Frank McMahon built the Trans-Mountain Pipeline across the Rockies to ferry Alberta oil to markets in B.C. and the U.S. west coast. And in 1957, American financiers, aided by a compliant Liberal government dominated by Trade and Commerce Minister C.D. Howe, launched one of the largest Canadian construction projects since the railroads: the Trans-Canada Pipeline – at the time, the world's longest – to carry gas across 2,300 miles of prairie, swamp and muskeg to markets in eastern Canada and the U.S.

Oil was one prop of the 1950s resources boom. The other was uranium. The rush began in 1952, when geologist and promoter Gilbert LaBine received a telegram from one of his field geologists in northern Saskatchewan: "Come quick," it read. "I've shot an elephant." The elephant in question was a uranium discovery which became the main property of LaBine's company, Gunnar Gold Mines Ltd. Gunnar's stock rocketed from 40 cents to $12 per share; and in the classic manner of Canadian mining booms before and since, dozens of other companies staked claims near Gunnar's discovery, and started selling shares to a public which was convinced that uranium was the fuel of the future, the peaceful servant of the atomic age. The excitement intensified in 1954, when a series of discoveries near Blind River, Ontario, led to the opening of 11 uranium mines, including Consolidated Denison's (the world's largest), a new town in the middle of nowhere called Elliott Lake, and, on the TSE, the wildest speculative action since the 1920s.

It was the heydey of the storefront brokerage office, an innovation that Ike Solloway had pioneered in the 1920s. Bay Street was lined with brokerage houses which, unlike today's high-rise sanctums, encouraged people to drop in, sit awhile, watch the stock quotations being chalked up on the big blackboard at the front of the room, and perhaps make a trade or two. One broker, Frank Leslie, heightened the appeal of this spectator sport by hiring only gorgeous young women as board markers. Some of the firms installed auditorium seating. When the market was running strongly, the places would be jammed. Trying to get rich on penny stocks became a form of lunchtime theatre. Upstairs, in barren little offices all around Bay Street, shirtsleeved men, some of them former carnival pitchmen, sat all day at banks of telephones, extolling the unlimited profit potential of Consolidated Moose Pasture to dentists in Dubuque and widows in Kansas City. In 1951, the U.S. Securities and Exchange Commission issued a report accusing Bay Street boiler rooms of bilking Americans of as much as $52 million a year. "These greedy, ruthless men . . . have been milking gullible Americans from Toronto for years," the SEC report charged. The Ontario Securities Commission, which in those days often seemed more anxious to nurture the stock-promotion business than to regulate it, was ready with a pious response: It wasn't $52 million; it was only $9 million or so.

The exact sum didn't matter. It was as academic as the number of nickels you spend at a carnival, throwing baseballs at milk bottles. The customers – known on Bay Street as "mooches" and "pooches" – were eager to gamble. The entry price was less than a dollar per share, and you just might get fabulously rich, or so the mooches and pooches were persuaded to believe. It didn't much matter whether the object of the excitement was uranium or oil; from around the world the money poured in to Bay Street. "I pray God," wrote a lady evangelist from Los Angeles to her Toronto broker, "who alone knows just what is under the ground in Alberta, Canada, to touch the hands of the drillers to place the drilling bit at the right place."

The euphoria continued on the TSE, practically without interruption, for more than a decade and a half. From Leduc in 1947 to the discovery of the fabulous Kidd Creek Mine, near Timmins, Ontario, in 1963, Canada experienced an extraordinary string of resource discoveries which boosted the country's petroleum and mineral production from 7.6 million barrels (worth $19 million) in 1947, to 189 million barrels ($423 million) by 1960. But the Kidd Creek rush was the end of the party in Toronto. That major discovery will forever be associated with the Windfall Oil and Mines affair, the scandal that finally prompted the Ontario government, and the industry itself, to clean up Bay Street's act.

Twenty years after the event, it is difficult to understand why Windfall, of all the hundreds of stock promotions that passed through Bay Street, should have been singled out for such copious regulatory scrutiny. Over the years, many other penny stocks had risen far higher, and fallen just as fast. Other penny stocks had been manipulated just as outrageously. Why, then, should Viola MacMillan, Windfall's president and promoter, be sent to jail? Why should her activities be the subject of an exhaustive and costly royal commission enquiry? Why, in fact, did the authorities appear so *surprised* at the revelations of the events surrounding Texas Gulf Sulphur Co.'s huge copper, lead and zinc discovery? Do the proprietors of dockside saloons assume that the ladies frequenting their establishments are working for the Salvation Army?

No, Windfall's notoriety was not due to its uniqueness. It was because of the vastness of the Texas Gulf discovery, which seized the imagination of the entire world; it was because of the personality of Viola MacMillan herself – as perennial head of the Prospectors and Developers Association, she was one of the most visible figures in Canadian mining. But perhaps it was the spectacle of so many people profiting so hugely from inside information that finally alarmed the public, the press and the government. The sheer moral sleaziness of a system in which brokers, promoters, exchange officials, highly paid corporation executives and even securities regulators conspired to make themselves rich at the expense of people who were probably just as greedy, but not so advantageously situated – well, it was all simply too flagrant. Something had to be done.

As the royal commission report by Mr. Justice Arthur Kelly later documented, people lined their pockets, either illegally or improperly, all along the line. Kenneth Darke, the young, UBC-trained geologist who originally staked the property as an employee of Texas Gulf, joined a secret syndicate that got rich peddling claims adjacent to the strike – claims which TGS had already rejected as geologically worthless. Practically the entire senior executive echelon of TGS started buying stock as soon as they learned the results of that first exploratory drill hole. One of those worthless claims near the TGS strike ended up as the principal asset of Windfall Oil and Mines Ltd., a company controlled by Viola MacMillan and her husband, George. They drilled a single hole early in July which indicated the property was worthless – and then maintained a studied silence for the next three weeks while Windfall stock, fed by rumors of a second major strike, went crazy.

While the MacMillans stalled, dropped hints, issued ambiguous news releases and resisted demands by the OSC and TSE that they announce the results of their drilling, Windfall stock climbed from 40 cents to more than $4, and then to a peak of $5.65. Finally, at the end of July, the MacMillans announced their drilling results: nothing. In a single day of pandemonium, the stock fell from $4 to 40 cents. "She allowed people to misunderstand what was going on by putting down another hole," explains one official who studied the case closely. "The first hole was a bust, so she put the drill core off somewhere, and put it under tight security, and then started a second hole. That's what you'd normally do if you had a hot find and were drilling to confirm it. But by the end of the game, the short sellers were flying helicopters over the property, and discovered that the rig was not drilling in a way that would confirm the first hole. The drill was searching – they'd got nothing. The whole thing happened through a failure of securities regulation to insist on timely disclosure."

Viola MacMillan went to jail, convicted of fraudulent manipulation of the stock of another of her companies, Consolidated Golden Arrow Ltd., which also had claims near the TGS strike. But the report of the royal commission convicted not just a few individuals but an entire industry, as Mr. Justice Arthur Kelly compared the TSE to "a private gaming club," and recommended sweeping reforms of the system.

Windfall was a watershed. It marked the beginning of Vancouver's emergence as the premier resource exchange in North America. It marked the end of Bay Street's frontier phase. From 1964 onward, Toronto became much less dishonest, but much less venturesome. Many of the flim-flam merchants who were no longer welcome in Toronto found life more congenial on the west coast, and so did many legitimate mining entrepreneurs. "It wasn't all bad, all that old stuff," notes a securities regulator with long experience on Bay Street. "The mining promotions were very cheap to do, and lots of honest guys were involved. They would raise money with very little aggravation and expense, and spend it putting holes in the ground. When the regulations get complicated, when you get a lot of lawyers involved, you find a lot of honest people thinking, 'Gee, the risk is too high now – I'm spending so much money on lawyers and accountants that I'm not going to bother.' It's wrong to characterize the old days as the Bad Old Days and the new days as just wonderful. Unethical financings go on any old time."

It may be sheer coincidence, but Toronto hasn't found or developed a single significant mine since 1964. Vancouver's promotional community, many of its members refugees from Bay Street, has developed several. After 1964, Bay Street's main activity became the reshuffling of wealth, rather than its creation. Fifty years earlier, the Montreal Stock Exchange had been the arena of established wealth, Toronto the upstart. After 1964, Toronto came to occupy the Old-Money role once played by Montreal; and the Vancouver Stock Exchange became the arena of New Money and the frontier.

6
The
Montreal Exchange

A tour of Montreal's St. James Street and its environs, once the resonant heart of Canadian finance, is an exercise in cultural archeology. The facades are still magnificent: huge, colonnaded temples of commerce, built of stern Protestant granite, designed to last a thousand years. There are stone lions and polished brass nameplates; there are whole forests of leafy Corinthian columns; there are offices with fireplaces and private vaults; there are carved stone coats-of-arms above wrought-iron doorways and banking halls the size of nineteenth-century railroad stations. From here, the lords of Montreal finance once controlled an empire of wheat and cattle and infant cities. From the green farms of Ontario to the frightening vastness of the north, from the grassy inland ocean of the prairies to the lumber villages at the edge of the Pacific Ocean, the wealth of the young Dominion flowed like the St. Lawrence through the counting-houses of St. James Street.

A Private Government

Never before in our history has so much of the nation's wealth been commanded by so few. The tightly interlocked little cabal of Montreal finance, dominated by the holy trinity of Sun Life, the Bank of Montreal and the CPR, functioned as a sort of private government. The CPR, with its holdings of about 36 million acres of freehold land in western Canada, its scheme to populate the prairies with sturdy old world peasants, its transportation system that spanned the globe, probably exerted more direct influence over the lives of more Canadians than did the Laurier government itself. The Bank of Montreal (which had issued its own currency until 1866) was Canada's first and largest bank, and regarded itself not merely as a business, but as a self-appointed guardian of the entire national economy. In 1907, for instance, sensing the current instability on Wall Street,

70

and without consulting anybody, the bank grandly hiked its interest rates. This willingness to enrich itself at its customers' expense was not, of course, based on any sordid desire for private gain; it was done for its customers' own good – "not so much with a desire to increase our profits," explained the bank's general manager, Sir Edward Clouston, "but more to give a practical indication to our customers of our expectations of the trend of financial affairs, and to impress upon them that in the conduct of their business they must bear it in mind, and govern themselves accordingly." If Clouston sounded like a nonelected minister of finance, it's because that's pretty much what he was.

Made in Montreal

St. James Street was riding the crest of one of the greatest economic booms the world had ever seen – a boom that was characterized by the immigrants who poured into the west, and the wheat that came pouring out. Canada's population almost doubled between 1891 and 1916; during the same period, wheat exports rose from 2 million to 150 million bushels. Montreal was the indispensable funnel for this two-way traffic of humanity and wealth. Between the turn of the century and 1910, it was the fastest-growing city in North America by far; its only rivals were Detroit, home of the infant automobile industry, and Cleveland. Montreal's population didn't rise above 100,000 until 1870; but by 1911, with nearly 600,000 people in the Greater Montreal area, it ranked twenty-sixth among the cities of the world. It was larger than Brussels, Manchester, Cairo, Bangkok, Naples, Amsterdam, Pittsburgh, Birmingham, Dresden and even Madras, India.

About one-sixth of everything manufactured in Canada was made in Montreal. There were five textile mills, employing more than 5,000 people; there were three huge bridge and ironworks companies; there was Mr. Molson's brewery (and, until it was absorbed by the Bank of Montreal in 1924, Mr. Molson's bank), and Mr. Redpath's sugar monopoly and Mr. Ogilvy's flour mills. There were the rows of ornate Victorian mansions along Sherbrooke Street and up the mountain, inhabited by the likes of the CPR's Sir William Van Horne, or the Bank of Montreal's Lord Strathcona, one of the founders of the CPR, who remained as the bank's president until 1905, despite the fact that he'd been living in London since 1896 as Canada's High Commissioner.

The Entrepreneur and the Establishment

The securities firms of St. James Street functioned as adjuncts to the great pools of capital commanded by the banks and insurance companies, or as convenient vehicles for the promotional schemes of entrepreneurs such as Max Aitken, the future Lord Beaverbrook. Aitken founded Royal Securities Corp. in Halifax in 1903 and moved the firm to Montreal in 1906. He'd come close to his first million before he was 25 by buying up companies from their aging proprietors, selling bonds through Royal Securities to finance the purchases, then installing fresh managements to turn the companies around. Aitken made his money from the sales commissions on the bonds and preferred shares, and by hanging on to the common shares that were issued as part of each transaction. Usually he sold them years later at a large profit.

Most of the companies he bought were utilities in the Caribbean – tram lines, electrical companies, small railroads. Describing his honeymoon in Cuba in 1906, Aitken wrote to a friend: "I bought the Puerto Principe Electric Light Co., for the sum of $300,000. I bought 200 acres of land in the city of Camaguey, and 217 acres north of Sir Wm. Van Horne's car works. I bought the old Mule Tram franchise, and I acquired the electric railway franchise in an almost completed condition. When the tram lines are constructed they will pass through the lands I have purchased. On account of the congested condition of the population of the city, I expect to make a very large profit out of selling business lots."

Aitken's four-year stay in Montreal was dazzlingly successful – or would have been considered so by anyone less furiously ambitious than the future Lord Beaverbrook. When he moved to the city from Halifax, he was worth about $700,000; when he left four years later, he was worth about $5 million. His first triumph was the amalgamation of 13 regional cement companies into Canada Cement, thus imposing a fixed, coast-to-coast price on a commodity which, until the merger, had been subject to the disorderly forces of competition. His second coup was the purchase of Montreal Rolling Mills, which he merged with several other steel mills to create The Steel Company of Canada. It was a classic "flip"; before he actually handed over the $4.2-million purchase price, Aitken resold the mill to the new syndicate for a $2-million profit; 50 years later, Stelco's common shares were worth 60 times what he'd paid for them.

In spite of these triumphs, Aitken still felt rebuffed by the Montreal Establishment. He once confessed that they'd made him feel "something of an Ishmaelite." They prevented him, for instance, from buying the *Montreal Gazette*, then controlled by the Bank of Montreal and the CPR. He also failed in his attempts to buy into the *Montreal Herald* and the *Montreal Star*. Miffed, he left for England via New York in June 1910, travelling in a car "as big as a house." Although he did further Montreal deals, he never again lived in Canada as a permanent resident. The British Establishment made room for him as the Montreal Establishment never had; within a year he was sitting as a Unionist MP in the British House of Commons and by 1916 had bought *The Daily Express*, the foundation of his British newspaper empire. "What might have been my future," he wondered 50 years later, "if the *Montreal Gazette* and the *Herald* had come under my control?"

In 1915, Aitken sold Royal Securities to his junior partner, Izaak Walton Killam, a fellow Maritimer who became one of the lions of Canadian finance. Through the 1920s and 1930s, Killam put together a dazzling series of combinations, mostly in pulp and paper and hydro-electric power, including Calgary Power, Ottawa Valley Power, Bolivian Power, Newfoundland Light & Power and Venezuela Light and Power. He also briefly owned the *Toronto Mail and Empire*, before its 1936 merger with the *Toronto Globe*. He died in 1955, an erect, silver-haired old gentleman who used to carry an egg down to the barbershop of the Mount Royal Hotel, in order to be shampooed in the manner to which he'd become accustomed. The taxes on his estate provided part of the $100-million seed-money for the establishment of the Canada Council. But, like his old partner, Killam was never fully accepted by the Montreal Establishment; his mansion on Sherbrooke Street was kitty-corner from the Mount Royal Club, an institution he was never invited to join.

Killam's influence was perpetuated after his death by his widow Dorothy, a magnificent eccentric who once, while holidaying in New York, instructed one of the senior officers of Royal Securities to book a first-class railroad suite for her pet dog; the animal, she was careful to specify, must occupy a *lower* berth. "I went to her house once when she was entertaining a bunch of young bankers from the City of London," a former minion at Royal Securities recalls, "and, my God, it was like central Europe! There were at least three footmen standing around the dining room, and the old girl was practically *manacled* with jewels. It looked like about $200,000 sitting on her wrists and neck. She must have been in her seventies then, and I found her lively, bright and amusing. She took an active interest in the firm until the day she died."

Vanished Glories

English Montreal played together, slept together, worked together and intermarried, in a social round that seemed as foreordained, and yet as unpredictable, as the cycles of the stock market. Everyone not only knew everybody else; they were frequently related. "You couldn't say anything catty about anyone," says Gordon Ball, whose father was president of the Bank of Montreal, "because it would always turn out you were talking to their cousin or uncle. I finally learned to keep my mouth shut." In the summer, there was the annual hunt ball on the Pitfield estate in Senneville, outside Montreal, where, one participant recalls: "We all wore hunting pinks and drank from stirrup cups. One year somebody got drunk and accidentally broke the Pitfields' big crystal punch bowl. I wonder what ever happened to the poor bastard? Probably had to move to Toronto."

In November, there was the St. Andrew's Ball at the Mount Royal Hotel, a roaring celebration of Scottishness, complete with pipers, haggis and the presentation of debutantes to some Scottish laird who'd been flown in to preside over the festivities. At one St. Andrew's Ball in the 1950s, the fourth Viscount Hardinge, an English expatriate who'd married a Molson and ran the investment firm of Greenshields Inc., dazzled the assemblage by performing a wild dance across several tables.

What *happened* to all these vanished glories? The simplistic answer is that they were swept away in the Quiet Revolution that has been transforming Quebec since the early 1960s. But other Establishments, in other countries at other times, have ridden out greater waves of change. Why didn't Montreal's? If the Rothschilds can survive French socialism and the British aristocracy can come bumbling through successive Labour governments with their privileges and aplomb largely intact, why is St. James Street – or Rue St Jacques, as it's now known – virtually a museum? One man I know, who grew up in that vanished world of Anglo-Saxon privilege, understands exactly why: "In Toronto," he says, "you find the current generation of Old Money working their asses off to build on what their fathers left them – the Galen Westons, the Conrad Blacks, the Ken Thomsons. In Montreal, you won't find the Old Money on St. James Street. They're out in Cartierville or someplace, clipping their coupons and playing polo."

You can almost pinpoint the moment which marked the beginning of the end of that old world. It came in May 1963, when the Quebec government of Jean Lesage, egged on by his fiery

Minister of Natural Resources, René Levesque, nationalized 11 of the province's privately owned power companies, including the largest and haughtiest of them all, Shawinigan Water and Power Co.

In B.C., in the same year, Premier W.A.C. Bennett had seized the privately owned B.C. Electric Company without negotiation, paying the current market price for its shares and passing a law forbidding any court challenge of the transaction. Levesque's $600-million takeover, by contrast, was a model of moderation. With help from St. James Street itself, he simply bought a majority of the utilities' shares on the open market, and borrowed money on Wall Street – with the aid of Douglas Chapman of A.E. Ames – to pay for them. The firms were then merged with Hydro Quebec, which had been operating since 1944. "You shouldn't underestimate the enemy," Levesque said afterward, "but it was really quite easy."

It turned out to be just as easy for St. James Street to vote with its feet. The parade of armored cars that rolled across the provincial border on the eve of the 1976 Quebec election, ferrying the gold of St. James Street to the safety of Anglo-Saxon Ontario, was a dramatic demonstration of the petulance of privilege. But it also underlined how amazingly skittish large pools of capital can be. As every Swiss banker knows, nothing is so cautious as a million dollars, except perhaps a billion dollars.

Financial Refugees

And so, when capital began fleeing Montreal in earnest after Levesque's 1976 election victory, it was only a question of time until the people who owned and managed that capital would follow. Within months of the Parti Quebecois victory, the trickle of financial refugees became a flood. The decision in 1978 of Sun Life Assurance Company of Canada to shift its head office to Toronto was only the most visible of these head-office defections. Sun Life, with its mausoleum-like building on Dominion Square, had been a symbol in Montreal of stability, and of Anglo-Saxon dominance, since 1865. But after the PQ victory nothing – neither the private urgings of Canada's prime minister nor the protestations of some of its own influential shareholders – could deter Sun Life's management from getting out.

The company's departure elevated the exodus to the status of a cultural phenomenon. It wasn't just people and bank accounts that were moving to Toronto; it was the entire culture of St. James Street – the analysts, the brokers, the underwriters,

75

the fund managers, the dealmakers, the young up-and-comers and the established gentlemen who settled billion-dollar bond issues over lunch at the St. James Club. A financial community is a network of skills, sentiments, contacts and shared memories; like any other tribal culture, it is as fragile, as vulnerable to shocks from the outside world, as a band of New Guinea tribesmen or some rare species of arctic lichen. Levesque's brand of Francophone nationalism, combined with a vast expansion of the provincial bureaucracy and a corresponding increase in taxes, accomplished what many Montrealers would have considered an impossibility; it made Toronto seem like an attractive place to live. Between July 1977 and July 1982, according to Statistics Canada, some 140,000 English-speaking Quebecers left the province. That number – which represents one of the largest mass migrations in postwar Canadian history – included almost everyone who mattered on St. James Street.

A New Generation

What's emerging in the place of that departed tribe of Anglos is a genuine Francophone investment community, which is beginning to outgrow its regional roots and become a national force. One manifestation of the revolution is the Caisse de Depot et Placement du Quebec, a provincially controlled investment fund which invests the pension savings of Quebecers, and has used its billions to buy a seat at the boardroom tables of some of Canada's most powerful corporations. Another is the emergence of Levesque, Beaubien Inc. as a major national investment house. But perhaps the most visible manifestation is the Montreal Stock Exchange itself – or, as it's been renamed, The Montreal Exchange.

Under an intense, pipe-puffing workaholic named Pierre Lortie, the Montreal Exchange is becoming an important element in the industrial strategy of the new Quebec. The old exchange, housed in a nineteenth-century building off St. James Street that looks like a small Greek temple, rivalled the Mount Royal and the St. James as the city's best gentleman's club – complete with a well-stocked bar off the trading floor which operated during business hours. It was founded as the Montreal Stock Exchange in 1874 and, for much of its history, was operated largely as a convenience for Sun Life, the banks, the CPR and the great old monied families. This clubbiness persisted well into the 1960s. "You could only be a full-fledged trader on the ME if you were a member," recalls one veteran floor trader, "and the members were the sons and brothers and so on of the old families. This is where the club atmosphere came in."

For many decades it was the country's most active arena for buying and selling the stocks of solid, blue-chip, industrial companies. Bay Street, with its sordid preoccupation with penny mining stocks, was regarded as a disreputable upstart. But at some point in the 1930s or 1940s – historians can't agree exactly when – Toronto surpassed Montreal in terms of the value of shares traded. Montreal's relative decline has continued, practically without interruption, ever since. In 1980, the value of trading on the Vancouver Stock Exchange exceeded Montreal's for the first time. Since 1975, when the Anglophone exodus began, the ME's share of national trading has slipped from 24 per cent to about 7 per cent – an accurate barometer of Montreal's reduced status as a financial centre.

There have been a few upticks in this downward curve. In 1965, the exchange moved from its Greek temple on Rue St François Xavier (the old building is now used as a theatre) into glittering headquarters in a new office tower on Place Victoria. Exchange officials marked the occasion with a ticker-tape parade and rode to their new home in a procession of antique cars and an open carriage, drawn by four dappled grey horses, which had been used for the visit to Quebec City of Queen Elizabeth and King George VI in 1939. In the mid-1970s, the exchange flirted briefly with penny mining stocks. But a series of stock-fraud scandals triggered a wave of reform. The Securities Act was amended and the Canadian Stock Exchange was merged into its parent exchange. Ever since, Montreal has been happy to leave the penny-stock trade to Vancouver.

Lortie, who was only 33 when he was hired in 1980 as the seventh president in the exchange's history, is running hard to arrest the ME's decline. An engineering graduate of Laval University with an MBA from the University of Chicago and a postgraduate degree in economics from the University of Louvain, he exemplifies a new generation of bright young Francophone MBAs whose careers, in the vacuum left by the Anglophone exodus, have taken off like rockets. For the past decade he's moved easily between the private and public sectors, assembling contacts and influence on St. James Street, in Ottawa and in Quebec City. In the 1970s he served as executive assistant to Raymond Garneau, who became Robert Bourassa's finance minister, and built business contacts as the exchange's director of development in 1975 and 1976.

In that job, he stage-managed the exchange's entry into the options market, the fast-growing branch of the securities business which allows investors to make heavily leveraged bets on the future prices of various stocks and commodities. The options business, conducted in partnership with the Toronto and Vancouver exchanges, now covers 430 listed stocks, plus gold, silver and various currencies. It's been so successful that in 1981 Lortie expunged the word "stock" from the exchange's name. He also chaired a committee to advise federal Finance Minister Marc Lalonde on how to revise the tax system to encourage Canadians to become stock-market investors; Lalonde adopted most of his proposals in his April 1983 budget.

In concert with the Quebec government, Lortie has also been working hard to persuade young Quebec companies to raise expansion capital by selling shares on the ME, instead of borrowing from the bank. "Going public" is a process that many businessmen don't understand, he discovered; so he set up a new department to explain the procedure to businessmen, and to woo their companies to the exchange. On the other side of the equation, the Quebec government is making it easier for Quebecers to become shareholders. Through a stock-savings plan that gives generous tax breaks to investors who buy shares of Quebec-based companies, and a package of grants and subsidies which reduces the costs of going public, the government is working in the same direction. In 1983, some 28 companies were listed on the ME for the first time; that's more new listings than in the previous five years. And since the Quebec Stock Savings Plan came into effect in 1979, more than 200,000 Quebecers have become stock-market investors for the first time.

Quebec used to be known as a province of mattress-stuffers – cautious savers who preferred to keep their money in the local credit union, or even hidden away at home. Today, thanks to Lortie's innovations at the Montreal Exchange, and the tax regime ushered in by the Levesque government, it's becoming a province of stock-market players. As a financial centre, Montreal may be only a pale shadow of its former self. But in the end, the new Rue St Jacques may turn out to be a far more democratic capitalist conduit than was the old St. James Street.

7

The Vancouver Stock Exchange

The tenants no longer remark on it, but it's the first thing that visitors notice: The elevators of the Vancouver Stock Exchange Tower go whooooooooooooooooo – a mournful, aeolian backdrop to the activities of the building's occupants. The vast majority of them are stock promoters, stock traders, stock underwriters, stock salesmen or people who serve them, from securities lawyers to consulting geologists to at least one masseur. These people, and the sighing elevators which they ride all day, give the building a unique ambience, a mixture of extravagant expectations, broken dreams and expensive cigar smoke. If the shades of long-vanished stock promotions could make a noise, they would sound exactly like the ghostly murmurings of those elevator shafts.

Penny-Stock Capital

Nothing is exactly what it seems in the VSE Tower and, if possible, nothing is ever called by its real name. To begin with, the building is now the spiritual centre of a stretch of Vancouver real estate known as "Howe Street," even though the VSE Tower is located a block away from Howe, on the corner of Granville and Dunsmuir. Howe Street, in turn, is the centre of what its proponents like to describe as "North America's premier venture-capital exchange." That means it's the penny-stock capital of North America, if not the entire world. But since many of the VSE's stocks now trade for more than a dollar, one no longer speaks of "penny stocks" in Vancouver. One speaks instead of "financing junior resource exploration," which is a far worthier pursuit than flogging worthless moose-pasture to the greedy multitudes. Nor should one refer to these mul-

79

titudes as "mooches" and "pooches." Those terms were once used on Howe Street, and on Bay Street too, back in the bad old days, to describe the guileless souls who will happily line up for the privilege of allowing a stock promoter to deprive them of their savings. Today, on North America's leading venture-capital exchange, one speaks instead of "clients" and "investors."

For most of this century, at least until the Beatles transformed the business in the mid-1960s, a shabby Manhattan office tower called The Brill Building was the centre of the American popular music industry. The place was a legendary honeycomb of song-pluggers, agents, touts, publicists, composers and shadowy music-publishing houses, all living out of one another's pockets, all doing their best to steal one another's ideas. The VSE Tower, despite its up-to-the-minute marble lobby and its tasteful decor, is Canada's financial equivalent of The Brill Building.

There are many striking parallels between Tin Pan Alley and Howe Street. The products of both are nearly always ephemeral. Like all those long-forgotten songs of yesteryear, the value of Howe Street's products is almost wholly dependent on the vagaries of public fancy. Most Vancouver stocks, like most songs, take off briefly, then vanish. Everyone who has so much as mastered three chords on the guitar dreams of writing a smashingly profitable hit song. Similarly, there are millions of North Americans (and, increasingly, Europeans and Asians) who dream of making a small score, or a large one, on some penny stock which will quintuple in price the day after they buy it. The main function of Howe Street, of the Vancouver Stock Exchange, of the VSE Tower and of all its denizens is to create and sell pieces of paper which will satisfy this natural human craving for swift and effortless reward. If, in the process, someone finds a mine or a new oilfield – well, that's wonderful. It makes it easier to sell more stock. But mine-finding is an almost incidental by-product of the VSE Tower's main activity, which is selling stock.

Brokers in Toronto or New York tend to shake their heads and chuckle when the VSE is mentioned, as if they were hearing about the escapades of a naughty but particularly endearing child. The VSE, and the people and rules and attitudes and folklore surrounding it, are indeed naughty and endearing. In some ways, the place is a throwback to the palmy days of American capitalism – the 1890s, say, or the 1920s: risky and rapacious, but also visionary and audacious, glorying in its own potential.

You will find exchanges like the VSE in Tokyo, Hong Kong,

Sydney, Sao Paulo, Denver – wherever in the capitalist world the economy is growing faster than the bureaucracy. These exchanges specialize in trading the shares of young, untried companies, instead of established, widows-and-orphans stocks such as Bell and IBM. Speculative stock exchanges are associated with young, developing economies in which the emphasis is on creating new wealth rather than reshuffling existing assets.

What makes the VSE unique among North America's 15 stock exchanges is its intimate connection with the resource industries of Western Canada and the U.S., and the permissiveness of its regulation. In the U.S., trading on all exchanges is carefully governed by the Securities and Exchange Commission. In Ontario, the Ontario Securities Commission is equally intolerant of the excesses of the stock-promotion business. But in Vancouver, the VSE revels in what its officials proudly describe as a "positive regulatory climate." This means that the exchange is largely self-regulating, and that the B.C. government's official watchdog, the Superintendent of Brokers, attacks only the most flagrant abuses. Because the superintendent's office is chronically understaffed, its attacks tend to be sporadic and not terribly effective. The present incumbent, Rupert Bullock, an amiable ex-Mountie, sometimes sounds more like a professional booster than a government watchdog. "The whole objective of the superintendent's office," he once declared in print, "is to make Vancouver the junior financing centre for North America and Europe."

This combination of "positive" regulation and a sporadically active resource-based economy has transformed speculative trading from a marginal activity into a major B.C. industry. In terms of the amount of money raised for new resource ventures – about $1 million every working day in the boom year of 1980 – the VSE is first in North America. In terms of the number of shares traded, it's second, behind only New York. But in terms of the *value* of shares traded, it's North American's seventh-largest exchange, far behind senior exchanges such as Toronto or New York, but far ahead of junior ones such as Denver and Chicago. In terms of the dollar value of trading, the VSE does about one-eighth as much business as Toronto.

Five days a week, starting very early, the VSE Tower starts to hum. The exchange itself, with its banks of computers, its trading floor, its staff of 180 and its securities depository (with a vault whose door weighs 70 tons), occupies four floors of the building. On the second storey, where the VSE's trading floor is located, the traders have shed their suit coats well before

7 a.m., have donned the colored jackets which, when combined with their expensive shirts and jewelled cufflinks, make them look like the world's best-tailored grocery clerks, and are already milling around the trading area, waiting for the opening bell that signals the beginning of the session. The VSE opens for business at this ungentlemanly hour because of the three-hour time difference with Toronto and New York, where the exchanges open at 10 a.m.

The VSE's trading floor is like any trading floor anywhere, but boasts of a few distinguishing features. For one thing, there's an inconspicuous door leading directly from the trading floor to the adjacent lounge of the Four Seasons Hotel. For another, the VSE still clings to the antique custom of employing board-markers – young people who pace back and forth along a cat-walk mounted in front of a vast expanse of blackboard, chalking up the numbers that record the interplay between would-be buyers and willing sellers of more than 1,550 listed stocks. The chalkboard numbers are then punched into the VSE's computer system by women located at various points around the trading floor, who sometimes use binoculars to double-check illegible scrawls. Minutes later, the numbers are swimming across electronic tote boards throughout Vancouver's financial district.

Booms and Scandals

The electronics may be more sophisticated, but the essentials of natural-resource financing haven't changed much since the VSE's founding in 1907. Remarkably little is remembered about its early days – a deficiency that was compounded a few years ago by a PR woman who, in a bid to polish up the VSE's image, threw out all its old archives. Its first home was simply a large room in a storefront building on Hastings Street.

By the time Harold Lefever joined the business in 1924, the VSE was in the middle of a mining boom. Lefever is an erect and honorable old gentleman who remembers the names of long-vanished mining stocks the way some schoolteachers remember the names of old pupils. His first firm was R.P. Clarke & Co., founded by a World War I general whose partners included many of his fellow-officers. In those days, the firm employed three telegraph operators who sat in the office, wearing headphones and green eyeshades, writing down stock quotations which came down the wire in Morse code from New York and Toronto. That's why Black Tuesday in 1929 didn't really arrive in Vancouver until the following Thursday; the panic selling on the New York and Toronto stock exchanges was so voluminous that it took nearly three days for the wire to catch up. "None of us was aware of what was going on until it was too late," says Lefever. R.P. Clarke & Co. expired a few months later, the inadvertent victim of a 1930 Toronto stock scandal that sent 27 brokers to jail.

But the 1930s weren't all bad for the brokerage business. A boom in gold stocks began in 1931 and endured for most of that desperate decade. By the mid-1930s, Ontario gold stocks such as Teck-Hughes, Wright-Hargreaves and Little Long Lac were trading a million shares a day. Lefever remembers buying shares in a BC gold stock, Lorne Mines, for 75 cents in 1929, and watching it run all the way up to $18 in 1934. The gold boom ended in Vancouver in 1937 with a resounding scandal: It was discovered that someone had "salted" the drill cores on a property owned by Hedley Gold Mines. The resultant collapse killed the market. The few brokers who didn't enlist in 1939 spent the war years selling Victory Bonds.

The Godfather of Howe St.

It wasn't until 1947, the year of the Leduc oil discovery, that happy days returned to Howe Street. The 1950s and early 1960s – with the exception of a nasty downtick when U.S. President Dwight Eisenhower had his heart attack – were boom years for base metals, oil, gas and uranium. The godfather of Howe Street was John McGraw of Continental Securities Ltd. McGraw made so much money underwriting B.C. mining stocks that he was eternally grateful that he'd once turned down C.D. Howe's invitation to become president of Trans-Canada Airlines. He was president of the VSE in 1938, and again in 1954 and 1955, and more or less ran the place as an extension of his office. One of his triumphs was Bethlehem Copper Mines, a penny stock which became a major B.C. producer; Continental sold Bethlehem's first stock issue to the public at 75 cents per share. When John F. Kennedy was assassinated in 1963, there was panic selling on the VSE, which stayed open for an hour after the news flashed through from Dallas, while other exchanges shut down immediately. During that fateful hour, when everyone else was clamoring to sell, McGraw bought heavily – and pocketed a small fortune when, a few days later, the markets reopened stronger than ever.

The Day the Lid Blew Off

The best thing that ever happened to the VSE, however, was Ontario's decision to impose stiff new regulations on mining promotions in the wake of the 1964 Windfall Oil and Mines scandal. The new regulations made it almost impossible to promote any kind of a junior mining deal, good or bad, in Toronto. The promoters, crooked and otherwise, started doing deals in wide-open Vancouver. Some of them were shysters, but some were mining men of world-class stature, such as Norman Keevil Sr., the founder of Teck Corp.

On Monday, November 1, 1965, it became stunningly apparent that Vancouver had replaced Toronto as the centre of the speculative universe. That was the day when, in the words of the *Vancouver Sun*, "the lid blew off the Vancouver stock market." The object of all the excitement was Pyramid Mining Co. Ltd., which owned claims near the huge Pine Point lead-zinc mine being developed by Cominco. Pyramid had been trading in the $1 range only a few weeks earlier. But on Friday, October 29, the company's consulting engineer, Henry Hill, reported that they'd struck commercial ore. The rumors flooded Vancouver all weekend. Before dawn on Monday morning, crowds lined up in front of the brokerage houses and cars were double-parked at Howe and Hastings Streets. When the VSE opened at 7 a.m., Pyramid, which had closed the previous Friday at $4.45, opened at $10. By the end of the day it had touched $15. The stock of more than a dozen other companies with claims near Pyramid's strike also went crazy. More than four million shares traded that day. "Here's the Pyramid story in words of one syllable and six figures," wrote Jack Wasserman, the *Sun's* streetwise gossip columnist, the next day. "The mooches made $10 million on paper Monday alone. Little old ladies in tennis shoes, bartenders and bootblacks, rogues and remittance men, cabbies and call girls, sewer diggers and socialites, shared in a bonanza that outdid the Irish sweepstakes."

Some 20 million shares changed hands on the VSE during the month of November 1965. All this hysteria was based on a single drill hole. Pine Point, the successful mine next door, had drilled 1,200 holes to define its ore body. But Pyramid did indeed have a mine and, within a matter of months, had sold the property to Cominco for more than $30 million. Alex Lenec, Pyramid's original promoter, says Cominco eventually dug half a billion dollars' worth of lead and zinc out of the property. Dynasty, another VSE penny stock that was buoyed upward by the Pyramid madness, also made a mine. But none of the other stocks issued during the Pyramid boom was worth the paper its certificates were printed on.

Vancouver's Turn

But it didn't seem to matter. The VSE, which had existed for more than half a century as a little-noticed financial subculture, had become the focus of the fantasies of an entire city. "Toronto's had it for 25 years," said an exultant broker named James McKissock at the height of the Pyramid mania. "It's B.C.'s turn now."

Pyramid established the VSE's ability to generate excitement, but it was another ten years of ups and downs before the VSE began to transcend its origins and become, in a phrase that exchange officials are perhaps excessively fond of using, "the premier venture-capital exchange in North America." The man who initiated that transition, who has made an enduring fortune from it, and who now dominates the exchange the way John McGraw dominated it in the 1950s, is Peter (the Rabbit) Brown.

The Rabbit

People in Vancouver simply can't stop talking about the Rabbit. Still in his early forties, he practically personifies today's VSE – the perfect combination of raffishness and respectability, shrewdness and flamboyance.

The Rabbit's flamboyance has often been chronicled: the 70 pairs of Gucci loafers he keeps in a specially built closet in his Shaughnessy mansion; the $200,000 Rolls-Royce Corniche he had flown over from England; the time when, lazing beside a pool in Las Vegas, he calmly ordered 150 triple bullshots for a few friends. Each of his three homes, naturally, has its own hot tub; the latest residence is a mansion-sized cottage on Bowen Island, B.C., that grandly reflects his flair for the excessive.

Brown has always had baroque relationships with established authority, from headmasters to headwaiters to securities regulators. He was bounced from several private schools as a boy, flunked his freshman year at the University of B.C. three times and refuses to join the Vancouver Club, where his father, uncle and brother are all members. Traffic cops have always given him trouble. In 1982 he was stopped late at night on the highway between Vancouver and Whistler, B.C., where Brown is a major shareholder in the ski resort development. When the officer asked him to lock his Cherokee Chief jeep and accompany him to the police station, Brown responded with badinage along the lines of: "Come on, Sergeant Preston, where's your dog King?" The Mountie didn't think this was funny, and Brown spent Saturday night on the concrete floor of a prison cell. "I saw him on Monday morning," says a friend, "and he was so stiff and hunched over he could hardly walk. Peter told me it was the first night he'd ever spent in jail – which, you know, sort of surprised me."

It would surprise anyone who'd known the Rabbit in his younger days. After university and a four-year stint with Greenshields Inc. in Toronto and Montreal, Brown returned to Vancouver in 1968 as sales manager of a small but furiously active investment firm called H.H. Hemsworth & Co. Ltd. Its salesmen were not always paragons of fiscal rectitude, and the Rabbit has spent the last decade trying to live down the reputation he acquired during those halcyon years. "We weren't crooked," he says, "we were inept."

The Hemsworth firm virtually collapsed in 1972. Brown and a broker named Ted Turton revived the company, renamed it Canarim and started rebuilding. Brown applied to the VSE for approval of the firm's new structure – a mere formality, he thought – and to his horror discovered that Mike Ryan, a respected and influential member of the board of governors, was strongly opposing the application.

"He turned me down, for no other reason than he thought I was a bad guy," Brown recalls. "He had to change his position in the end, because the board didn't have the legal right to reject my application. But Mike did me a great favor. He made me ask myself: 'How could I have got myself into a position where I could allow a guy like that to interfere with my career in that way?' I told myself that I must have an awful lack of credibility."

From that day forward, Brown has been working 13 hours a day to build Canarim into the best, the smartest, the most respected firm on the street – a firm so rich, so successful, so *excellent* that his old detractors will be sick with envy. The firm's offices in the Stock Exchange Tower reflect this upward mobility: puce carpets, a mirrored circular staircase, a Riopelle canvas in the boardroom, rain-swept Toni Onley watercolors everywhere you look. The Rabbit serves on all sorts of boards and committees, and Canarim hands out more than $1 million a year to worthy causes, which probably makes it the province's largest corporate donor. Brown has even been mentioned as a plausible successor to Bill Bennett as Premier of B.C., and he no longer bothers to deny that he'd be interested in running the province the way he runs Howe Street.

A New Credibility

There's no question that Brown has been instrumental in up-grading not only Howe Street's image, but the very way it does business. The reform process started in 1975, when Brown led a polite rebellion against the VSE's board of governors, the same set of gentlemen who'd tried to put him in his place four years earlier. By demanding that nominations be received from the floor of the exchange, rather than from a self-perpetuating nom-inating committee, Brown managed to get himself and three allies elected to the VSE board. Spurred by this ginger group, the VSE hired a new president, a former securities regulator from Alberta named Bob Scott, to police the exchange's activ-ities.

The new board of governors drafted new rules which, al-though they still allowed ample scope for abuse, were an im-provement on their predecessors. They bought more computers and hired more staff. They set about cultivating harmonious relations with the regulators in Victoria. Most important – and this is probably Brown's major contribution – the exchange stopped trying to imitate Toronto and began rejoicing in its own identity. "Once we made that decision and stopped apol-ogizing for what we were," says Brown, "that was the start of regaining a new credibility."

It was more a change of attitude and semantics than of di-rection. People started referring to the VSE as a "venture cap-ital" exchange instead of a "speculative" one. Salesmen started referring to their customers as "clients" instead of "mooches." These semantic nuances reflect a recognition of the VSE's pe-culiar role as a vehicle for raising money for small but hopeful resource companies. Financing mining and oil companies is a vastly different game from trading the shares of established companies. It involves a frank recognition that finding mines and oil wells is inherently a gamble, and that those who gamble on such long-shots should be prepared to lose it all. It acknowl-edges that scams and shysters are an inevitable part of this process; and that totally eliminating the larceny from such a market means eliminating the market itself.

Eager Money

Equipped with this new ideology, Howe Street, and especially Canarim, was in a position to profit hugely from the next bull market, which began around 1978 and lasted until late in 1980. Canarim dominated VSE trading more thoroughly than any single firm ever had. With 150 salesmen at the peak of the boom – about a dozen of whom called themselves millionaires – and with speculators clamoring to buy in a rising market, Canarim was in a position to sell almost anything it offered. The firm became Vancouver's leading underwriter; that is, Canarim would buy an issue of stock from a promoter, then resell it at a slight premium to the public. At the market's height, Canarim was churning out new stock issues like a sausage-machine – as many as $250 million worth in 1980 alone – and was responsible for about 20 per cent of the exchange's trading volume. (The company's dominance was slightly less massive than it appeared, since some of the underwritings which bore Canarim's name were put together by older, Toronto-based firms that did not wish to sully their good name by underwriting one of those flaky Vancouver deals.)

This was an energy boom, and many of the companies Canarim backed really were finding oil and gas – not only in Alberta and British Columbia, but throughout the United States. American oilmen discovered that it was often easier to raise money for new drilling ventures in Vancouver than it was at home, and they crowded into Brown's office, seeking his blessing and his access to eager money. Foreign investors came calling too – from West Germany, Hong Kong, London and Geneva. VSE officials estimate that, of the $5.7 billion which poured into the VSE in 1980 and 1981, only 30 per cent came from B.C. The rest came from elsewhere in Canada, the U.S. and abroad.

A nagging question intrudes: Did all those people get a fair shake for their money? That question went unanswered until 1978, when the B.C. government commissioned a study of VSE trading patterns. Brown, Farris & Jefferson Ltd., a respected Vancouver firm of financial consultants, carried out the study, and only 11 copies of their report were printed, each bound in a binder of a different color to facilitate the detection of leaks. For years the report sat behind locked doors in the Ministry of Economic Development, its contents deemed unfit for public consumption. But an enterprising *Vancouver Sun* financial reporter named Der Hoi-yin got hold of a copy in 1981 and published the highlights. They are not reassuring for anyone who might be thinking about taking a flyer on the VSE.

The study examined what happened to the $1.2 billion invested by the public in 1,623 VSE-listed stocks, nearly all of them mining companies, between 1965 and 1977: how much of this sum was spent on exploration; who got the rest; how much equity in mining companies the public received in return; how much equity the insiders received for the money *they* invested; and what rate of return the public received on its investment. Among the study's findings:

* The 1,623 companies received only $624.5 million of the $1.2 billion invested by the public. The rest – almost half the money – went to brokers, to promoters and to those who originally sold property to the mining companies.

* Mining companies tend to spend between half and three-quarters of their available money on exploration. Thus, for every $10 that the public invests on the VSE, no more than $3.75 goes into the ground.

* It's the public that takes the greatest risk by investing in exploration at the earliest stages of a mine's development. The later stages, when the property's potential has been established and the risks are lower, are usually financed by large, established mining companies. Yet the public usually ends up paying far more for a piece of the successful companies than do the original insiders, or the large companies which bring the new mines into production.

* The study also examined in detail the 10 producing BC mines which had been partly financed on the VSE between 1975 and 1977. The public shareholders received about one-sixth as much benefit for their investment as did the promoters of these winning deals.

* If you compare all the dollars invested on the VSE in 1965 with what all those shares were worth in 1977, the results are particularly horrifying. "Over the whole period of the study," the authors comment, "all dollars combined lost 13.2% of their value in each year after the initial outlay."

* Losers consistently outnumber winners on the VSE by a margin of roughly five to one. "The odds of losing, overall, are 84%," says the report – "about five times out of six. A full 40% of the financings are now worthless."

* The study estimated that promoters and vendors – there can't be more than a few hundred of them – pocketed $268.5 million over a 13-year period. The brokers who underwrote the share issues and made commissions by trading them pocketed a further $335.6 million.

* To explain why the returns to the public are so low, the study analyzed what happens in a typical mining financing. In

the early stages of the company, after the first public issue of shares, the public has put up 79 per cent of the money but owns only 21 per cent of the shares; promoters own about 60 per cent of the shares, for which they paid practically nothing. A year later, if the property looks promising and the company sells further shares to pay for further development, the public ends up owning about 32 per cent of the company, in return for having provided about 80 per cent of the funds. If the promoters sell some of their shares – as often happens if a property is successful and the stock is a high flyer – the public shareholders recover almost three times their original investment. The insiders, because they picked up their shares for almost nothing very early in the game, get more than 33 times their money back.

The situation today probably isn't *quite* as bad as it was painted by Brown, Farris & Jefferson Ltd.. For one thing, the study examined rates of return over a period of years. And everybody is supposed to know that the only way to win on the VSE is by buying in a rising market, and then getting out fast. Proximity and contacts have a lot to do with how successful you are; that's why thousands of Vancouver-based clients of the major speculative houses made huge gains in 1980-81. It also explains why so many speculators from Dusseldorf and Hong Kong lost heavily. It's still true that the vast majority of the VSE's offerings are rubbish. But that also happens to be true of the publishing and film industries, among others.

It's also true that today's rubbish might become tomorrow's billion-dollar orebody. It doesn't happen very often, but it happens often enough to keep the VSE rolling from the trough of one speculative wave to the crest of the next – and it happens often enough, I believe, to justify the entire crazy game.

8
Hemlo And
The Pez

Murray Pezim's office is a cross between a Jewish delicatessen and the cockpit of a Boeing 747. His desk is an information clearing-house, crowded with electronic instruments that deliver instant readouts of the state of markets around the world. There's a closed-circuit TV monitor that slowly pans back and forth across the huge blackboard on the trading floor of the Vancouver Stock Exchange, giving the viewer an over-the-shoulder view of the board-markers chalking up their quotations. There's also a computer terminal which can summon these numbers, along with stock quotations from Toronto and New York and a lot of additional statistical information, at the touch of a few keys. A digital clock on Murray Pezim's desk constantly reminds him of time's swift passage. A hissing teleprinter whispers the latest financial intelligence from around the world. A loudspeaker system, piped directly from the exchange floor, nine stories below Pezim's office in Vancouver's Stock Exchange Tower, informs him every few minutes that a "cross" has taken place – some investment house has matched a client's buy order with another client's order to sell, thus bypassing the floor traders. And of course there's the telephone, which Murray uses constantly as an extension of his nervous system; and of course there are all Murray's hundreds of friends and hangers-on, who seem to wander in and out of his office like extras in his own private movie.

Pezim is perhaps the most colorful stock promoter this country has ever produced, and one of the most successful. He has the air of a standup comedian who, like his good friend Bob Hope, is very crafty and very rich. He's a man of large appetites: He loves to talk and eat and smoke and fly his friends to Las Vegas where, he says, some of the swarthy gentlemen running the casinos are his boyhood friends. He's in his mid-sixties and his hair is thinning, but it still stands up all over his head like Art Garfunkel's. He has the face of an amiable but experienced turtle. He works in short-sleeved shirts that have PEZ mono-

91

grammed on the pockets. His office is full of yes-men, including a body-builder named Stan – a former Mr. Poland whom The Pez has hired full-time to make salads and act as his personal masseur. On a shelf above his desk is displayed a shiny architectural model of a hotel that he wants to build on land he owns near Victoria, B.C. If Murray gets his way, the hotel will have stock-market monitors in every room, and it will be called Chateau Pez.

Some of Pezim's friends describe him as a manic-depressive. Whether or not that's clinically accurate, it's true that his relationship to wealth is peculiarly intense. When Murray feels rich, his voracious ego seems to swell like a barrage balloon, until his mere physical presence can dominate entire ballrooms. But when he's broke, something inside Pezim collapses; he looks old, sad, broken. Vast wealth and humiliating poverty seem to alternate like conflicting leitmotifs in Pezim's up-and-down career. He's been wiped out in the market several times. And he's been a multimillionaire, at least on paper, more often than he can count.

In 1981, at the height of the energy boom, he felt flush enough to pay $630,000 cash for a luxury condo beside Vancouver's English Bay. Then the stock market collapsed, and Pezim, by his own casual reckoning, was worth $15 to $20 million less than he'd been at the market's peak. To compound the misery, he was facing stock-fraud charges which threatened to send him to jail. But a year later he'd been acquitted of the fraud charges and, through a fortuitous chain of circumstances, was revelling in the wealth and wild acclaim he'd been seeking all his life. After 30 years as the clown prince of Canadian stock promoters, after decades of touting stocks that usually turned out to be worthless, Murray Pezim finally, incredibly, brought in a mine – not only a mine, but an entire gold field, one of the greatest North American gold discoveries of the postwar era. By 1983, his fortune was estimated at a debt-free $40 million, with the prospect of untold wealth still to come. He controlled about 60 VSE-listed companies and was influential in dozens more.

Drillhole 76

The source of The Pez's new assurance is his part-ownership of a tract of scrubby bush that stretches for several miles on either side of the Trans-Canada Highway, about 220 miles east of Thunder Bay, Ontario.

For nearly a century, the ground had been staked repeatedly by successive generations of prospectors. But in 1980, a series of events and personalities converged, almost accidentally, to create something miraculous. Two vastly experienced prospectors staked new claims on the property, and refused to stop believing in it. Then a brilliant young geologist looked at the property with fresh eyes and spotted geological virtues which had eluded previous generations of gold-seekers. The deal then passed from hand to hand, as the prospectors and a series of go-betweens tried to raise money for further exploration in Toronto. Rebuffed, the go-betweens then looked for money in Vancouver. Almost inevitably, the deal crossed Pezim's cluttered desk, one of dozens of such deals he looks at every week. Pezim passed it on to a remarkable young associate, Nell Dragovan, who risked her own money to keep the deal afloat. When, on the basis of early exploration, the deal looked more promising than ever, Pezim gambled millions of his own and other people's money to pay for continued exploration.

It wasn't until the seventy-sixth drillhole that the young geologist, David Bell, confirmed that they'd uncovered a major orebody. From that point forward, the Hemlo find followed the classic pattern of all Canadian gold rushes: a furious staking contest; the formation of more than 200 companies with claims near the discovery, with the stock of each bouncing up and down on the VSE according to the latest drilling rumors; billion-dollar lawsuits over disputed land claims; and a wave of gold-plated euphoria that swept across the country, touching hundreds of lives with magic, turning welders and housewives into would-be millionaires.

For once, the enthusiasm was well-founded. By the end of 1983, after dozens of companies had drilled hundreds of holes, the broad outlines of the new goldfield were firmly established. On the International Corona property alone, a pay zone almost a mile square by a mile deep had been delineated. Neighboring properties, owned by Lac Minerals Ltd. and by the joint venture of Goliath Gold Mines Ltd. and Golden Sceptre Resources Ltd., were part of the same bonanza. The drilling had conservatively established more than 55 million tons of commercial-grade ore, containing between 0.18 and 0.5 ounces of gold per ton.

In terms of actual production, the claims could work out to 15 million ounces of gold produced by three separate mines. Assuming a price of $US350 per ounce, in other words, the Hemlo deposits were worth upward of $5 billion. The Kirkland Lake-Larder Lake region, with 20 separate mines, has been producing gold since shortly after the First World War; and in all those years, the region's total production has been about 35 million ounces, worth less than $2 billion – about one-third the value of what Hemlo is apparently capable of producing. Hemlo is the kind of deposit which, in the past, has created family dynasties and caused cities to spring up in the wilderness. No one, it seemed, would ever again fail to take Murray Pezim seriously. And never again would he be poor.

The Poverty Years

Pezim's father was a Romanian-born Jew who owned two Toronto drugstores. In those prohibition years of the 1920s, sales of medicinal alcohol were very brisk, and Pezim's father was prosperous enough to live in a mansion on Palmerston Avenue, then a private thoroughfare with iron gates at each end. "We had guards on the street, would you believe it?" Pezim recalls. "I remember my father used to bring home the silver coins from the drugstore and put them under the carpet, so we always knew there was money. But then, after 1929, it was a big home and we didn't have heat and light. We couldn't afford to pay the bills.

"What I remember most about the Depression," Pezim recalls, "was how hungry we were, how we had to fight to stay alive." At 14, he dropped out of Harbord Collegiate, where his classmates had included Johnny Wayne and Frank Shuster, and started to hustle. "In 1935 there was a police-protected gambling joint called the Brown Derby in Port Credit," Pezim recalls. "We'd go out there and be car jockeys, hoping that whoever we'd park the car for would throw us a quarter. If we got the quarter, we could eat the next day. It was that serious."

After the failure of his drugstores, Pezim's father started two butcher shops in poor Toronto neighborhoods, and that's where Murray worked until he enlisted in the army in 1940. His war consisted mainly of serving as a truck-driver (and running a few crap games on the side) in a prison camp for German POWs in Jamaica. "It scared the hell out of me. Those Germans were huge bastards from the Afrika Corps. One little Jew looking through the fence at all these guys, and if they ever got loose, I'd be chopped liver."

After the war, it was back to 100-hour weeks in the butcher shop. The place was left unheated in winter to save on refrigeration bills. Pezim used to keep a bucket of warm water beside his chopping-block; every few minutes he would plunge his bloody hands into the pail to thaw them out. One day deliv-

94

erance arrived in the person of a stockbroker named Max Guthrie, who walked in to buy some lamb chops. "This was 1949 or 1950, and I had $15,000 saved up from hard, hard work. Guthrie introduced me to a stock called Duvay. I kept buying the stock as it went up and up, dreaming I'm going to be the bull of Wall Street. Six weeks later they pulled the plug on the stock and I lost every cent. When I found I'd lost all my money, I thought: 'Geez, I've got to learn this business.' I figured that if I'd lost it, somebody else had made it."

Pezim spent nearly a year studying the market, hanging around Bay Street brokerage offices, watching the board with the other pooches, and working for six months without pay in a New York brokerage house. Finally, at age 30, he was hired by E.T. Lynch & Co. as a salesman and, 18 months later, joined the firm that was to employ him for the next 17 years, Jenkins, Evans & Co., a now-defunct Bay Street company which specialized in penny-stock promotions.

Within five years, Pezim was rich. A young Czech-born promoter named Steve Roman, who'd got his start sweeping floors in a General Motors factory in Oshawa, was trying to raise $40,000 to drill for uranium near a place called Blind River. Pezim helped him raise the money. "Well, you know the rest of the story," he says. "It was Denison Mines and it was trading at 40 cents. My people and I made fortunes, even though I sold my stock at $17 and then watched it go to $85 a share." Pezim paid $497,000 for a 22-acre estate near Ocho-Rios, Jamaica, that had three houses on the property. "I started to invite my friends down and, needless to say, the party went on for a year and a half. It was a wild scene. Women? Sure, in those days I loved to screw. Jamaica is a great island – your pecker goes up as soon as you get off the plane."

The First of His Fortunes

Some of his new friends suggested tearing down all three houses to build a hotel, the Carib Ocho-Rios. "This was 1957, money was tight and the Bank of Montreal ended up owning it. We blew our brains out." That was the beginning and end of Pezim's first fortune.

Then came an era of buying large or controlling positions in various companies and, with remarkable frequency, running them into the ground. By this time, Pezim was working in partnership with another Toronto promoter named Earl Glick, who'd drifted into the stock market via the costume-jewellery business. First came Delta Electronics, a Toronto company that manufactured co-axial cable. Then they bought Spartan Air Services, which owned 40 fixed-wing aircraft and 30 helicopters. That deal, too, ended badly. Then came a U.S. firm called Leland Publishing. "The stock was $12, and I had 300,000 shares," Pezim recalls. "One morning the president phoned me before the market opened and said, 'Murray, we're going into receivership this morning.' I said, 'Can't you wait until noon?' So that one didn't turn out very well either." Then came Phantom Hosiery. "We started selling in supermarkets, and that was a deadly error, since it was a high-class product." Hundreds of shareholders lost money on most of these deals, but Pezim and Glick usually came out a little richer than before. In 1964, at the height of the Texas Gulf Sulphur madness on the Toronto Stock Exchange, they were major players. "I remember one day the TSE traded 28 million shares – and of that volume, 14 million was ours. National Explorations, one of our companies, traded three times its issued capital in a single day."

The 1964 Windfall scandal, a by-product of the Texas Gulf Sulphur boom, launched a wave of regulatory attacks against Bay Street's stock-promotion practices. Pezim and Glick started doing deals in Vancouver, and soon they were virtually commuting between the two cities. In 1967, through a Vancouver-listed company called Stampede Oil and Gas, whose stock went from 50 cents to $27, Pezim actually discovered a major Alberta gas field, the Strachan-Ricinus field. It was a totally accidental bonanza, since Pezim had been drilling for sulphur. But it generated enough attention to force the Toronto authorities to consider whether they wanted Murray Pezim doing business on Bay Street.

Chased out of Town

In 1967, he was summoned to the office of William Somerville, executive vice-president of the TSE. When he walked in, Somerville didn't even look up. "He didn't even say 'hello' to me," Pezim recalls with bitterness. "All he said was: 'Make up your mind: east or west?' I said, 'What do you mean?' He said, 'Where do you want to work – east or west?' I said, 'Are you *telling* me where I can work?' And Somerville said, 'That's exactly what I'm telling you.'" Angry and humiliated, Pezim resigned from Jenkins Evans the next day and moved permanently to Vancouver.

His departure was a matter of symbolic and historical importance. The Windfall scandal had convinced the Bay Street Establishment that its future prosperity depended on running a market that was honest, and was perceived to be honest. To this new way of thinking, Pezim and his ilk were worse than sleazy; they represented an economic threat. By making them unwelcome in Toronto, Bay Street believed it was securing its own future as a senior securities exchange. But Pezim's move to Vancouver reflected the start of a cultural shift. The whole subculture of mining finance – the brokers, the promoters, the prospectors, the publicists, the salesmen, the touts – constituted an infrastructure which, for all its wastefulness, fraud and excess, had helped develop one of Canada's major industries. It took Bay Street another 20 years to discover that in the process of stamping out fraud, they'd also managed to stamp out an important ingredient of the mining industry's success. Between 1964 and 1984, the VSE, with Pezim as one of its reigning godfathers, financed many genuine, producing mines, along with hundreds of duds. Not a single new mine was financed by Bay Street during the same period. And when Hemlo came along, it was a source of acute embarrassment to Bay Street that Ontario's greatest mineral find in a generation had been financed, not from Toronto, but from Vancouver – and by people whom Bay Street had almost literally chased out of town.

Prospecting as a Profession

The term "prospector" still evokes an image of some grizzled old party leading a donkey through the bush, like Gabby Hayes. In northern Ontario, however, prospecting is simply everybody's other business. Barbers, hardrock miners and high-school students spend their weekends prospecting as routinely, and for much the same reasons, as other people dabble in real estate. But there are also prospecting professionals. And Don McKinnon and John Larche, who first staked the Hemlo property, are regarded as two of the finest.

McKinnon is a high-school dropout from Cochrane, Ontario who taught himself geology by tramping through the bush, looking at rocks, and reading everything he could get his hands on. When you're hunting gold, formal training isn't always an asset. "With gold," he says, "you have to bang rocks. You almost have to be able to smell it. That's why a knowledge of prospecting and a limited knowledge of geology is a real good combination, versus strictly knowledge as a graduate geologist." He and Larche were at the forefront of the 1963–64 staking rush near Timmins, in the wake of the Texas Gulf discovery, and made enough money selling claims to live on for the next 20 years. In fact, it was McKinnon and Larche who staked the claims which became Windfall Oil and Mines – the source of the scandal which transformed Bay Street and sent Pezim packing to Vancouver.

McKinnon does almost as much prospecting in the library as in the field. Since the early years of this century, the Canadian Shield has been minutely picked at, staked, surveyed and drilled by generations of prospectors and geologists. Much of what they discovered, or failed to discover, is on the public record. By carefully examining what his predecessors found, McKinnon gathers geological evidence that is as useful as anything he could find by smelling rocks.

Digging into the Records

It was the historical record which attracted him to the Hemlo area. A prospector named Moses Pe-Kong-Gay discovered two veins near the present town of Heron Bay, not far from Hemlo, in 1869. The discovery led to the opening of a small mine in 1872. A CPR station agent at Hemlo sunk several test pits in the 1920s. In 1931, J.E. Thompson, a geologist for the Ontario Department of Mines, mapped the entire region and recommended the Hemlo area as a promising field for further exploration. In 1944, a prospector named Peter Moses found gold in the area, and a Maryland resident, J.K. Williams, staked the claims. In 1947, a group of weekend entrepreneurs from Thunder Bay, operating as a company called Lake Superior Mining Co., drilled some holes on what is now the International Corona property and proved up 89,000 tons of ore averaging 0.27 ounces of gold per ton. They even sold an option on the property to Teck-Hughes Mining Co., the predecessor of what is now Teck Corp. But in 1947, with gold pegged at $35 per ounce, the find was deemed uneconomic.

Largely on the basis of this history, McKinnon staked 12 claims in the Hemlo area when they came open in 1979. Working independently, Larche staked seven claims just east of McKinnon's. In 1980 they joined forces and canvassed Bay Street for risk capital to finance further exploration. "For a year and a half I tried to sell that ground to almost every major company in captivity, with no success," says McKinnon. "In fact, the worst part about it was they never even had the courtesy to check out some of the work we'd done. That was the worst part. They just turned it down flat because Teck had already been there. That's the part that hurts."

In October 1980, McKinnon brought a thick file of mining prospects to David Bell, a bright young geologist who, partly because of McKinnon's encouragement, that very month had quit a promising job with a big mining company, setting himself up in Timmins as a consultant. One of the prospects was the Hemlo claims, and they immediately caught Bell's eye. McKinnon's maps showed where Teck had drilled in the 1950s, and what they'd found. Bell realized that Teck's 30-year-old ore estimates – 89,000 tons, grading 0.27 ounces per ton – needed to be revised in light of the current price of gold.

Because gold was $35 per ounce in the 1950s, Teck's geologists hadn't been interested in ore grades of less than 0.25. But Bell knew there must be such deposits nearby. With gold at $400 per ounce, the whole package might add up to a mine. He took the available information home with him that evening. "I calculated everything out and figured there must be something like 250,000 tons of 0.12- or 0.13-ounce material on the property," Bell recalls. The next day he told McKinnon: "This is too good to pass up. It looks as if there's a larger, lower-grade situation here which should be re-drilled and shaped up."

McKinnon had already tried, without success, to find financial backers for a drilling program. So Bell, with McKinnon's permission, turned to an old friend who'd become a stockbroker and small-time mining promoter, Don Moore. Moore, in turn, passed the deal on to an old university classmate named Steve Snelgrove, another former stockbroker and part-time mining promoter. Snelgrove, in turn, flew to Vancouver from Toronto and tried to interest a fellow-promoter, Doug Collingwood, in buying the claims. Collingwood declined, but sent Snelgrove over to Murray Pezim's office – which is where, as luck would have it, he met Nell Dragovan.

Dragovan now controls or is active in 22 VSE-listed companies, and according to Howe Street scuttlebutt is a millionaire several times over. But in November 1980, she was a nervous young woman who had stumbled into the stock-promotion business more or less by accident. While working as a restaurant hostess after graduation from Simon Fraser University, she'd drifted into journalism, helping some friends with a magazine they'd started called *Canadian Shareholder*. It made no money, but it did give her a string of contacts on Howe Street, and taught her how the stock-promotion business worked. She also

99

discovered that there were few barriers to entry, and that dozens of ex-cops, ex-newspapermen and ex-insurance salesmen were calling themselves resource financiers and running VSE-listed companies. Dragovan decided to take the plunge herself.

Tristar, Jetstar, Corona – and Dragovan

With the aid of a young lawyer and budding promoter named Ken Gracie, she put together a company called Tristar Resources, talked a few of her Howe Street contacts into practically giving her some oil and gas claims that no one else wanted, and steered the prospectus through the regulatory maze. This meant she had permission to sell 250,000 shares of Tristar at 20 cents each, to raise a total of $50,000. So Dragovan trudged around Vancouver, selling Tristar shares to friends and relatives. Some of her Howe Street contacts felt sorry for her and, mostly as an act of charity, bought a few thousand shares each. "I heard later there was some difficulty about getting Tristar listed," she says, "because there were so many brokers' names on the shareholders' list that the VSE thought there must be something kinky going on, which wasn't true at all."

At the end of the four-month period which the law allows for selling the issue, she still had 50,000 shares unsold. On the final day, she borrowed $10,000 to buy them herself. Tristar was duly listed on the VSE, and Nell Dragovan, ex-publisher, ex-restaurant hostess, was now a resource financier. A few months later, fortune smiled: Bob Lamond, a high-flying oil and gas promoter from Calgary, bought the company for one of his own promotions, largely because he liked the name. Under Lamond's control, Tristar hit $7.25 before flaming out. Dragovan made a lot of money on the deal – a little by selling her piece of Tristar to Lamond, and a lot more by trading the stock on the way up and on the way down. She was learning the business.

"Then I formed a company called Jetstar. Then some friends of mine started forming companies too, and put me on their boards. I just kept forming more and more companies." One of her companies was called Corona Resources Ltd., which raised money to drill for oil and gas in Manitoba. Nothing was found, and Corona joined the VSE's vast population of corporate has-beens – that ghostly gallery of depleted companies which have raised and spent money on exploration, have found nothing, and then exist in a sort of corporate limbo – a few hundred dollars in the treasury, perhaps, or a few thousand dollars coming in every month from a piece of a producing oil well – until they either vanish completely or are magically resurrected by some new promotion.

Corona's resurrection occurred because Nell Dragovan was in Pezim's office the day Snelgrove dropped by. "Nell just happened to be in the office," Pezim recalls, "and I said I needed a dormant, VSE-listed company to take on Snelgrove's Hemlo claims. Nell said: 'What about Corona?' It was as simple as that. I said, 'Fine,' and we agreed to do a financing. That's how it all began."

At this stage, Corona didn't exactly belong to Dragovan, or to anyone else. But as part of the resurrection process, Pezim made her president of this worthless, orphaned little company. Such dealings were by now routine for Dragovan. "To me, it was just another property. Some work had been done on it in the past and it had a showing. So what? There are lots of them."

At Snelgrove's suggestion Dragovan hired David Bell to manage the exploration program. He needed money to get started, but funds from the underwriting weren't expected until January 1981. "So, I decided," says Dragovan, "well, I'll send David $10,000 of my own money; and if he steals it, it'll be a $10,000 experience." She needn't have worried. As a geologist, Bell is a promoter's dream; he is methodical, conservative, almost painfully sincere, and he looks like a Methodist choirboy. "David appears so honest that I believe he's the greatest promoter on this earth and he doesn't know it," says Dragovan.

Bell began drilling in January. A generation earlier, Teck-Hughes had established the existence of a "pod" of high-grade ore on the property. What Bell was trying to discover through drilling was the extent of the lower-grade ore surrounding it. The drill cores themselves showed little visible gold, but when the assays of these core samples came back from the lab, they showed that the gold was distributed throughout the ore-bearing zone with remarkable consistency, like the sugar in a cup of well-stirred coffee.

"Dip your fingers in an inkwell, then flick the ink against the wall; that's the way gold is usually distributed," Bell explains. "Then close your eyes and throw a dart at the wall. How many times will you hit the ink-splatters? That's the problem you usually have in diamond drilling.

"But in Hemlo, the pattern was completely different. It's more like flicking the ink into a bathtub. Instead of leaving splotches, it spreads out into a uniform distribution. You have a harder time seeing the ink, because it's evenly distributed. But it's there."

101

Bell's confidence kept growing as hole after hole was completed. In April, when he examined the drill cores from the seventy-sixth hole, his confidence changed to genuine excitement. Until then, all the drilling had been on the west side of a region of barren rock known as a diabase dike. The seventy-sixth hole was on the other, eastern, side of the dike, and revealed the existence of a similar gold deposit. The Corona deposit, in other words, wasn't just a localized showing; the fact that it continued across the diabase barrier indicated that it might be something huge.

The actual moment of discovery, in keeping with Bell's cautious nature, was very low-key. When the core segments from Hole 76 were laid out in their boxes in the core shack, Bell examined them with his assistant, John Dadds. "Gee," said Dadds, "these look a lot like some of the stuff we've been getting in the west zone." That was the moment Bell became a true believer. "But despite what I was telling Murray and Nell," he says, "they didn't really believe they had a mine. You know, they'd never had anything like this in their lives before."

The Vancouver market was heating up on the strength of the rumors emanating from Hemlo. Prospectors were rushing in to stake claims near the site of the rumored strike, and companies were being formed by the dozen to exploit them. Before Hole 76, Corona's shares were trading in the $1.50 range. By July they had risen to around $2. That's when Pezim pulled out all the stops, riding the telephone 12 hours a day, whipping up enthusiasm among investors all over the continent. Corona kept rising as the conviction grew that Pezim had at last discovered an honest-to-God goldfield. By autumn, atop a wave of speculative madness which must be experienced to be believed, Corona reached a peak of $32.

Then the recession hit. The VSE fizzled like a punctured balloon, and by late 1981 Pezim was feeling the financial squeeze. He'd been buying Corona shares heavily for himself on behalf of several companies he controlled, and had been busy floating other companies with claims near the Corona strike. But the money from the initial Corona underwriting, plus an additional cash infusion in mid-year, had already been spent on drilling. Millions more were needed, and with the market collapsing around his ears, Pezim couldn't raise the money.

From Speculator to Financier

So, in December, he did the logical thing. He made a deal with Teck Corp., a major mining company, to explore and develop the property at its own expense, in return for a major interest in Corona. David Bell and Don Moore were both Corona directors, but they learned of the agreement with Teck only because they bumped into a broker in Thunder Bay who'd seen it announced on his news ticker. They were horrified. Pezim, in effect, had given away control of their company without consulting them. They phoned Nell Dragovan, who was in tears, and caught the next plane to Vancouver. "It was desperation," says Bell. "It was a shame. In return for spending $1 million, Teck got 55 per cent of Corona's shares. And we'd already spent $1.6 million ourselves."

Through Don McKinnon, they tried to find another buyer. Imperial Oil was approached; they expressed some interest, but couldn't give an immediate commitment. Besides, Pezim said, he'd given his word to Teck, and that was that. Moore and Bell, disgusted at what they regarded as a sell-out by Pezim, resigned from the board and flew back to northern Ontario.

That was the end of one phase of the Hemlo story and the beginning of another. Two seasoned promoters, Frank Lang and Dick Hughes, with the aid of David Bell's geological insights, discovered another huge gold showing nearby; their companies, Goliath and Golden Sceptre, soared from pennies to the $25 range. Lac Minerals, a major Toronto mining group, got control of a third set of productive Hemlo claims. There were squabbles and claim-staking disputes and then, in 1983, Noranda Mines made a commitment to spend $100 million on a mill to process the ore. Geologists and prospectors across Ontario were taking fresh looks at scores of abandoned properties, trying to apply the lessons learned from Hemlo.

The Hemlo discoveries have transformed Pezim from the clown prince of Canadian stock promotion into something approaching the status of Corporate Statesman. He was being invited to speak at *Financial Post* seminars and to sit on the Vancouver Ballet Guild's board of directors. He was being interviewed with a new deference by financial reporters. People didn't kid with him the way they used to; instead, they listened respectfully to his opinions on anything from bagels to the price of gold.

At one conference where Pezim had spoken in Toronto, a senior official of Wood Gundy, the ultra-Establishment investment dealer, greeted him warmly and invited him to drop around for a chat.

"Are you kidding?" The Pez replied. "You guys won't let me in the front door."

"Oh, no," the Wood Gundy man answered earnestly, "We'd *love* to talk to you about what you're doing."

103

Hemlo, and Hemlo alone, was the reason for this sudden and unaccustomed deference. For Pezim, being wooed by those haughty Bay Street financiers, those people who'd hounded him out of Toronto and always disdained him, was the sweetest accolade of all. "Sure it makes you feel great," he says. "After taking all that abuse for all those years, with the East against you, with the Establishment against you, calling your deals bullshit and moose pasture – it was a bloody battle.

"I started out in this business as a broker. Then they called me a promoter. Then I went from speculator to entrepreneur. And now they're calling me a *financier*! That's the evolution of The Pez. It's a great feeling, it really is."

9
The Commodities Game

The difference between trading stocks and trading futures and options is the difference between Chinese checkers and three-dimensional chess. Futures and options are also far riskier and – if you're both brave and lucky – vastly more rewarding. In the stock market, the absolute worst that can happen is that you'll lose every nickel you invest. And that hardly ever happens; in all but the most disastrous stock-market debacles, investors can usually get back most of the money they put into the market.

Traders of futures and options inhabit a world that is far more savage and intense. Because they're borrowing heavily to gamble on the future price of a commodity, they risk losing every penny of their original investment – and, in the case of futures, even *more* than their original stake. In the commodities business there are countless stories about credulous amateurs being forced to sell their homes to cover their trading positions. In New York and Chicago, the world centres of commodities speculation, billions of dollars, most of them borrowed, are gambled every day on the price of wheat, or heating oil, or hogs, or sugar, or frozen orange-juice concentrate – or the most seductive commodity of all: money itself.

A Massive Side-Bet on the Market

Unlike the stock market, it is a zero-sum game; whatever you lose, someone else makes. The more wrong you are, the more money you lose; that's why the losses sustained by the billion-aire Hunt Brothers of Texas totalled more than $900 million when, in 1979, they tried and failed to corner the silver market. It's this life-or-death quality that lends the commodities game its peculiar intensity. During a heavy trading session in New York a few years ago, one commodities trader keeled over dead from a heart attack. His colleagues had no trouble choosing

105

their priorities; with as much solicitude as they could muster, they pushed his stiffening corpse over to the side of the pit, and continued trading until the final bell. "In this game," says a former Toronto commodities trader named Manny Batler, "you've got to have stainless-steel balls."

The trading in futures and options represents a massive side-bet on the market – a tail which threatens to end up wagging the entire bull. In 1983, some $1.2 trillion worth of shares were traded on North American stock markets. In the same year, some $5 trillion was gambled – there is no other word for it – on 11 U.S. commodity exchanges on the future prices of everything from frozen orange juice to the Mexican peso. The value of the side-bets, in other words, now vastly exceeds the value of the main market – and most of the side-bet money is borrowed money.

People have been betting on the future prices of commodities since the nineteenth century at least. The original rationale was that it allowed farmers and manufacturers to lock in prices through hedging on the commodities markets. The chocolate-bar manufacturer, by buying contracts for the delivery of so much cocoa by a certain date at a certain price, could insure himself against a sudden rise in the price of his main raw material. The producer, in turn, was happy to sell the contract; it protected *him* against a fall in commodity prices and ensured that he could repay his bank loans. In order for the system to work, of course, there had to be additional speculators involved in the process, buying and selling contracts between the time they were written and harvest time. Only one party to such a transaction can be right – and the winner takes home all the loser's money.

Historically, commodities speculation goes back much further than stock-trading. It was big business on the Toronto Stock Exchange in the 1850s, when trading beef and grain futures far outweighed the occasional transactions in the handful of available railroad and bank stocks. It was also an important ingredient of the speculative mania which culminated in the market collapse of 1929. In those days, the speculators tended to be professionals; the futures traders of Chicago or Winnipeg were never far from the smell of the stockyards or the sound of the shunting freight trains laden with prairie wheat.

But since the 1970s, trading in options and futures has become a popular middle-class preoccupation, routinely conducted by people who can't tell one end of a hog from the other. The Chicago Board Options Exchange, which accounts for more than half of U.S. options trading, has grown explosively since its founding in 1973. Its new headquarters, with a trading floor almost one and a half times as large as that of the Toronto Stock Exchange, has a cloakroom that's larger than the CBOE'soriginal trading floor.

A Quick Killing

The boom in options and futures has happened for a variety of reasons, but the principal one seems to be that the major stock markets have become less appropriate as vehicles for the credulous multitudes who want to make a quick killing. You could trade stocks on as little as 20 per cent margin in 1929; that is, you could buy $100 worth of stock by putting down only $20 in cash. Today's margin requirements are 50 per cent or more, and the prices of good stocks are higher than they used to be. So are most brokerage commissions. Unless you're playing a high-risk market such as the Vancouver Stock Exchange, it's difficult to buy a meaningful position in the stock market for less than $10,000 or so. But in the futures and options markets, $10,000 buys you a chance to gamble in the most exciting casino in town, sometimes at margins as high as 100 to one, and the potential profits can be enormous.

Pork Bellies in Pinstripes

Financial communities around the world, sensing a large, un-tapped market, have made the game easier to play by inventing new and more accessible vehicles. "Mini-contracts," which enable a speculator to bet on the price of 50 or 100 ounces of silver instead of 500, have become increasingly popular. In addition, they've invented ways for speculators to bet not only on the future price of actual commodities, but on the future direction of interest rates, on the future price of specific stocks and, with index futures, even on the future level of the stock market as a whole. The development of these financial futures (which have been dubbed "pork bellies in pinstripes") may turn out to be one of the most significant financial developments of this century. Says Richard Sandor, the Chicago Board of Trade's former chief economist: "We're where the computer business was in 1963. We haven't even gotten to the Apple and the Peanut."

This plethora of new "products" offered by the world's exchanges is so pervasive that it's now reflected in their names, and sometimes in the very architecture of their trading floors. Chicago, home of the Chicago Board Options Exchange, the Chicago Mercantile Exchange and the Chicago Board of Trade, is still the world's largest arena for trading options and futures. But stock exchanges around the world are doing their best to grab a piece of Chicago's business. The Montreal Exchange has dropped the word "stock" from its title to reflect its hoped-for status as a sort of financial supermarket, rather than as an arena for trading only stocks. The Toronto Stock Exchange's new logo has the words "The Exchange" in large type, with the words "Toronto" and "Stock" deliberately de-emphasized. Its new trading floor, opened in 1983, has ten trading posts. But only five are devoted to trading stocks. Three similar posts have been reserved for options trading, with room for a fourth; and another two are used for trading futures. Huntly McKay, the TSE's vice-president for markets and market development, believes that, by 1988, about 30 per cent of the exchange's business will be in options and futures.

Exchange officials argue that these new financial vehicles are needed as protection against an increasingly uncertain world. In an era of bouncing interest rates and wildly fluctuating stock prices, some mechanism is needed to enable traders to hedge their bets. Interest-rate futures, for instance, enable a corporate treasurer to insulate his company against a sudden hike in interest rates. If the rates go up, his profits on the futures contracts partly compensate him for the extra interest charges he must pay. Through hedging, in other words, a company has protected itself against the unpredictable – just as farmers have done for generations.

The TSE used this hedging argument in 1982 when it sought permission from the Ontario Securities Commission to introduce trading in stock index futures. Using this vehicle, traders can buy and sell contracts for future delivery of cash, based on the level of the TSE 300 index. The OSC grudgingly approved the new vehicle, but expressed doubts that it would be used extensively by legitimate hedgers.

One gets the impression that the TSE doesn't much care who does the trading, just so long as there's plenty of it. The exchanges are so anxious to get new products onto their trading floors that, on occasion, they've even lapsed into unseemly displays of competitive behavior. In 1975, the TSE was negotiating with the Montreal Exchange to set up a stock-options market that would be owned jointly by both exchanges. Then, one morning, TSE officials read in the newspapers that Montreal had decided to open an options market on its own. "I can tell you," says Huntly McKay, "we were very upset."

The TSE set up its own rival options market in 1976. In 1983, at the insistence of regulatory authorities in both provinces, the Montreal and Toronto options markets were merged and linked by computer, and the Vancouver Stock Exchange was later added to the network. Around the same time, the Montreal and Vancouver exchanges joined forces with an exchange in Amsterdam to offer options contracts on various currencies, and on gold in 10-ounce units. The TSE fired back with its own plan for trading silver options in 1,000-ounce units (now changed to 100-ounce units). The TSE has also been trading futures contracts on short- and long-term bonds and treasury bills since 1980 – offering investors a chance to bet on interest rates – as well as trading on the aforementioned stock index futures contracts, which allow speculators to bet hard cash on the ups and downs of the stock market itself. These financial futures are bets on a number instead of a commodity; or, as one New York investment banker explains it: "They're bets on nothing, on a feeling about the future trend of the market as a whole. You're betting on someone else's bet. It's crazy."

Options or Futures

At this point, you may be wondering about the difference between options and futures. They're related vehicles, in the sense that in both cases the trader uses a small down-payment to bet on a future price. "Both futures and options," says McKay, "are a recognition of a fundamental fact of life: that life is time, and time has value. These new vehicles make it possible to merchandise them."

Options (also known as puts or calls) are simply pieces of paper which entitle you to buy or sell something specific – such as 50,000 Canadian dollars, or 100 shares of Gulf Canada, or 10 ounces of gold – at a specific price by a specified date. Suppose, for instance, that today is April 1 and gold is trading at $400 per ounce. If you think the price is going to rise, for $230 you can buy a call option on 10 per cent margin, giving you the right to buy 10 ounces of gold in May for $3,750; or, for $430, you can buy the right to purchase 10 ounces of gold next November. Now let's suppose your hunch is correct and gold rises to $450 by next November. If you'd bought 10 ounces of gold directly, your profit would be $500. But since you paid only $43 for the *right* to buy 10 ounces of gold on the November contract (the rest of your $430 bet was borrowed from your broker) you'll benefit from the magical effects of leverage. Because you gambled $43, you're now entitled to buy 10 ounces of gold, worth $4,500 on the open market, for only $3,750 – a profit of $750, or better than 1,700 per cent. That $750 comes out of the hide of someone you've never met: some unfortunate who thought gold would drop below $400, and backed his conviction by buying a put contract. If gold is still trading at $400 next November, of course, your option will be worthless when it expires, and you've lost $430. That's a drastically oversimplified example of an extraordinarily subtle game.

The futures game is even riskier, since it's possible to lose far more than your original stake. Options contracts merely give you the *right* to buy or sell; futures contracts *commit* you to buy or sell on a specific date, at a specific price. The most terrifying aspect of futures trading is "limit moves," a rule designed to cushion wild fluctuations in prices. If a commodity rises or falls by more than a specified amount, trading is shut off for that day – which means that, during crisis periods, such as a Florida freeze that wipes out half the orange crop, not every speculator who wants to buy or sell *can* buy or sell. Several days of successive limit moves can thus deprive you of far more than your original stake. Losing $10,000 on a highly leveraged $500 gamble isn't unusual. That's why commodity brokers insist that new clients deposit at least $10,000 in a brokerage account before they're allowed to play; and that's why amateurs by the hundreds are routinely cleaned out in a twinkling.

In Toronto, financial futures are traded in a smallish area separated from the Toronto Stock Exchange's main trading floor by a tall wooden wall. In contrast to the cacophony next door, the atmosphere in the futures pit is quieter, almost deliberative. On the other side of the wall, equity traders are shouting themselves hoarse, behaving the way stock traders have always behaved. But the futures traders, because there are so few of them, seldom need to shout at one another. Instead, they stand around in attitudes of rapt bemusement, like sidewalk superintendents, or strollers in a park watching a game of outdoor chess.

Two Steps Down into the Pit

This is the trading area of the Toronto Futures Exchange, a TSE-sponsored institution that is part casino, part insurance mart, part bear-pit. Its most notable architectural features are two circular indentations in the floor, each the size of a child's wading pool. The traders stand around these pits, reading paperback novels or watching the changing numbers on an overhead electronic quote-board. When they want to make a trade, they walk two steps down into the pit and call out their orders.

Some of these traders are from the large banks or the large brokerage houses, such as Merrill Lynch, Wood Gundy and Richardson-Greenshields, whose commodity departments are becoming important profit-centres. A few others are professional stock traders from the other side of the wall. Although most stock traders ignore the futures pit because they don't understand it, a few have learned to use it to hedge their minute-by-minute bets on the stock market. Still other futures traders are known as "locals" because, when the TSE set up the TFE as a separate entity, it bought advertisements to *invite* people to become TFE members. Some 260 seats were sold at $6,500-$8,500 each, and about 25 of them were bought by individuals, including a secretary, a bus driver, several lawyers, an airline pilot, a Canadian Forces helicopter pilot and a real-estate salesman. These individual TFE members are trading for themselves, not for clients; and their function is to try to make a living by betting against the corporate hedgers, thus providing liquidity to the market. "Toronto is a thriving commodity town," says Andrew Clademenos, the TFE's secretary and general manager, "and most of that business is going to Chicago. If we took just a portion of that business, and repatriated it, we would have a thriving exchange."

Five products are traded: contracts on government treasury bills and long-term bonds, which allow traders to bet on interest rates; contracts for cash settlement on the TSE 300 index, which allow traders to bet on the future level of the stock market; 100-ounce silver contracts; and U.S. dollar contracts. Bill Bell, a real-estate salesman who bought a seat and now spends most of his mornings buying and selling futures in the TFE pit, succinctly summarizes the risks of the game: "In real estate," he says, "if you have a bad year, you don't make any money. In this business, if you have a bad year you give a lot of money back."

One morning in 1984, a youngish man with horn-rimmed glasses and a precise, almost scholarly manner stepped into the futures pit and began trading – glancing at the numbers on the board, calling out his bids and noting the trades on his clipboard. The other traders watched him carefully, for the spectacle of Al Freidberg in the pit was a little like watching Alfred P. Sloan descend from the executive suite, roll up his

111

sleeves and run a welding machine on the General Motors assembly line.

Friedberg is not only the founder of what is probably Canada's largest commodities-trading firm, the Friedberg Mercantile Group; he virtually invented the business as it's played in Canada today. Until the 1970s, options and commodity futures were the preserve of a handful of specialists. It was Al Friedberg, more than any other individual, who made the Canadian game accessible to the multitudes. Few traders have been as richly rewarded. In 1983, it is whispered, the Friedberg Mercantile Group, owned through holding companies mainly by Al Friedberg and his father Fred, made a cool $18 million.

Friedberg's office is on Bay Street. But once or twice a week he walks over to the TSE building, clips an identification tag on his lapel and personally performs the kind of belly-to-belly trading that executives of most investment firms would delegate to juniors. "Al just wanted to get the feel of it on his own," explains a fellow-trader. "He's been coming in here and making money scalping – you know, like selling contracts and then buying back at a profit a few minutes later. He's been doing quite well, as a matter of fact. The other traders appreciate him because he usually comes in here and does a bit of size. He'll trade 10, 20 or even 50 contracts at a time. Most of the guys only do one or two."

There is something alien and faintly mysterious about Friedberg, some hint of foreignness that you can't quite place. He seems too smooth to be a Canadian, too North American to be European. He was, in fact, born in France and raised in, of all places, Uruguay. Growing up in that once-prosperous country taught him a priceless lesson. At an early age, he acquired a visceral understanding of a truth that Canadians are only beginning to understand: that currencies are fragile, confidence is ephemeral and that if people are greedy and stupid enough, they can make prosperity disappear.

The Supremacy of Uruguay

As recently as the early 1950s, Uruguay was a sort of transplanted Switzerland: prosperous, democratic and sane, the envy of Latin America. The world paid well for its wool, hides and beef. The sort of embedded poverty that afflicts most of Latin America was almost unknown. Its capital, Montevideo, was a pleasant city of 1.2 million, with broad boulevards, a baroque opera house, fashionable hotels, and an elegant social life. Not the least of its attractions were a delicious climate, stable prices and a strong banking system, modelled after Switzerland's. People from less well-managed countries in Latin America used to salt away their money in Uruguayan numbered accounts.

It all began coming apart around 1951, the year that Fred Friedberg, a refugee Austrian Jew, settled in Montevideo. Friedberg is a survivor. He had fled his native Vienna the day the Nazis seized power in Austria in 1938, spent the war years in Vichy France and, in 1946, when European currencies were still in a shambles, set himself up as a money dealer in Lyon and later in Antwerp, mastering the intricacies of currency markets that came in at least three colors: black, grey and white.

In Montevideo, although he'd come seeking stability, Friedberg found the beginnings of monetary chaos. Uruguay had been one of Latin America's pioneers in social legislation. But, by the mid-1950s, Uruguay was losing its traditional overseas markets, and had embarked on a costly but futile plan to replace imports with goods of local manufacture. In addition, government handouts had become the subject of bidding contests among the country's splintered political parties. The president had no veto power, so congress could vote as much spending as it wanted; and Uruguay's central bank was subject to political control, so the temptation was irresistible to print money to pay for the social programs the country couldn't afford. The inevitable result was a storm of triple-digit inflation which ruined the country's economy, destroyed its democratic institutions, debauched its currency, wiped out the savings of the middle-class, beggared the poor and triggered a wave of urban terrorism. In the 20 years he spent there, Fred Friedberg witnessed the destruction and impoverishment of one of the world's richer countries – partly through external causes, but also because of stupidity and greed and an internal lack of political discipline.

Fred's son, Al Friedberg, watched it happen too. He was only four when the family emigrated to Uruguay. As a teenager he attended private school in Baltimore and, after graduation, studied economics at Johns Hopkins University and international banking at Columbia. But on his regular visits home, he could see the changes in the Montevideo he'd known as a child. "Life went on, even during triple-digit inflation, but everything deteriorated," he recalls. "The streets became filthy. Montevideo's a place where people enjoy looking good. But year after year, when I'd come back for visits, the people you knew looked seedier and seedier. Their suits weren't as good, the stuff in the stores wasn't as good. You couldn't get foreign merchandise because of import restrictions. Everybody drove old cars and kept them in perfect condition. Even in the 1960s, my uncle was driving a black 1928 Austin."

Once, during a visit home when he was still in high school, Al Friedberg saw a long queue of people on one of Montevideo's main streets. The country's second-largest bank had collapsed, and the depositors were lining up in desperation, vainly hoping to reclaim part of their savings. "It was a revelation for me," he recalls. "It was as if the Toronto Dominion Bank had gone down the tubes."

With an MBA in international banking, Al Friedberg moved to Toronto in 1969, worked as a securities analyst on Bay Street for two years and then, in 1971, spotting a vacuum in the financial market, set up his own small commodities-trading firm called Friedberg & Co. His family emigrated from Uruguay to join him, and Fred Friedberg once again set up shop as a foreign-exchange dealer. Father and son sat facing each other across a huge wooden desk, in the style of the Rothschilds in the nineteenth century. With telephones and ticker machines instantly relaying commodity prices from around the world, they began to trade for clients and for themselves.

It was a time when the price of gold was still pegged at $35 per ounce, and when the U.S. and Canadian dollars were as sound as – well, as sound as a dollar. Hardly anyone in North America could imagine anything else, but the Friedbergs knew better. I interviewed the 25-year-old Al Friedberg for the *Toronto Star* late in 1971. His words, in retrospect, sound eerily prescient: "Canadians and Americans firmly believe their currencies are strong and that there's no need to hedge. They haven't yet adjusted to the fact that their own currencies can suffer the way some European currencies have suffered. But over the next few years we're going to see a change. North Americans are going to start asking themselves, 'Where can we get protection?' And then they'll start buying gold or silver, and socking it away."

Canadians began doing exactly that, and Friedberg & Co., with its storefront office on Bay Street, became part of a quiet revolution in economic behavior. It was the first Canadian firm to specialize solely in commodities. On the ground floor, Fred Friedberg still practises his old trade, running an affiliated company which specializes in trading currencies and precious metals. Upstairs in a suite of offices tastefully furnished in mahogany and brass, Al Friedberg runs the commodity-trading operations from a glass-walled office, where he often works standing up at a desk that resembles a preacher's pulpit. On the other side of the glass wall, Friedberg's dozen-odd traders are grouped

114

around the trading desk, their eyes glued to the Reuters electronic terminal which, second by second, relays the price movements of commodities around the world. The atmosphere is cheerful, noisy and cosmopolitan. Clients sometimes wander in with their kids in tow. Some of the traders wear yarmulkes and speak in thick Germanic accents. "Albert, iss rising, der gold!" shouts one. Friedberg has a knack of finding talent in improbable places. One of his best traders, a red-haired woman named Gari Brick, was on welfare and training as a chef when he hired her. Another trader, David Rothberg, was a playwright; "I hired David because he had such a romantic notion of the futures business," Al Friedberg explains.

Friedberg believes that no one who trades commodities, not even the great grain-trading companies such as Dreyfus or Cargill, has an advantage through inside knowledge. "I don't think anyone in this business has an edge in information," he says. "The trick is to interpret the information more correctly than somebody else." Most of Friedberg's market triumphs have come through betting on unconventional interpretations of well-known events. Gold, which Friedberg began recommending to his clients at $42 per ounce, was the prime early example. "Gold was very cheap then," he says. "Most of the production was going into private hands – buyers who thought gold was cheap. On top of that, there were the monetary considerations." In the early 1970s, the U.S. and other Western nations abandoned the international system of currency controls, based on a pegged price for gold which had been forged at the Bretton Woods conference in 1944. They moved instead toward a system under which currencies floated freely against each other.

"That was the beginning of the great inflation of the 1970s," says Friedberg. "We lost the anchor. We lost the discipline. Our central banks were mindlessly increasing the money supply to finance government deficits." Few Canadians realized what was happening. Friedberg, who'd seen the crowds of ruined depositors lining up at the bank in Montevideo, knew exactly. He and his clients rode gold all the way from $42 to $375, started selling in January 1980, when the price reached $600 per ounce, then watched it soar to $825 in another few weeks, before it collapsed.

He also bought platinum in the early to mid-1970s at $110 per ounce, then watched it soar to $170 because of its use in catalytic converters for cars. He bought cocoa when it was trading in the 30-cent range, rode the market to the mid-70s, started selling, and then resumed buying until the price broke $2. Sugar went crazy in 1973-74, and Friedberg saw it coming. In his newsletter, he advised his clients to "mortgage your house and buy sugar."

"Our clients had about 10 per cent of the world futures market in sugar," he says, "and the price went from seven to 20 cents. Then we sold." Too soon, as it turned out; sugar later broke 60 cents before collapsing. But then it was Bernard Baruch, the legendary Wall Street speculator, who explained his success by saying, "I always sold too soon." Friedberg also predicted the devaluation of the Mexican peso in 1981, two years before it happened. "We [meaning Friedberg and his clients] held almost half the open positions in the Chicago futures market on the short side of the peso. That's close to 2,500 contracts, each worth $40,000. So we were short about $100 million." In other words, Friedberg's 500-odd clients, many of them rich and sophisticated investors, playing on 5 per cent margin, gambled about $5 million on the proposition that Mexico, with its sagging oil revenues, would be forced to lower the value of its currency. Because of this 20-to-one leverage, they profited hugely when the peso fell.

On occasion, however, Friedberg can be spectacularly wrong. Early in 1983 he predicted that the OPEC cartel would collapse, and the world price of oil would fall from $29 to as low as $10 per barrel. OPEC held firm through the year and into 1984, as did the price of oil. In 1980, copper was another miscall. Friedberg said it would climb from 90 cents to $1.40; it fell instead.

What is the effect, one nervously wonders, of gambling all those borrowed trillions? Friedberg is convinced that it's a healthy development, and that the new crop of financial futures represents a useful and productive tool. One of his clients, a widow who had inherited stocks worth about $3 million, was in a rush to sell her holdings because of tax complications. The market was declining and, if she'd tried to dump her stocks in a hurry, she would have depressed their price even further. Instead, through Friedberg, the estate's trustees immediately bought $3 million worth of puts on the stock-market index. As the market declined, and as they sold the stocks over a two-week period, the puts correspondingly increased in value. "She sold her portfolio for $2.6 million instead of $3 million," says Friedberg, "but in the meantime she made $400,000 on the index futures, and came out even. This sort of thing is happening every day now. Index futures are one of the greatest inventions in the financial markets in the past 100 years."

But won't all those speculative side-bets make the market more volatile? "No way," says Al Friedberg. "In the futures market, for every buyer of a contract there's a seller. You literally have the same number of longs as you do shorts. It makes for a better market. Sure, there's a lot of leverage built in. But if both the longs and the shorts are borrowing money, it isn't destabilizing. The trouble with 1929 was that there weren't enough short-sellers. As a result, when the market went down, there was very little cushion. Very few buyers came in to support prices. When you have short-sellers in a market, it smooths out the upward moves, and cushions the declines."

To those still imbued with the work ethic, there is, nevertheless, something faintly repellent about all those speculators winning and losing fortunes on the price fluctuations of things they never see or touch or cause to grow. For if you're clever, you can make a far better living gambling on the price of soybeans than you can by actually growing them.

10
How The Pros Pick Stocks

The stock market is often pictured as a marketplace in which tens of thousands of individual investors come together in a daily contest of wits. That's only half true, in the sense that only about half the value of trading on the country's largest stock exchange represents the decisions of individual investors. The rest of the Toronto Stock Exchange's trading decisions are made by professional investors on behalf of various financial institutions. There are probably fewer than 1,000 people involved in these decisions; and of these, there are probably fewer than 500 who really matter.

The Golden Circle

The influence of this golden circle extends far beyond the stock market. Their hunches and perceptions also play a substantial role in the movement of the bond, commodity and real-estate markets. In fact, this handful of professional investors is in charge of nearly $100 billion of other people's money that accumulates in pension funds, insurance funds, individual estates, mutual funds and Registered Retirement Saving Plans (RRSPs). Their job, depending on the investment objectives that are established by the people who own the money, is either to make these savings grow, or to prevent them from shrinking. Their approaches range across a wide spectrum, from the wearily bureaucratic to the zestfully entrepreneurial.

Professional investors appear in a variety of guises, calling themselves securities analysts, portfolio managers or investment counsellors. They range all the way from junior trainees in insurance company investment departments to investment counsellors who earn huge incomes by managing billions of dollars' worth of other people's money. And they represent a vast diversity of approaches to the problem of knowing the unknowable. Some work like snoopy investigative reporters, prowling supermarket aisles to gain insights into the marketing strategies of a grocery chain, or drinking beer late into the night with frustrated computer programmers to discover the bugs in an electronic company's latest product. Some work like nine-to-five spies, scanning company reports and technical journals for clues to the next hot technology or the next swing in the price of palladium. Some work like diplomats, chatting up company representatives to gather insights into next year's hot microchip or the next quarter's earnings estimate. Some get much of their information simply by being members of the corporate Establishment. A number of successful analysts talk to no one; the market's secrets, they believe, can be divined only by studying the statistical behavior of the market itself. Others, including a number of floor traders, have learned to "smell" future movements in stock prices, using instincts they can neither understand nor explain; they simply watch the tape all day and *feel* what's happening to particular stocks, the way an animal senses a change in the weather. Still others admit that they're less than brilliant at picking individual stocks, but are geniuses at predicting overall economic and market trends.

Regardless of their methodology, there are really only two kinds of stock-pickers: those who play the market and those who don't. The former usually work for brokerage firms; they're paid to generate ideas for the firm's clients, but they seldom take financial risks themselves. The other type of analyst is a market participant. He acts on his own judgments by investing his own or other people's money. All these people, whether they're onlookers or participants, constitute a sort of Greek Chorus in the stock market's endless drama: a priestly caste that analyzes, comments, warns, recommends and predicts – and also acts out their predictions and encourages other people to do the same.

Taken together, they are an awfully bright group of people. But you mustn't suppose that their brains, their knowledge and their discipline necessarily make them right. Analysts, fund managers and investment counsellors come in such a variety of shapes and sizes, such a diversity of opinions and attitudes, that most of them, at any given moment, *must* be wrong. Collectively, they're probably no smarter than the public as a whole. Collectively, they may even be less bright. Some investors, in fact, base their investment strategies on doing the exact opposite of what most analysts and fund managers are doing and recommending. "If an analyst is consistently wrong," says Sandy Boyd, a portfolio manager with The Permanent, "he's valuable because you just read him backwards."

119

Go-Getters and Plodders

How good are they at managing other people's money? There's no pat answer to that question. A portfolio manager's success in making your money grow doesn't seem to bear much relationship to how much you pay him. You might suppose, for instance, that a firm of investment counsellors – a hyper-ambitious group of individualists who are out to earn a million a year by selling their investment expertise – would perform better than a group of salaried plodders in the bowels of some insurance company's portfolio-management department. But according to Don Ezra, principal of a Toronto company called Pension Finance Associates Ltd., which methodically measures the investment performance of hundreds of Canadian fund managers, there's no significant difference between the long-term track records of the bureaucrats and the entrepreneurs. "Some years, the trust-company returns are better than those of the independent investment counsellors," he says. "Some years the counsellors are best." Ezra thinks the notion of go-getters outperforming the plodders is largely a myth, but a very seductive one. "That's why the trust and insurance companies are losing business to the counsellors," he says. "The big corporations think these guys with a stake in their own companies are bound to be more successful investors. In fact, I think it's just because they feel more comfortable with go-getting types of people. The counsellors' actual performance isn't necessarily a part of it."

It's important to note that there is no such thing as the "best" fund manager. "That's like asking which is the 'best' stock," says Don Ezra. Some fund managers are terrific in strong markets, but falter badly in weak ones. Others soldier on through good markets and bad, often ending up with stronger performances in the long term. The point is: Who's doing well, considering the *objectives* that have been set for them? Some funds are designed to protect capital, and therefore the managers pursue very conservative investment policies. Others – often the ones with "growth" in their title – attempt to score large gains in return for accepting greater risk.

Fundamentalists and Technicians

Among people who make their living trying to predict the stock market, there are two main schools: the fundamentalists and the technicians. Like most such sweeping distinctions, this one ignores the overlapping, the fuzziness around the edges, the honest human ambiguity which makes every fundamental analyst at least partly a technician, and every technician at least partly a fundamentalist. Yet the distinction really does exist. Some analysts try to predict a stock's future movement *primarily* by looking at the hard facts about the company, its management, its industry, the economic environment in which it operates and its prospects for future earnings. Others rely *primarily* on an abstract consideration of that same stock's past behavior – how much of it has changed hands, and at what prices.

Fundamental analysis tends to deal in hunches, subjective judgments, balances of probabilities. Technical analysis purports to operate in the icy realm of pure reason: The numbers say what the numbers are telling you, nothing more and nothing less. Hard-core chartists believe it's futile to attempt to divine a company's future earnings, to psychoanalyze its management, to monitor the new technologies emerging from its laboratories, to assess its competitive position – because all those factors are already reflected in the trading record of the stock. "Who knows why the buyers are buying and the sellers are selling?" asks Ian McAvity, editor of a technically-oriented investors' newsletter called *Deliberations.* "The only real evidence you have is the evidence they leave behind on the tape."

Fundamentalists, on the other hand, tend to dismiss technical analysis as the worst sort of pseudo-scientific mumbo-jumbo. As early as 1906, an American financial writer named Thomas Gibson warned that technical analysis "is founded wholly on repetition, regardless of actual conditions. The idea is untrustworthy, absolutely fatuous, and highly dangerous." As late as 1983, Dr. Morton Shulman, the millionaire physician, speculator, media pop star and devoutly fundamentalist stock-picker, was able to describe technical analysis in the following terms: "I think it's nonsense to look at squiggles on a chart of what's happened in the past and, in that way, forecast the future. I think it would probably be more reliable to use the comic books, or the stars, or the state of your bowels."

It is one of the investment industry's more endearing quirks that the fundamentalists – those Enquiring Reporters of capitalism – tend in their personal lives toward the coldly rational, the buttoned-down; and the technicians, whose discipline supposedly calls for the merciless application of pure logic, turn out to be among the goofiest, most loveably eccentric people on the street.

Financial analysis is a relatively new discipline. Although Bay Street has always teemed with people with their own systems for picking stocks, most retail investment houses didn't have their own research departments until the 1960s. Twenty years ago, technical analysis was the preserve of only a handful of devotees, and nobody paid them much attention. But the growth of mutual funds in the 1960s, and the accompanying "cult of performance" which turned some U.S. fund managers into celebrities, brought a new emphasis on the art of picking stocks. It was no longer enough for stockbrokers to recommend stocks on the basis of tips, rumors and whatever the firm happened to be underwriting that week; their retail customers wanted facts, statistics, stories, background, ideas. Today, almost every firm on Bay Street either has a research department or – in the case of the so-called institutional boutiques – *is* a research department.

The In-House Analyst

In most large investment firms which deal with the public, the research department exists to generate ideas for the salesmen, and to answer customers' questions. The in-house analyst thus functions as an arm of the sales department. So how reliable is his advice? That depends, but it's a truism of the business that investment-house analysts almost never tell you to sell a stock. This is regrettable but understandable, especially if the firm is active in the underwriting business. A firm that sold you a new issue of Consolidated Widget last April is unlikely to advise you to dump the same stock in September. "The reason they won't tell you to sell," says Ed Eberts, president of Rapport Ltd., a financial consulting firm which keeps close tabs on the analytical community, "is that corporate executives hate to hear someone saying their firm's shares are overvalued and should be sold. These executives apparently have very long memories."

The public, luckily, doesn't. Investment houses mail out research reports by the ton to their customers, blithely confident that their predictions will never come back to haunt them. Most analysts are happy to remind their readers of successful recommendations but grow forgetful when it comes to the duds, so it's difficult to track the losers. When *Toronto Star* reporter Diane Francis asked several large brokerage houses for back issues of their investment letters so she could scrutinize their recommendations, she was told they weren't available. "Why should I help you make us look bad?" she was told. The investment houses often file their research reports with the

Toronto Stock Exchange, but the TSE won't allow the public to peruse them, on the novel grounds that these documents, which were distributed by the tens of thousands to anyone who asked, are "private property."

There is no particular moral to any of this. Some analysts, and some fund managers, are better than others – some of the time. But anyone who tries to outguess the market is bound to be wrong a lot of the time. A seasoned market observer named John Train once contemplated the torrents of information to which he was subjected – the bulletins, the excited phone calls, the stories, the opinions, the forecasts, the figures, the computer printouts and the analysts' reports – and offered a zen-like insight into the meaning of it all. "Is it all true?" asked Train."No. Is it all false? No. It is, so to speak, the murmuring of the forest, the sounds each creature makes as it pursues its function in the larger design."

A closer look at some of these forest creatures, accordingly, may help you to interpret the market and its murmurings.

Norman Short:
The Investment Counsellor
As Skeptic

Rags-to-riches stories are unusual in the money management business, but Norman Short, a Scottish parson's son, qualifies in every respect except the actual rags. The investment-management company he and his partners founded in 1960, Guardian Capital Group, began as an informal investment club – just three friends meeting once a week in one another's living rooms. Today, although practically no one outside Bay Street has heard of the firm, Guardian is an international financial conglomerate that runs more than $1 billion of other people's money.

Guardian is respected for its methodical, almost scholarly, approach to investment management. Its brains consist of a handful of people, grouped into three-person teams. One group, known around the office as the "free-to-roam team" (John Bak, Peter Briegher and Anthony Munk) scouts the world for investment bargains; another, consisting of Jim Cole, Lewis Jackson and Catherine Delaney, specializes in Canadian stocks. A third group, working with London-based consultants, looks for opportunities outside North America. After 25 years, Guardian's investment philosophy has boiled down to a deceptively simple formula: "We try to decide where the major trend is," says Short, "and to be in tune with it. Then we try to pick five classes of stocks which make common sense and good value and adapt well – and then we watch those five classes very carefully. If one class seems to get overpriced, or if the trend of value becomes doubtful, or if the fundamentals are fine but the stock isn't acting well for some reason, then we chuck it out and either go to cash or find something better. So it's really very simple: Where is the tide flowing? And, having decided that, what are the five best things you know about?"

Methodical Patience

Short got into the business in the late 1950s with the same methodical patience that has characterized his investment performance. Raised in London and educated at Fettes College ("a strong emphasis on rugger and cold showers") and at Oxford's Worcester College*, he came to Canada in 1953 because his father had moved to Toronto to become pastor of St. George's United Church. After a stint as a trainee in George Weston's food empire, he spent four years at Confederation Life as a junior investment analyst and then, in 1960, moved to one of Canada's first investment-counselling firms, Andrew Cole & Co. Ltd. There, with another young analyst from the same firm, Ralph Horner, and a chemical engineer named Alan Grieve, he started something called the Speculative Value Fund as an after-hours business.

Essentially, the fund was nothing but a three-man investment club which had chosen to incorporate itself. Its first investment, of about $50,000, involved a complicated manoeuvre with a stock called Kilembe Copper. The details, which involved shorting Kilembe common stock and simultaneously buying its rights and warrants, were complex; but the bottom line was that the warrants, which the fund bought for 30 cents, later went as high as $3, and the stock itself doubled from $2.50 to $5. Friends started putting money in, and then friends of friends joined in. Speculative Value nearly doubled its money in 1961 by buying warrants on Alberta Gas Trunk Line Ltd. stock and other investments.

---

* At Worcester, there were only four students in his economics tutorial. One was a cocky Australian named Rupert Murdoch, who later assembled one of the world's great newspaper empires, including *The Times* of London and New York's *Village Voice*; another was John Silcock, now a director of N.M. Rothschild & Sons Ltd., the London merchant bank. The fourth became a tea-taster.

That was when the three partners decided to take the fund out of their living rooms and into the world. In 1962, renamed Guardian Growth Fund, it began selling its shares to the public. By 1965, still as a part-time venture, Guardian was running more than $4 million of other people's money. That's when Short quit his job as a research analyst at Bache & Co. to run the fund full-time out of a small office on Yonge Street.*

It was an auspicious time to start a fund. The so-called "go-go" years were just beginning. Mutual funds, and the "gun-slingers" who managed them, were becoming Wall Street's new folk-heroes. The 1960s was a time of almost limitless expectations. So-called glamor stocks – which, in practice, meant almost anything with the words "computer" or "systems" in its name – sometimes doubled on the same day their shares were issued to the public. Guardian, with its mandate to invest in hot, speculative stocks, suddenly found itself as one of the leading Canadian exponents of go-go investing. By 1969, the year the go-go market finally ran out of steam, more than half a million Canadians owned shares in mutual funds, many of which were heavily invested in glamor stocks. Guardian's performance was one of the hottest; every dollar invested in the fund in 1960 was worth $10.19 by March, 1969.

Guardian's shares rose roughly 10 times as fast as the market during the go-go years. But when the party ended in 1969, they fell almost as hard – down 23 per cent, versus a general market decline of 10 per cent. The shakeout had a chastening effect on Short and his partners, who by this time were managing more than $50 million. They were still on the lookout for little companies with hot prospects, but by this time they had learned that stocks can go down as well as up. I tape-recorded one of their regular investment meetings in July 1970, and the dialogue aptly captures some of the flavor of the period. The preoccupation with cute little companies with hot ideas still persists; but Short displays a salutary skepticism.

At one point in the day-long meeting, John Bak was pushing a stock called Olla Industries Ltd., which was trying to put together a resort development in Honduras. Here, in part, is what was said:

Bak: So British Honduras is a game, and maybe it's lousy,

---

* The office was sublet from Sinclair Stevens, who was then trying to launch the first new Canadian bank in several generations, the Bank of Western Canada. Despite the fact that James Coyne, a former chairman of the Bank of Canada, was its president, the venture collapsed in a blaze of headlines and recriminations. A chastened Stevens went on to become a Conservative MP and one of the Trudeau government's fiercest financial critics.

but they've already sold 30 cents a share so far worth of un-developed land, for *cash*, which is almost unbelievable. See, they only paid $100,000 for that Salt Creek Estates down in British Honduras. The guy was down there from Scheinman, Hochstin and Trotta in New York, and he said it was fabulous land and everything else, and it reminds him of Hawaii, and there's no mosquitoes, and it's great, and it's got a great big barrier reef and beautiful blue water and skin diving and it's the next great tourist attraction, and it's only an hour and a half from Miami, and if they do land sales continually and if they build the Holiday Inn, and if they get the casino licence, which Olla says he's *definitely* got, it's just a matter of getting the official . . .

Norman Short: The only thing, it sounds a bit me-too. You know, casinos and development? Christ, who needs it? They'll be franchising hot-dog stands in Guatemala next. That's all we need to guarantee a no-good story.

Murray Sinclair: According to people I know who've been down there, one of the big problems is the lack of accommodation. There are very, very few fine hotels where you won't, you know, get violently ill after you've been there 24 hours.

Short: Speaking personally, it doesn't turn me on. It sounds like last year's idea in a new country that's going to take years of fighting swamps and God knows what, construction costs and so on, to drag tourists down there. You know, if you want to go into the gambling-tourist business, I would have thought there were about 85 easier, probably better-value ways to do it. But if you want to sponsor it as a stock, then sponsor it. How would it compare in value to Inter-Island Resorts, for instance?

It was the same world-weary caution, plus Short's intolerance of bad manners, which saved Guardian's partners from becoming involved with Bernie Cornfeld's Investors Overseas Services (IOS) Group. Cornfeld, a former New York social worker, had started in the late 1950s selling mutual funds to U.S. servicemen in foreign postings. By 1969 he had 85,000 commission salesmen scouring the far corners of the earth, scooping up spare cash from investors in more than 100 countries. But he wanted a stronger presence in North America, and offered to buy Guardian for $25 million.

Short and his partners knew that the IOS empire was shaky. But $25 million, in those days, was still a lot of money. So Short flew to New York to see Ed Cowett, Cornfeld's chief lieutenant.

"I spent four hours in his office in the Carlyle Hotel," says Short. "He was a devious, unpleasant and probably quite clever lawyer. I suppose in those four hours I talked to him for about half an hour. The rest of the time he was on the phone shouting at people all over the world about something they'd done that he didn't like, or about some disaster, or the Brazilian sales force had just been put in jail, or a hotel in Mexico was on fire – I just came back and said, 'Who needs to be one of those guys on the end of a telephone being shouted at by Ed Cowett?' " The Guardian partners declined to sell.

IOS collapsed, of course, but Guardian continued to grow. Today it consists of a whole battery of investment funds and financial services, both here and abroad. But it's run on decidedly conservative principles. When you've been in the business as long as Norman Short, when you've seen hot markets come and go, when you've seen the Bernie Cornfelds of the world rise and fall, the world holds few surprises. Norman Short is a survivor, and that's the way he likes it.

Stephen Jarislowsky:
The Investment Counsellor
As Insider

"He can be an awful pain in the ass sometimes," remarks an admiring rival, "but he sure is good." That's the sort of comment which Stephen Jarislowsky would accept as an appropriate tribute from his inferiors. As the founder and senior partner of Jarislowsky, Fraser & Co. Ltd., a Montreal and Toronto investment-counselling firm that either manages or advises on about $6 billion worth of pension-fund money, Jarislowsky is an object lesson in the art of getting rich by doing precisely as one pleases.

He is one of those deliciously arrogant people who can scarcely imagine the possibility of ever being wrong. And he has been right so often that his clients, which include some of the country's largest pension funds, plus the endowment funds of several major universities, are torn between awe and irritation. Jarislowsky is supremely indifferent to both responses. He has an aristocrat's disdain for approval, as befits the son of a German merchant banker whose earliest memories are of ornate Berlin drawing rooms and vast Bavarian hunting lodges. The shipyards in Gdansk, Poland, where Lech Walesa's Solidarity movement was born, once belonged to his family, as did the coal mines near Katowice. He speaks German, Dutch, French, Japanese and European-accented English. He is, in point of plain fact, a true aristocrat; another branch of the family included a banker who was named a baron by Napoleon III. "I'm the only male descendent in the collateral branch," he explains, "so I'm entitled to use the title." But he never does.

Jarislowsky came to North America in 1941 (his stepfather was a bureaucrat in the Vichy French government), attended a prep school in North Carolina, studied engineering at Cornell University, and took an MA in oriental studies at the University of Chicago and an MBA in 1949 at the Harvard Business School. He spent three years with Alcan in Montreal, and then, fed up with the slowness and bureaucracy of a large company, he set up his own investment-counselling firm in 1955. Two years later he was joined by another budding analyst, A. Scott (Scotty) Fraser. Those were the days when Canadian uranium and copper stocks were hot, and the new firm began peddling advice on Canadian stocks to a string of British and U.S. fund managers, including Loeb Rhodes in New York and Samuel Montague in London. "Some of them stumbled on our doorsteps. Others sent analysts here, found us and, instead of coming here, hired us on a retainer," says Jarislowsky.

The firm's growth was quiet and methodical. Jarislowsky and Fraser simply continued providing sound investment advice, and word got around. By 1984, after 29 years in the business, the firm manages more than $3 billion worth of pension-fund assets, and advises on accounts worth another $3 billion. Their pension-fund clients include a string of pulp and paper companies (Abitibi, Consolidated Bathurst, International Paper) and no fewer than eight Universities (McGill, Concordia, Queens, Toronto, Alberta, Saskatchewan, Wilfrid Laurier and McMaster). There is nothing flashy about the firm's performance, or about Jarislowsky's investment philosophy; he makes it sound almost easy.

Investment Common Sense

"I just operate on what I consider to be investment common sense," he says. "If you buy companies that are growing faster than the economy, you'll do better than the market. And if you buy them when they're cheap, you'll do better than if you buy them when they're average or high. If you know your companies well, you'll have a better chance than if you don't know them well. If you buy cyclical stocks only when they're down, you won't have to ride them up and down. Since the market is usually down when you're scared, you've got to buy when you're scared. And since the market is usually up when everybody's happy, you've got to sell when everybody's happy. Those are really the simple benchmarks of what I've discovered over the years. It brings you better results than a lot of the prima donnas get. It's like playing tennis on the base line; you don't rush the net.

"Doing better than the average is what this business is all about. If you can consistently do better than the average, then in eight or 10 years you'll be among the very first. Some of the funds we manage have done better than average for nine consecutive years and, in one case, for 10 consecutive years. If you can do that, you're obviously doing something right – something over and above what normal luck could have brought you. And that's what a good investment counsellor is all about. If you hire me to manage your estate while your children are still young, you want somebody who will make that money last through the years of their childhood and education and beyond. You don't want anybody spectacular, who will make half a million one year and lose it all the next. You want somebody who keeps ahead of inflation, gives you an above-average stream of income and is totally reliable throughout the piece. That's what you're looking for. That's what investment counsel are hired for. There's no sense in being the greatest guy in '83 and '84, and a bum the next year. In the end, for whom have you done favors? You haven't done you or your associates any favors. And you certainly haven't done your clients any favors – you've lost all their money."

Getting to know companies, Jarislowsky believes, is something like the process of courtship. "Looking at a company's balance sheet," he says, "is like looking at the skeleton of a pretty girl. I think most of us like to see a bit more than that. So you have to flesh this girl out – find out what she's all about."

Jarislowsky knows the companies he invests in because he knows the people who run them. "If you really understand management's thinking or lack thereof, you have a pretty good idea of what they might and might not do. And if you meet a couple of hundred of these executives in your lifetime, you don't fall for the ploys that the average analyst falls for – reading about the company in the newspaper, and then meeting the great man for the first time. If you sit on the guy's board, you know what a stupid bastard he is, how he deals with his family and all the rest."

Jarislowsky sits on a lot of boards, including an Abitibi subsidiary called Intercity Paper, a subsidiary of the Steinberg's grocery chain, the Canadian branch of Swiss Bank Corp. and SNC Ltd., Quebec's largest privately held engineering firm.

He's also president of a German-owned manufacturer of fire-bricks called Didier Refractories, and a director of a prefab concrete company, an office-equipment company and a firm of auctioneers. All these connections pay off in terms of information. "It gives me a tremendous listening-post. To be a director of a world-wide engineering firm gives you tremendous knowledge of what goes on in the economy. To be the director of a world-class bank's Canadian subsidiary and mix with their top people internationally gives me a tremendous amount of information. To be president of Didier Refractories gives me knowledge of what happens in the steel industry, the copper industry, the glass industry, the cement industry, et cetera."

But he's not merely a passive sponge for information. As a director, he's actively and deliberately obnoxious, asking all the tough questions and demanding answers. He's also involved, almost continually, in battles with the managements of companies in which he's bought major positions. "When I find that someone is trying to gyp me or rip off my clients, I feel somebody has to stand up to the bastards and say, 'We don't go for that.' He's prevented at least half a dozen mergers or takeovers which managements had contemplated, but which Jarislowsky felt would undermine the value of shares he or his clients owned. Perhaps the most notable occasion was in the late 1960s, when Jarislowsky led a shareholders' revolt which forced BP Petroleum to restructure its takeover offer for Supertest Petroleum. He also led a battle which toppled the president of Cartier Sugar Ltd.; that one went all the way to the Supreme Court of Canada. There is also the famous court case of Jarislowsky versus Dominion Glass Ltd.: "Paul Desmarais [of Power Corp. fame] took over the company, squeezed out the minority shareholders and ordered a study which told him the stock was worth $16, but that he should pay a $4 premium for control. We went to court and won $36 per share."

Despite their battle over Dominion Glass, Desmarais and Jarislowsky are still friends – or, perhaps more accurately, friendly rivals. Once, when they were having lunch at the Mount Royal Club, Jarislowsky compared their two lifestyles – Desmarais, the isolated captain of industry, whom hardly anyone gets to see; and Jarislowsky, the independent gadfly.

"I manage just as much money as you do," Jarislowsky told Desmarais, "and I don't need a security guard to walk me to work. As a director of all your companies, how much more do you know about them than I know as a securities analyst? Whether the money is yours or your clients', what difference does it make?"

Desmarais's reply is not recorded.

Ian McAvity:
The Analyst
As Guru

Canada's best-known technical analyst is a fast-talking, hyper-active, utterly independent analyst-entrepreneur named Ian McAvity. With his instantly recognizable Vandyke beard, his highly individualistic lifestyle, his excessive fondness for cats and his capacity for dispensing 25 inflammatory opinions per minute, both McAvity and his views on the financial scene are highly marketable commodities.

They have become so marketable, in fact, that McAvity no longer confines himself to selling his advice on paper. He now sells it as an advisor, and part-owner, of several major precious-metal funds, which invest other people's money in gold and silver. In what he regards as an exciting mid-life career shift, McAvity the outside spectator has become McAvity the inside participant.

The son of a former president of Seagram's, McAvity grew up in Montreal's wealthy Westmount, attended Trinity College School in Port Hope, Ontario and, after dropping out of the University of New Brunswick after six months, joined the Bank of Montreal as a $2,050-a-year teller. (His father's firm was one of the bank's biggest clients.) By the time he was 23 he'd gravitated to a job in the securities business as an analyst in Dominick & Dominick Inc.'s New York office. After five years with Dominick and two years with the now-defunct Mead & Co., McAvity in 1972 joined Draper Dobie & Co., a Toronto-based firm, then controlled by Montegu Black, which was later absorbed by Dominion Securities Ltd. McAvity set up Draper Dobie's technical analysis department and started a newsletter, *Deliberations*, for the firm's clients. (He picked the name out of the dictionary because it started with D, as did Draper Dobie. "I've always been a nut for alliteration," he explains.")

Draper Dobie's *Deliberations* became a well-regarded source of technical comment, but in September 1975, there was an explosive parting of the ways. McAvity resigned from the firm, he says, because he wanted to go into business for himself.

He continued to spend time in the Draper Dobie offices, because he was managing his family's portfolio, which was trading through his old firm, and he regarded himself as a valued customer as well as an ex-employee. One day, however,

131

a former colleague informed him that it was the firm's wish that he not come around any more. "They literally told me to get off the premises, because they were sure I was still getting data from their computer," says McAvity. "What they didn't realize was that, for the past 18 months, I'd been weaning myself off that computer because it wasn't doing me any damned good at all. I never had a high opinion of Monte Black to begin with. But after that, my opinion of him went straight into the sewer. Monte didn't even have the balls to tell me himself; he had to use somebody else to do it. I've never forgiven them for that."

McAvity's former colleagues decline to discuss the manner of his parting, but some feel it may have had something to do with his shoulder-length hair (it's shorter now), his impatience with those he deemed less clever than himself, and with his habit of sleeping until noon and then working through the night. The bitterness was compounded by the firm's insistence that the newsletter he'd started belonged to them, not him. McAvity won that battle, and has been publishing *Deliberations* ever since – first from his home, later from a small, cluttered office above a pinball parlor on Toronto's Parliament Street.

It is an odd location for what is becoming an international clearing-house for investment advice. Parliament Street, on the border of a fashionable neighborhood of renovated town houses, is still a street that belongs to the urban poor. Instead of urgent men carrying briefcases and squash racquets, the sidewalks are occupied by mumbling old bag ladies, welfare moms shopping for day-old bread and winos trying to score enough spare change for their next bottle of muscatel. McAvity's office is thoroughly in character with these surroundings: Every horizontal surface is stacked with books and moldering newspapers, three secretaries struggle with a surfeit of incoming calls, and OC and Maxi, the two office cats, prowl the corners in search of fresh vermin. The only evidence of modernity is an Apple computer, which McAvity uses to compile his mailing lists (*Deliberations* has about 4,000 subscribers at $215 a year), but not his charts; McAvity insists on maintaining them in the traditional manner, with colored pencils and sheets of graph paper.

He charts the Dow-Jones Industrial Average on an *hourly* basis; he tracks the fluctuations of the yen, the Deutsche mark, the Swiss franc, the U.S. and Canadian dollars and the British pound; he monitors the trend of stock markets in London, New York, Tokyo, Sydney and Toronto; he tracks the movement of precious metals – and crams the results into 16 pages twice a month, along with salty, image-ridden commentary that is as distinctive, in its own quirky way, as Hemingway's prose: "Downside airpockets in some recent glamors, and correctional dips amongst recent leaders, are worrisome . . ." Or: "Today's 60.22 is just a snick below the May '82 peak, and also not so far from the 60.54 top last November. Get above that latter level, and you will have an *extremely* bullish confirmation that a bull market is underway in bonds . . . and that's bullish for stocks."

People pay McAvity to talk like this, as well as to write. He's lionized on the North American investment conference circuit, and has been interviewed four times on television's most influential business program, *Wall Street Week*, with its weekly audience of 12 million. He made headlines in February 1981 when, appearing on Dr. Morton Shulman's interview show on Toronto's CITY-TV, he bet the multimillionaire fundamentalist $1,000 that gold would drop below $400 (US) an ounce. A few months later gold did exactly that. Shulman, during a subsequent McAvity appearance on his show, manfully paid up.

His clients also pay him to talk on the telephone. Much of McAvity's day is spent taking calls from investors in Europe and across North America. McAvity talks; they listen. What they hear is partly a regurgitation of his latest letter, and partly a rehearsal for his next one. Some of these monologues, when you play back the tape months later, seem remarkably prescient. Here, for instance, is what he told a telephone caller one morning in August 1982, when the market had just begun what turned out to be one of the longest, strongest climbs in its history. "If you look at this current surge in relation to the beginnings of past bull markets," McAvity said, "that first surge is an indication of how powerful the whole thing is going to be. The worst thing you want to do is to put a rein on a rampaging bull. We're already incredibly overbought by any measure, but there's no limit to how overbought you can get . . . In last week's issue I talked about the fuel tanks that are necessary to get a rocket off the ground. What we're seeing this week is that those goddam fuel tanks are even bigger than I thought they were. Somewhere in the 920 area this thing has got to start running into some sort of churning. But I'm still waiting for the momentum to ebb, let alone for the prices to reach a peak . . ."

The Effects of the Full Moon

McAvity was among a handful of analysts who accurately predicted the bull market which began in August 1982. Few fun-

133

damental analysts called it; but technicians including McAvity, Iain Fraser and Leon Tuey of Dominion Securities Pitfield Ltd., at the crucial moment just before the market hit bottom on August 12, 1982, all sent out unequivocal bulletins urging their readers to start buying. McAvity cheerfully admits that he almost blew it: "My last July issue was very bullish. Then, when the market broke to a lower low, I got really mystified. So I said it could go either way. Then the market proceeded to keep going down for eight days in a row. I was sitting there debating whether or not I should send out some sort of bulletin telling people to bail out completely. I finally decided that the market wasn't accelerating enough to hit the panic button. There was just something missing; the trap door was yawning open, but people weren't jumping. And so, as a result, I stayed bullish."

McAvity, like many technicians, is a fearless intellectual adventurer. He is not one to reject an idea merely because it seems outlandish. Thus, with a perfectly straight face, he has examined the effects of the full moon on the stock market, and informed his readers that its impact, though slight, is real enough to be of value to heavily leveraged investors, such as options traders, for whom even a minor uptick in the market can generate significant profits. Testing a hunch, McAvity studied lunar cycles between February 1977, and December 1981, and compared them to movements in the Dow-Jones Industrial Average. His conclusion: "The market shows a tendency to drop in the three days following a full moon; and on average shows losses for the 10-day span. For a new moon, the market averaged gains over the ten-day span." Would he advise buying and selling stocks on the basis of lunar cycles? No, because McAvity never makes trading decisions on the basis of a single indicator. "But I would consider the full moon's bearish bias to be an indicator worth noting, and in the event that other tools were prompting me to go long for a trade over the full-moon period, this record would probably keep me from doing it; unless my case was overwhelmingly strong."

He doesn't use phases of the moon, however, to guide his investment decisions as advisor to two of North America's largest precious-metal funds. He's on the four-man advisory committee to Central Fund of Canada Ltd., which uses its shareholders' money to invest in gold and silver bullion and precious-metals stocks. In 1984 he also bought a 2 per cent interest in United Services Gold Fund, the largest precious-metals fund in the United States, for which he also acts as advisor. McAvity's high-profile success demonstrates an important rule of the analytical game and, perhaps, a rule of life: It's no good having a great product unless you promote it.

Tony Reid:
The Analyst
As Tuning-Fork

Tony Reid, like his father before him, has been following the stock market since he was 13. Today, after more than three decades spent contemplating its moods, its petulances, its spurts of manic euphoria, he is so attuned to its mysterious rhythms that he believes his very body responds to the market, just as the strains of a well-played violin will set up sympathetic vibrations in a crystal goblet. When the market goes up, Tony Reid gains weight. When it drops, Tony's weight drops too. He has kept track of the fluctuations in his own body weight for the past 20 years, comparing it to the ups and downs of the Dow-Jones Industrial Average, and there is an uncanny correlation. "I'm at my highest now," he announced early in 1983, after the market had staged one of this century's strongest six-month recoveries. "I was down to 235 at the bottom of the market in July of '82. Since then I've gone back to 251."

Rhythms and Repetition

Like McAvity and Fraser, Reid is a technical analyst – what's known in the trade as a chartist. He believes that the stock market – and indeed, the very mechanics of the universe – are rhythmic and repetitive in nature. By studying what the market has done in the past, and meticulously recording its behavior by drawing lines and graphs, he tries to figure out what it will do in the future. Lots of people believe in the efficacy of technical analysis, but Reid believes it in his very marrow. His large and – at times – rather plump body seems to vibrate in response to cyclical laws. When he spent a week in hospital after an appendectomy, he used to crawl out of bed and peer at the temperature chart hanging at the foot of his bed. "I'd look at the figures, and I'd say, 'Gee – I didn't know I was this sick.' Then I'd see that my temperature had topped, and I'd tell myself: 'Aha! I'm going to get better.' "

Reid has even discerned certain statistical correlations between his productivity as a financial columnist (for 25 years, he has written regularly on stock trends for the *Financial Times*, *Investors Digest*, *The Financial Post* or the *Toronto Sun*) and his romantic life. "In 1971 I only wrote 18 columns. The next year only eight. In 1973, the year my marriage broke up, I wrote exactly two. Since then I've been climbing. Six in 1974, nine in 1975, then 10, 20, 30 – 26 last year, but that didn't include 12 *Digests* and 52 columns for the *Toronto Sun*. So I'm now writing more than 90 columns a year, and I've never felt better in my life – better adjusted, healthier, everything else." His sex life is fine too.

Like a surprising number of people on Bay Street, Reid learned about the market inside his own family circle. His father, Alexander Gordon Kissam Reid, was one of the pioneers of the Canadian mutual fund industry, and an avid chartist. Reid senior learned the investment business on Howe Street in Vancouver in the 1930s and, by the time World War II came along, had made a small fortune financing the exploration efforts of junior oil companies, in return for a percentage of future production. In 1949 Reid senior formed his own company, Mutual Funds Management Corp., to sell and manage the mutual funds that were just beginning to become a feature of the Canadian investment scene. By the time he sold the firm in 1963, it was managing about $100 million worth of assets.

The senior Reid was also obsessed with teaching the public about the virtues of thrift, and extolling the miraculous, loaves-and-fishes nature of compound interest. This prompted him to invent a board game called "It's Your $5,000." "It was almost the Monopoly of the financial business," his son recalls. "You had a stock ticker, you had stock market news and you had four main properties: industrials, rails, oils and golds. By spinning the ticker, the stocks would go up or down. The game even came with a little blackboard and a piece of chalk for marking up your stock quotations. Dad really promoted that game around B.C. He had 'Millionaire's Nights' all over Vancouver, with little girls in costumes, and games nights in Elks halls across the province. That's how I got interested in the stock market."

At 16, Tony Reid drew his first stock-market chart as a class project at Vancouver's Prince of Wales High School. He still remembers the name of the stock: Trans-Mountain Pipelines.

At 19, deciding to skip university, he went to work for his father's firm and began keeping the charts which, since early childhood, he'd watched his father draw on large sheets of graph paper. At that time, his father wrote a monthly market letter for an old-line Vancouver brokerage house called The Western City Company. When his father was especially busy, Tony would write the letter for him.

That's roughly what he's been doing ever since. Reid has moved from job to job, from his father's firm to Midland Osler to The Western City Company in Vancouver, from Bolton Tremblay to Greenshields in Montreal, and from D.D. Creighton & Co., to Brawley Cathers Ltd., to F.H. Deacon, to MBA Securities and back to Brawley Cathers again, and then to Walwyn Inc. in Toronto. Between MBA and Brawley Cathers, he even had his own firm for a couple of years, and fulfilled a boyhood ambition that would have pleased his father: He owned a seat on the Toronto Stock Exchange. He's also owned several restaurants and a computer software company. But what he's basically been doing, at all those jobs, in all those cities, for all those years, is sitting in small, tucked-away offices, drawing lines on sheets of graph paper and telling other people what he thinks those lines mean.

Reid was strongly influenced, early in his career, by a year-long stint at the Montreal investment firm of Bolton Tremblay Ltd. One of its partners, the late Hamilton (Hammy) Bolton, was an intellectual who studied all sorts of obscure factors in his attempt to figure out why the market fluctuated: the money supply, bank deposits, the level of bank credit – indicators which, in the period of Milton Friedman's monetarist ascendance, became much more closely watched than they were in the 1950s. Bolton's pioneering work was still being carried on 30 years later by Donald Storey and Tony Boeckh, two of his early protégés. They're co-editors of an influential publication called *The Bank Credit Analyst*, which Bolton founded, and whose subscribers include international financiers, White House economists, Swiss bankers and reclusive multimillionaires.

Most technical analysts have pet theories and secret formulae which, each of them firmly believes, give them an edge on their competitors. At Bolton Tremblay, Tony Reid discovered the technical indicator that has been his main stock-in-trade ever since: the market's *rate* of change, as measured by a special weighted index developed by Tony's father. The most commonly used index of the market's overall performance is the Dow-Jones Industrial Average (DJIA), which is a composite number formed by averaging the prices of 30 key stocks traded

137

on the New York Stock Exchange. Reid found that by monitoring the *rate* at which the Dow-Jones rose and fell, he could predict future rises and falls; and by substituting the weighted index his father devised for the DJIA, he found that his system worked even better. Reid's index is a composite of the Dow and a number of TSE-listed stocks, weighted to give greater importance to some industrial groups (Reid won't tell anyone exactly how his weighting system works) and lesser importance to others. "The market may still be rising, but its rate of increase may be declining. Therefore the cycle is starting to turn," says Reid.

Although computers can easily be programmed to perform the necessary calculations for any form of technical analysis, and can even be instructed to draw the resultant charts in glowing technicolor, many technical analysts prefer not to use them. Like medieval monks hand-copying manuscripts, they find something meaningful and rewarding in the very act of drawing lines and squiggles on sheets of graph paper; it somehow brings them closer to their subject. Reid – who finally started using a computer in 1984 – once spent an entire summer drawing a chart that involved 20,000 separate calculations, plotting the ups and downs of the Dow-Jones Average back to 1871. The chart is fully 30 feet long, and Reid has dazzled more than one gathering of investors by pulling out his chart and rolling it open to its full length across the expanse of a boardroom table. "You ask me about any week for the past 93 years, and I can give you the exact market index, *and* the relative strength, *and* the momentum. Sure the Dow has changed; they keep taking out some stocks and adding new ones. But it's the cycle that's important."

A slowdown in the market's rate of ascent precedes its fall; a slowdown in its rate of decline presages an upward trend. That rather unremarkable insight is really the only thing that Tony Reid has to sell. Most technical analysis, when stripped to its bare essentials, is just about that simple. The rest is common sense, showmanship and – probably most important – a flair for self-promotion.

Beutel, Goodman:
The Investment Counsellor
As Entrepreneur

Beutel, Goodman & Co. Ltd. is more than a firm of investment counsellors. It's easier to think of them as a sort of private merchant bank, which pulls in money from institutions and well-heeled individuals all over North America, and deploys these billions in dozens of different directions. The firm's five partners don't merely invest their clients' money in the many deals that cross their desks. Through various combinations of their own money, their company's money and their clients' money, they're also active investors themselves, in everything from oil companies to pizza restaurants to radio stations to factories that make roller casters. Although at times it's difficult to tell whether they're investment counsellors or a venture-capital factory, no other investment-counselling firm, with the possible exception of Sarlos and Zukerman, has such a large and well-founded reputation as creative deal makers.

But then, Austin Beutel and Ned Goodman, who founded the firm in Montreal in 1967, had some excellent basic training in the care and feeding of young companies. Both men spent at least four years as in-house portfolio managers for Edward and Peter Bronfman, the immensely wealthy scions of one branch of the Seagram's clan, and principals of Edper Investments Ltd., now one of Canada's most powerful family-owned conglomerates.

When they decided to set up their own investment-counselling business in 1967, although they had impressive credentials they hadn't much in the way of money or prospects. Goodman was a graduate geologist with a knack for picking underpriced resource companies. Beutel, a graduate of McGill and the Harvard Business School, had already demonstrated an entrepreneurial streak. The year after he graduated from Harvard he'd set up his own investment fund – grandly titled the Dynamic Fund of Canada – which at first was nothing more than an investment club for Beutel and a few of his buddies. But then he decided to go public. At Edper, Beutel had become accustomed to investigating young companies which came seeking Bronfman money, and he understood what could happen when you connected bright young managements with an infusion of cash.

Beutel, Goodman's first couple of years were lean ones. Although Edper gave them enough business to pay the rent, it was three years before the firm landed Imasco as their first institutional account. Their investment performance was good, however, and word got around in the investment business. By 1977, the year they moved the company from Montreal to Toronto, they were managing about $400 million of other people's money.

Looking for Bargains

Today, Beutel, Goodman is one of the country's largest independent investment-counselling firms, and probably the busiest. With more than 50 employees, it's still a relatively small shop; but it manages about $2.4 billion in pension-fund money, including $170 million in real-estate investments, plus another $175 million in various pooled funds which are sold to the public as RRSP investments, plus another $170 million worth of U.S. money that is managed by a two-man subsidiary in Houston. Among the various funds is Austin Beutel's old investment club, the Dynamic Fund, which is now sold to outside investors and whose assets have thus grown to more than $100 million. Another is BGR Precious Metals Fund Ltd., which specializes in trading gold and silver bullion and the stocks of precious-metal producers. Early in 1984, Beutel, Goodman launched yet another fund to invest in high-risk resource stocks; it's called the Dynamic Prospectors Fund, and when it was underwritten by McLeod Young Weir, the shares were deliberately priced at $1 each (minimum purchase 1,000 shares) to attract the kind of investors who like to take a small flutter on the Vancouver Stock Exchange.

As portfolio managers, the firm's four equal partners – Beutel, Goodman, Dave Williams and Seymour Schulich, and a fifth partner with a smaller interest, Owen McReery – tend to be "aggressive," a Bay Street buzzword which means they like to make a lot of money in a hurry. "Our criteria for the investments we make on behalf of clients are very simple," says Beutel. "A stock should return a minimum of 50 per cent in two years in order to qualify." The firm's six portfolio managers spend much of their time looking for potential bargains, which they present and defend at the firm's regular Monday meetings. If the majority agrees, the stock is bought on behalf of various clients.

But what gives the firm its unique clout in the marketplace is the partners' willingness to put their own money into deals they've recommended to clients, or into deals they find attractive, but which are too risky to qualify as pension-fund investments. "We've chosen to defend the investment counsellor's role as an active participant in business, and not this pure, holy guy who sits in an ivory tower" says Beutel. "To those who question our position, we say that it's a hell of a lot better to know what's going on by being in the boardroom and on the firing line than just looking at numbers. It's a two-barrelled thing. It makes us better businessmen, and it stimulates our guys – gives them an opportunity to invest their own bucks.

140

"The only thing we have to observe, of course, is that there's no conflict. So we've defined our areas. We'll never buy on a discretionary basis anything in which we're involved as beneficial owners and directors. If the client wants to invest along with us, we ask him to give us a letter directing us to do so."

Some of these investments are made through a holding company which the firm set up in 1969 called New Ventures Equities Ltd. New Ventures is partly owned by Trucena Investments Ltd., the Canadian investment arm of the Brenninkmeyer family of Rotterdam, who own retail chains throughout northern Europe; and Trucena also owns 10 per cent of Beutel, Goodman. New Ventures has about $55 million invested in various up-and-coming resource companies. About 70 per cent of this money comes from Beutel, Goodman's pension-fund clients; the rest comes from Trucena, from individual clients, or from the firm's partners.

The investments are seldom passive ones. When New Ventures takes a large position in a small company, they usually want a seat on that company's board and a say in how it is being run. In 1979, for instance, when Ned Goodman became dissatisfied with the management of Campbell-Chibougamou Mines Ltd., he mounted a proxy fight which ended in Campbell's management being turfed out. Since then, Goodman notes with satisfaction, Campbell's assets have grown tenfold. In the same vein, in the early 1970s, Seymour Schulich, on behalf of Beutel, Goodman and other shareholders, took control of a junior oil company called Trinity Resources. "We like to buy large positions in small companies where we can have an impact," Beutel explains. "That's where we can have fun, and that's where it doesn't conflict with our clients."

Anyone who puts money into small companies does so in the hope that a few glorious winners will more than compensate for all the losers. Beutel, Goodman has had more than its fair share of winners. In 1972, when the partners started buying into Guardian Trustco Inc., a small, Montreal-based trust company which specialized in trading foreign currencies and precious metals, its capital base was less than $2 million. By mid-1984, Guardian's capital had grown to about $20 million, and Beutel owned 26 per cent. Late in 1983, in the hopes of repeating their Guardian Trust coup, they bought 6 per cent of a small bank in Indiana. Beutel and Goodman, through New Ventures, have been half-owners since 1967 of Mike's Submarine Sandwiches, which started out as a single fast-food restaurant in Montreal, and is now a fast-growing chain.

"I've made my money investing in some very mundane

things," says Beutel. "My largest single investment success was acquiring the second-largest position in a small chemical company called Surpass Chemical. I bought the stock for less than $1, and sold it for $10." For a while, he was also the largest single shareholder in C & C Yachts Ltd. Beutel, Goodman has also done well in such mundane companies as Shepherd Products Ltd., which manufactures barbecues and roller casters, and in Delisle Yogourt, which was selling $500,000 worth of yogourt when the partners bought a piece of the company in 1967, and now has sales of $50 million a year. Early in 1984, Beutel, Goodman and an associate also bought 50 per cent of CKO Radio, the money-losing all-news radio network, in the hopes of an eventual turnaround.

The firm has been so successful, in fact, that Beutel and his partners now spend some of their time worrying about what might happen to the firm after they're gone. Some investment firms, if they survive their brilliant founders, grow very cautious and conservative. "There's a certain comfort in mediocrity," says Beutel. "There's a certain comfort in not taking risks. And that's the beauty of our system. When you're not hungry, you don't *have* to take risks. You can focus on conservation of capital, not aggressivity." That would be the supreme irony: If Beutel, Goodman, that extraordinary firm of dealmakers, turned into an investment bureaucracy.

Robin Cornwell:
The Analyst
As Investigative Reporter

The best securities analysts are like tough investigative journalists, or like big-city detectives who have seen it all. They read everything, notice everything and try to make connections between seemingly unrelated bits of data – connections which everyone else has missed. Like good reporters, they have a nose for detecting bluff and bullshit. They're hard to fool, and they're seldom victimized by their own enthusiasms.

By this yardstick, Robin Cornwell, a partner in a small Bay Street investment boutique called McCarthy Securities Ltd., could serve as the very model of the compleat fundamentalist. Using nothing but the telephone, published statistics and a finely-honed skepticism, Cornwell, single-handed, has deflated some of Canada's most expensive corporate images and, in the process, inconvenienced or alarmed some of the most powerful men in the country.

142

Tracking the Banks

Cornwell tracks the banks. He is one of an elite handful of investment analysts who follow the performance of Canada's reigning financial institutions, and try to predict which ones are doing as well as they say, and which ones are facing trouble down the road. Other prominent members of this exclusive club include Norman Heimlich, the garrulous, Montreal-based bank-watcher for Osler, Wills, Bickle Ltd.; Hugh Brown at Burns Fry Ltd. in Toronto; and Roy Palmer at Alfred Bunting & Co. Ltd. Often Cornwell seems to have a better fix on how these banks are really doing than do their own chief executives. "I've ruffled a tremendous number of feathers," he says, sounding not even faintly repentant. "You have to be right, but you should pursue an idea with zest and vigor. That can upset the Establishment – which can be amusing, and sometimes quite upsetting."

Cornwell has been in the business since 1972 and, like most analysts, has job-hopped frequently. He's a veteran of the research departments of Pitfield Mackay Ross (now part of Dominion Securities Pitfield), of Harris and Partners (now part of that firm too). At Harris he was assigned to follow trust companies, and soon turned to a discipline which is the closest Canadian equivalent to Kremlinology: studying Canada's chartered banks, the largest, richest and most arrogant financial institutions in the country.

His earliest coup was in 1979, when he published a report noting that several of the large banks, notably the Canadian Imperial Bank of Commerce, has seriously "mismatched" their loan and deposit portfolios, and predicted fairly dire consequences if interest rates rose – which they later did. The essence of successful banking is to ensure that the money you lend for longer terms is matched by correspondingly long-term deposits. Some of the Canadian banks, Cornwell discovered, had violated this fundamental rule; they had invested heavily in five-year mortgages, but these loans were matched with 60- and 90-day deposits. When interest rates rose, the short-term depositors withdrew their money because they could earn a better return elsewhere, and the banks were stuck with long-term mortgages which paid less than current rates of interest. "Some banks denied they were mismatched, but others later confirmed it," says Cornwell. "But I got totally frustrated, because the portfolio managers that we were selling research to wouldn't buy the concept." Subsequent events proved him right, in other words; but he'd failed to sell his story to the market.

An analyst cannot count himself truly powerful until one of his ideas causes a stock to rise or fall. Better still is to cause an entire group of stocks to move. Best of all is to move the market as a whole by the force and prescience of your perceptions. Economist Henry Kaufman of Wall Street's Salomon Bros. has been known to cause flutters in stock markets around the world with his oracular pronouncements on the future direction of interest rates. Joe Granville, whose newsletter once commanded a vast following of small investors, has done it more than once.

But Cornwell is one of the very few Canadian analysts whose pronouncements have been known to move an entire group of stocks. He's done it by spotting trends in the banks' performance before anyone else does. And he does *that* through a mysterious, almost magical, process that consists of buttressing a hunch with months of painstaking, foot-slogging research.

Early in 1981 for instance, he got a hunch that the banks, which were reporting profits so large that they'd triggered an enquiry by a Parliamentary committee, were saddled with a lot of bad loans. His interest was piqued initially by a rumor he'd heard from an American contact that a high-flying Calgary oil company called Turbo Resources Ltd. had reneged on a foreign-currency transaction. If Turbo was secretly in trouble with an American bank, Cornwell wondered, what was the status of the $800 million that Turbo also owed to the Canadian banks? And what was the status of similarly expansive Canadian energy companies such as Dome Petroleum?

Cornwell started digging — not by talking to the banks themselves, but by sniffing around their largest corporate customers. "I didn't even talk directly to the Turbos and Domes," he says. "Instead, I talked to their competitors. It took me two months, and I discovered that loads of companies weren't paying interest on their loans. In fact, I discovered more than $8 billion worth of loans on which interest hadn't been paid for 90 days. At that stage, not even the bankers were conscious of the magnitude of this trend."

In his report for McCarthy Securities, published in January 1982, Cornwell reduced the bad-loan figure to $5.33 billion in the interests of conservatism. But his revelations were enough to prompt the market to take a sober second look at the banks's prospects. Within three months of his report, shares of the Canadian Imperial Bank of Commerce had dropped from $25 to $16.25; of the Royal Bank, from $23 to $18; of the Bank of

Montreal, from $22 to $16.75. In all, the market's reassessment, initially triggered by Cornwell's report, lopped some $335 million off the share value of the five largest Canadian banks. "I even had guys from the U.S. Treasury Department fly up from Washington to interview me to find out what the hell was going on," he says.

William Bradford, the president of the Bank of Montreal, called Cornwell's report "grossly erroneous," and didn't speak to him for months. (In fact, the Bank of Montreal's loan losses turned out to be even worse than Cornwell had predicted.) By that time, the Parliamentary committee was no longer worried about whether the banks were making too much money; they were concerned instead about the stability of the Canadian banking system. And to advise them on the mysteries of the banking system, they hired Robin Cornwell as their chief economist.

Russ Morrison:
The Investment Counsellor
As Intellectual

"I have a great theoretical mind. I really do." Russ Morrison gazes at you earnestly as he says this, his freckled farm-boy's face shining with sincerity as he struggles to articulate the subtle mysteries of his genius. Among people who pick stocks for a living, Morrison has a large reputation as an intellectual. His approach to portfolio management is so resolutely cerebral that it seems to transcend mere braininess and flutter into some purer, platonic realm. His standing among his colleagues is similar to that enjoyed by the late Marshall McLuhan; they are awed by his brilliance, but often have trouble figuring out exactly what he's saying. "He's a real smartie, and he's picked out some real bargains," says Austin Beutel of Beutel, Goodman Ltd. "The trouble is, he's hard to make out. For the first 10 years of knowing Russ, I felt insignificant and stupid. I was sure he was delivering pearls and I didn't understand them. And I still can't figure him out."

There are plenty of investment counsellors who manage larger sums of money, and at least several who claim to have better performance records. But in the course of researching this chapter, I routinely asked the investment counsellors I interviewed who, among their number, was *really good*. Morrison's name came up almost every time. The source of his reputation may stem less from his unquestioned skill at making money grow

145

than in the disinterested manner in which he goes about it. In a world of fear and greed, Russ Morrison is a truth-seeker.

Morrison is one of the pioneering figures of Canadian investment management. At the age of 60, he has seen a dozen market cycles come and go, and he and his clients have managed to profit from most of them. But unlike stars such as Austin Beutel or Norman Short, Morrison has never become the focus of a major pool of investment talent. He has wandered for more than three decades around Bay Street and St. James Street, following his own interests, drifting from job to job like a mendicant medieval scholar. He was raised in Saskatchewan, educated at the Universities of Saskatchewan, Toronto and Chicago, taught economics for two years at Vanderbilt University in Nashville, Tennessee and, in 1953, joined Dominion Securities in Toronto as a securities analyst. He spent a further 13 years as an analyst at a now-defunct Toronto firm called Mills Spence, doing approximately what he wanted to do: "Trying to learn how the world works."

In 1966, the heyday of high-technology stocks, he moved to Montreal as vice-president of the Canadian branch of a U.S. investment-counselling firm, Canadian Channing Corp. Ltd., managing a group of investment funds. When Channing's parent company was sold in 1968, Morrison and his colleagues in Montreal bought the Canadian branch. A year later it was bought by Bernie Cornfeld's IOS organization, which needed Canadian investment expertise as part of its worldwide mutual-funds empire, and had already been turned down by Norman Short's Guardian Capital Group. Before IOS's collapse and Cornfeld's subsequent imprisonment, Morrison acted as an investment consultant to, but not an employee of, IOS's Canadian operations. In 1971 he began managing a group of funds sponsored by the Commercial Union Insurance group – in effect, freelancing. He's doing roughly the same thing today, although since 1977 his main clients have been Bolton Tremblay Inc., an investment-counselling firm that manages about $1 billion worth of pension funds, and Trimark Investment Management Inc.

Discovering What the Others are Ignoring

Every investment counsellor tries to discover investment situations that everybody else is ignoring; but Morrison is widely respected for having spotted more than his share. In the late 1960s, for instance, he was the first Canadian fund manager to spot the potential of the Japanese stock market, an involvement that has lasted well into the 1980s, earning tens of millions of dollars for his clients. As Morrison describes this multimillion-dollar triumph, it sounds almost accidental, like a fishing trip that just kind of happened one day because some of the boys down at the pub got to talking.

"I was visiting Toronto in the fall of 1967," Morrison recalls, "and talking with my friend Jim Cole [of Guardian Capital Group] in his office. I mentioned to Jim, remembering the Japanese market of 1960, in which we didn't do anything, 'What about Japan?' He said, 'Gosh, that might be fun,' and that's about all that happened. When I got back to Montreal I asked the other guys in the shop: 'Does anybody around here know anything about Japan?' Well, if they'd all said no, the chances are the idea would have been dropped. You get a hundred of those 'hey, what-do-you-think?' ideas, and if nobody salutes, you do something else.

"But Larry Davis just happened to have some files, okay? So that means you've got a live one in your shop; there can be some dialogue on the subject, involving at least two people. And that's enough to light a fire and have some fun. This was in October or November. At the January board meeting of Canadian Channing I suggested we should purchase a couple of million dollars' worth of high-quality Japanese stocks. One board member suggested, 'How about a million?' I agreed.

"I can remember spending the million pretty fast, then phoning up the executive committee to get authorization for another million, then a double, then another double. At the next board meeting, when we'd invested $8 million, the question was: 'Where does this end?' So we went for another double, to $16 million. It turned out that January 1968 was the exact moment to start to buy. It just went up from there. But you have to distinguish good luck from good judgment. If Jim Cole hadn't mentioned Japan, if Larry Davis hadn't reacted, if I hadn't reacted to Larry, if the board hadn't reacted properly – at any one of those stages, if anyone's ear had been put out of joint – know what I mean?"

In Morrison's mind, an investment portfolio is not simply a basket of stocks. It's a collection of *ideas* about what's going to happen; and the stocks are merely reflections of those ideas. An idea, under this definition, could be almost any theory of how the world will unfold. "An idea is when you perceive a difference between 'the truth' – how people are currently viewing a situation – and reality. For instance, suppose everybody thinks the car of the future is going to be made mostly out of plastic. Well, an idea might be: 'I think that's bullshit. The car

147

of the future is going to be made of nickel.' So you go out and buy nickel stocks." Thus, when Morrison describes what he does as "speculation," he means it in the classic sense: "the act of theorizing or conjecturing."

Each investment manager, he wrote in *The Financial Analysts Journal* in 1975, "should aspire to be a *speculative* man, able to achieve investment results – one who deals in ideas and only incidentally in securities; who understands how to combine ideas (speculations) into portfolios to provide a reliable investment result . . . Breadth of knowledge and enthusiasms, expressed via securities holdings, tempered by appropriate modesty, can and should result in diversified portfolios – automatically." This is pure Morrison. It sounds profound on first reading, and probably is. And yet one is left with a nagging suspicion that there may be less here than meets the eye.

There can be no second-guessing, however, of Morrison's best ideas. At the bottom of the bear market in 1974-75, he bought heavily into a U.S. company called Ryder System Inc., a large trucking and leasing operation, for less than $10 per share. "This is the biggest company in its field in the U.S.," he says. "Trucks! Lots of debt! Lots of people! And with 15 million shares outstanding at, say $5, that means the market says this huge company is worth only $75 million. Well, even the biggest company in *jelly beans* ought to be worth $75 million, let alone the biggest in truck leasing and rental! They were in financial trouble, but I decided they wouldn't always be in financial trouble, and they wouldn't disappear. I could have been wrong, but in fact I was right. In any case, the shares are now selling north of $40."

Russ Morrison actually sounds humble when he says this, and he genuinely is. A complex man, Morrison believes he is a theoretical genius, but also an ordinary individual. "I'm just a little guy standing on the corner," he says, in that cunning, aw-shucks manner that has become his trademark. "Just a little guy trying to understand the world."

La Caisse De Depot Et Placement: The Portfolio Manager As Political Activist

The Caisse de depot et placement, a Quebec government agency, has emerged as the largest single pool of capital in the entire country. The Caisse invests the pension funds of Quebec provincial employees. In 1983 it was managing more than $18 billion of these savings, allowing the Caisse to muscle its way into the boardrooms of some of Canada's most powerful corporations, including Domtar, Noranda and Canadian Pacific Ltd.

The Caisse's headquarters, on the eighth and ninth floors of a glass-and-chrome office tower on Montreal's McGill College Avenue, are an appropriate symbol of the New Quebec's financial strength. Under its canny, secretive president, a former stockbroker and government policy-maker named Jean Campeau, the Caisse has become Quebec's window on corporate Canada. Its influence, which extends from the cabinet chamber of Quebec City into the boardrooms of Toronto, is quiet, pervasive and – at least to Ottawa and Bay Street – disturbing. To Ottawa, the Caisse represents a challenge to federal power. To Bay Street, it represents creeping socialism in a maddeningly seductive guise: the pin-striped sophistication of the professional portfolio manager. Bay Street hates the notion of a vast pool of capital being deployed in ways that promote the aims of a separatist, social-democratic government. But there is a certain ambivalence to this aversion, for it is painfully difficult for any capitalist to argue with $18 billion of other people's money.

The money flows in to the Caisse, at the rate – in 1982 – of $1,219.93 every single minute, from the paycheque deductions of millions of Quebecers who never miss the money because they never see it – civil servants from all public sectors, municipal politicians, construction workers, motorists who subscribe to the province's auto-insurance plan, plus nearly every other wage-earner and employer in the province. It is invested, up there in the Caisse's silent broadloomed offices, by a team of French-speaking portfolio managers, most of them young, ambitious and MBAed, many of whom learned their trade in the investment departments of Anglophone firms such as Sun Life, which have since departed for Toronto.

The Lesage government opted out of the federal government's Canada Pension Plan in 1965, and set up its own pension plan, the Regie des Rente, whose revenues are deposited with the Caisse. Lesage wanted the Caisse to do more than merely husband the savings of Quebec workers until their retirement. "Funds of such magnitude must be channelled toward accelerated development of the public and private sectors, so that Quebec's economic and social objectives may be quickly attained with the greatest possible efficiency," he told the Quebec National Assembly. "In short, the Caisse must not be envisaged solely as an investment fund like any other, but also as an instrument of growth – a more powerful lever than any of those now available in this province."

149

Until Jean Campeau took over as Caisse president in 1980, Lesage's activist mandate was largely ignored. The Caisse, quietly and skilfully, invested about two-thirds of its assets – more than $10.3 billion by 1982 – in bonds and debentures of various governments and their agencies, mainly Hydro Quebec and the Quebec government. The rest of the money was invested in mortgages, real estate and stocks. The Caisse's professionalism attracted admiration from fellow money-managers. "It was one of the best-managed funds I'd ever laid eyes on," says Ross Archibald, a University of Western Ontario professor who is an expert on Canadian capital markets. "I remember wishing my money was in it. It certainly wasn't a mouthpiece of the government."

The climate changed in 1980, when Campeau was appointed chairman. He's a lean, greying, intense workaholic who looks like a scaled-down Gallic version of John Kenneth Galbraith. A 1955 graduate of Quebec's best business school, L'Ecole des Hautes Etudes Commerciales, he spent eight years as a stockbroker with René T. Leclerc Inc., the predecessor firm of Geoffrion Leclerc, and another eight years running an industrial company, Canada Flooring Limited, where he doubled sales and profits within two years. In 1971, while Lesage was still in power, he joined the Quebec Finance Department as manager of the provincial debt, much of which was held by the Caisse. By 1977 he was assistant deputy finance minister under Jacques Parizeau who, as a senior Finance Department official under Jean Lesage, had practically invented the Caisse.

One day, while Campeau was in Tokyo negotiating a loan for the province, his boss – now the finance minister and financial brains-trust of René Lévesque's separatist government – phoned him from Quebec City. He was looking for a new president for the Caisse. "I've put your name on the list," said Parizeau. "Is that okay?" Campeau agreed instantly; running the Caisse was a job he'd coveted for years. Campeau's accession to the top job amounted to a palace coup. Within two years of his arrival, a dozen of the Caisse's 29 senior administrators and portfolio managers had departed. To help replace them, Campeau hired two assistant deputy ministers from the Finance Department.

The Caisse has been a major player in the stock market ever since its inception, without attracting adverse comment from the private sector. But under Campeau, it began to take its mandate in earnest, buying heavily into companies with major interests in Quebec. Between 1979 and 1982, it more than doubled the value of its shareholdings to $2.759 billion, making it by far the largest stockholding institution in the country. Its reach is awesome. It is the largest single shareholder in each of Canada's seven largest banks, in CP Limited and in Bell Canada. With partners, the Caisse owns enough shares to give it substantial or controlling interests in Domtar Inc. (forest products); Noranda Mines Ltd. (a mining and forestry conglomerate, which the Caisse partly controls through its 30-per cent holding in Brascade Ltd.); Gaz Metropolitain Inc. (natural gas distribution) and Alcan Aluminium Ltd. Its shareholdings also make the Caisse virtually a partner in most of the largest Quebec-owned companies: 28 per cent of Provigo Inc. (grocery stores); 15 per cent of Trust General du Canada (financial services); 8.4 per cent of La Verendrye Management Ltd. (trucking and broadcasting); and 20 per cent of Prenor Group Ltd. (financial services).

Bay Street and even Wall Street have closed ranks against this strange and menacing new animal. *Barron's*, the influential U.S. investment weekly, warned its readers that "the managers of the Caisse are debauching the retirement savings of Quebeckers." Paul Desmarais, the powerful chairman of Power Corporation of Canada, which, along with associated companies holds a 6.7 per cent stake in CP, complained that the Caisse – which owns 9.9 per cent of the same company – had no business demanding a seat on CP's board. "They're nationalizing companies by the back door," he said. "The Caisse represents the state." The Conseil de Patronat du Québec, an employers' association, demanded that the Caisse be prevented from buying controlling interests in companies.

Government also got into the act. Both the Montreal Exchange and the Ontario Securities Commission insisted that the Caisse must file insider-trading reports like any other substantial shareholder. Campeau flatly refused, on the grounds that the Caisse, as a provincial government agency, wasn't bound by another province's regulations. But the most galling attack came late in 1982 from the federal government, which threatened to pass a law forbidding any provincial agency from owning more than 10 per cent of a private-sector transportation company – a blunt attack on the Caisse's growing involvement in CP. (The legislation died on the order paper in 1984, and Consumer and Corporate Affairs Minister Judy Erola told Parliament it will not be re-introduced.)

Others have attacked the Caisse on more cogent grounds: that it's making dumb investments, based on political considerations. Under Campeau, it loaned billions to the province and to Hydro Quebec at lower rates than those charged by the banks. It bought into Noranda at the top of the market, and watched the value of those shares plunge dramatically within a year. According to Marcel Belanger, an influential Quebec economist, the Caisse's performance ranking slipped from eleventh place among 100 Canadian pension funds in 1976 to ninety-ninth place in 1980, rising only to ninetieth place the following year.

Based on the stern yardstick of performance measurement, in other words, the Caisse went from being one of the very best-managed funds to one of the very worst. Quebec's pensioners may find themselves short-changed in the end. But that, apparently, is the price of national self-expression; and in the financial climate of René Lévesque's Quebec, it was a price the government was willing to pay – with other people's money, of course.

11
Morty
Starts
A Fund

By the summer of 1983, Dr. Morton Shulman – physician, speculator, TV star, ex-coroner, ex-politician, best-selling author, art collector, investment advisor to the millions – was dwelling in a state of existential boredom. He was rich and famous, and people often sought him out and tried to flatter him, for it was known that he had made some of his friends quite rich. Through his own individual speculative efforts, Dr. Shulman (or "Morty," as he is known to even slight acquaintances) had accumulated a fortune of about $40 million. He had roamed the exotic places of the world from Macchu Picchu, Peru to Katmandu, Nepal. He had soared in a hot-air balloon above Phoenix, Arizona and spent countless sun-soaked holidays aboard chartered yachts in the Caribbean. He had frolicked with nude starlets in his own indoor swimming pool. He had bought French impressionists and, at the top of the market, sold them at a profit to Japanese collectors. He owned a cellarful of the finest wines and a priceless collection of centuries-old watches carved out of solid blocks of crystal.

Morty's wife, Gloria, adored him. His friends were fiercely loyal. So were his patients – for, in spite of his wealth and his multitudinous commitments, he still cared for his old patients every morning in the same poky GP's office in the working-class neighborhood where he'd practised medicine for the past 34 years.

The ratings on Morty's syndicated TV interview show, *The Shulman File*, were good and getting better. Sometimes, when he drove downtown for lunch, parking-lot attendants would approach him shyly, as if he were a film star, and ask him: "Dr. Shulman, should I sell my Goldcorp warrants?" For, in addition to all the other hats he wore, Morty was probably Canada's best-known investment advisor. His two how-to-get-rich books, *Anyone Can Make a Million,* and *How to Survive and Profit from Inflation* had sold in the hundreds of thousands; and his monthly column in Canada's largest investment newsletter, *The MoneyLetter,* was devoured by nearly 100,000 readers. The mere rumor that Shulman was about to recommend a stock was sometimes enough to drive up its price. Tens of thousands of small investors were willing to rush out and buy whatever he recommended. His following was so large, his stock-market clout so massive, that his editors at *The MoneyLetter* had asked him to confine his recommendations to large, widely traded stocks. Otherwise, his tips might trigger a buying stampede which would immediately drive up the price, creating a self-fulfilling prophecy.

But money, power, fame and love apparently weren't enough. At 59, Morton Shulman felt restless, unfulfilled, weary. Sometimes, unwittingly, he revealed that malaise to strangers. At dinner parties, in conversation and occasionally even on television, the usual animation would sometimes vanish from his face; and in its place you could see the mask of a man gazing bleakly inward and not much liking what he saw. All his life he'd courted new challenges, and now there seemed to be nothing left. Could anything bring him alive again?

By August of 1983, Shulman had found his challenge, and was involved in what became the most intense, most exciting adventure of his eclectic career. The challenge consisted of a horserace between several of Bay Street's largest investment dealers, and Shulman was one of the horses. The object of the exercise was to persuade the public to invest in gold funds – or, more precisely, to invest in the skills of a handful of people, including Shulman, who are experts in the art of investing in precious metals. The race was over before the leaves were off the trees. In less than three months, Canadians invested an astonishing total of more than $400 million in the shares of a series of competing gold funds, each backed by a different investment house, each boasting its own high-profile guru.

This, accordingly, is the story of some of those gurus and how they think; of Morton Shulman's quest for diversion and further wealth; of the Canadian public's growing fascination with gold and the magic it represents. Finally, it is a serviceable example of the process that constitutes much of Bay Street's raison d'être: underwriting.

The Fine Art of Underwriting

In an underwriting, an investment dealer buys newly issued shares of a company that needs money, then resells those shares to the public.* It sounds simple, but it's actually a creative and competitive business.

Underwriting is not Bay Street's most profitable activity. Most firms make more money buying and selling stock, for a commission, on behalf of individuals and institutions, or by trading securities themselves. But brokers would kill, almost, to get a larger piece of the major bond and equity underwritings.**

In 1983, investment dealers raised about $6.3 billion through new common and preferred share issues, mostly on behalf of large and medium-sized companies. That sum represented tens of millions of dollars worth of underwriting commissions; and those commissions are the only thing Bay Street cares about. New jobs, creation of wealth, diffusion of the fruits of capitalism to an ever-larger segment of the population, support for native entrepreneurship – all that wonderful stuff really can happen as a by-product of the underwriting process, and sometimes does. But in the broker's simple-minded view of the world, there is only one important question: Will the issue sell? Can I convince my customers that they'll make some money if they buy this stock? The art of underwriting, whether the money is being raised for Bell Canada or for some two-bit mining prospect on the Vancouver Stock Exchange, is to structure the deal so that the stock will look attractive – even if that sometimes means virtually remaking the company.

If you're underwriting some relatively untried venture, it also helps to have some reassuring Big Names associated with the project. "It's much easier to sell a recognizable product than something that nobody's ever heard of," says Phil Holtby, president of Midland Doherty Ltd. "People find comfort in having recognizable names on pieces of paper they're going to buy. I

---

* If the dealer's customers aren't willing to buy the shares, the broker is stuck with them, except in the case of a "best efforts" underwriting, in which case the dealer agrees only to sell as much stock as he can. That's why so many junior underwriting deals get cancelled at the last minute. The broker agonizes continually over the state of the market, avoids setting a price on the issue until the last possible moment and frequently pulls back from the brink, leaving the client company high and dry.

** When an investment dealer underwrites a company's bonds it is, in effect, persuading people and institutions to loan that company money. Equity underwriting refers to the issuance and sale to the public of new shares in a company. What's being sold, in other words, is a piece of the ownership of the company that's issuing the shares.

155

mean, this business is no different from selling ties at Simpsons. We're in a marketing business. We're marketing products. If you don't dress them up and make them look good, like in the store windows, people aren't going to stop and take notice."

Holtby is not the only person on Bay Street who knows a hot product when he sees one. And so, in June 1983, when a newly formed mutual fund named Goldcorp Investments Ltd., brought a new issue to market and sold shares and warrants worth an astounding total of $175 million, the Street was electrified. The underwriter, Merrill Lynch Royal Securities, had expected to sell about $20 million worth. A gold fund? Why were all those people throwing so much money into a gold fund? Where did they come from? Funds that specialized in precious metals had been doing business for decades, without attracting much attention or much investor interest. But suddenly, out of nowhere, and at a time when the price of gold was stagnant, the Goldcorp issue had become one of the largest single stock underwritings in the history of the street. What had triggered this tidal wave of hitherto-unsuspected investor enthusiasm? And who, exactly, was Goldcorp?

Goldcorp turned out to be the inspiration of one of Bay Street's earliest gold bugs, a stockbroker named Don McEwen who was respected by those who knew him but was known by very few. With his kindly, self-effacing manner, McEwen reminds people of the favorite uncle they wish they'd grown up with. The tragedies in his life may have contributed to his reputation as a bit of a loner. He served with the RCAF in World War II, caught polio in northern India and returned to Canada as a paraplegic who could walk only with the aid of crutches. He's been a stockbroker all his life, but his career assumed meaning and direction only in 1965 when, as a salesman and analyst for a now-defunct firm, Equitable Securities Ltd.,* he developed an interest in gold – a passion that almost no one else on Bay Street then shared. "In those days," he says, "it was very difficult to find anyone to talk to about gold on this side of the water." A fact-finding trip to Europe and South Africa convinced him that gold's day was coming. North Americans who believed their currencies were "as good as gold," McEwen decided, were in for a rude shock.

The fruit of these insights was something called the Canadian South African Gold Fund, formed by McEwen under Equitable's auspices in 1965. It was a closed-end investment fund whose only assets were to be bars of gold and the shares of

---

* Which later merged with Montreal-based Levesque, Beaubien Inc.

gold-mining companies. McEwen spent two years trying to get the issue underwritten. But the timing wasn't right; no investment house he approached believed Canadians could be persuaded to bet money on gold. Discouraged, McEwen raised the money himself late in 1967. He and a few of his brokerage clients put $200,000 into the fledgling fund and, on March 7, 1968, bought $200,000 worth of gold bullion for $35.19 per ounce. About the same time, they converted it from a closed-end into a mutual fund, which meant that instead of issuing a limited number of shares, it would keep issuing new shares for as long as people were willing to pay for them.

The timing, in retrospect, turned out to be brilliant. That same weekend the International Monetary Fund, meeting in Stockholm, abolished the ten-nation gold pool which had been formed to hold the price of gold down to $35 per ounce, and established a two-tier system: an official price of $35, and a free market price which would be allowed to float higher. Gold accordingly moved above $40 and the Canadian South African Gold Fund – later renamed Goldfund Ltd. – started selling its shares to the public. By the end of 1968 it had sold about $700,000 worth. In the ensuing 15 years gold moved from $35 per ounce to as high as $850, and then fell back below $400. In spite of this setback, Goldfund's shareholders have seen their investment grow by 683 per cent during this period.

The Race for Gold Funds

McEwen has been launching and running small gold funds ever since. During the 1970s he set up his own brokerage firm and then, feeling hemmed in by administrative obligations when the firm began to grow, joined with John Easson and his company, Isard, Robertson & Co. Ltd., to form McEwen Easson Limited. In 1975 he launched Gold Trust Ltd., a fund which made it possible for Canadians to invest in gold through their Registered Retirement Savings Plans. In 1979 he launched another gold fund, aimed at U.S. investors, which eventually sold about $7 million worth of units. But he knew that the big money would always elude him unless he could figure out a way to get large institutional investors, such as pension funds and insurance companies, to put money into a gold fund.

In 1980, with the aid of the creative lawyers at Tory Tory DesLauriers & Binnington, McEwen found a way. He bought a solid little private mortgage company, Seigneury Investments, which had been quietly churning out profits for 25 years, renamed it Goldcorp Investments Ltd., and sought a listing on the Toronto Stock Exchange. This manoeuvre neatly circumvented two awkward regulations: one which requires pension funds to invest no more than 10 per cent of their holdings in commodities or in foreign securities; and another which says they must invest their money only in companies which have been profitable for at least five years. "If an account wanted to invest half its funds in South Africa, for instance, they could do it through Goldcorp, and it would still be a legal investment," says McEwen, "because Goldcorp is a Canadian company. We kind of launder the money. That's probably a dirty word to use, but in a sense that's what we're doing."

McEwen worked with Wood Gundy Ltd. to put together a Goldcorp underwriting, but a weak gold and stock market in 1981 forced them to postpone the issue. Late in 1982, McEwen decided to raise some money himself. He sold $500,000 worth of debentures to 130 of his own clients – including, interestingly enough, Dr. Morton Shulman – and used the money to buy gold bullion for Goldcorp's portfolio.

With a small but functional mutual fund up and running, McEwen renewed his efforts to put together an underwriting deal. Since Wood Gundy had lost interest, he turned to Merrill Lynch Royal Securities Ltd., the Canadian branch of the huge, U.S.-owned brokerage house. By the spring of 1983, the price of gold was falling – from $511 all the way to $400. "We held off until early April," says McEwen, "and then we said – 'No, the market is here. Let's get the deal going.' So we did. On May 3 we filed a prospectus; we got final approval for the issue from the Ontario Securities Commission a month later, and, on June 17, Merrill gave us a cheque for $175 million."

About one-third of the money came from the institutions for which Goldfund was designed. But the other two-thirds, more than $115 million, came from individuals – demonstrating the existence of a market which Bay Street hadn't suspected. Bay Street also noted that the sales commission for this massive underwriting, most of which was pocketed by Merrill Lynch, amounted to more than $10 million. The race was on. If people wanted gold funds, Bay Street would be happy to manufacture them.

The Least Humble of Men

Exactly three days after McEwen received Goldcorp's $175-million cheque from Merrill Lynch,* Morton Shulman made his

---

* From which he had to repay $10,062,500 for sales commissions and underwriting fees, plus about $300,000 in expenses.

move. "I decided – to hell with it, I'm not going to wait any longer," says Shulman. "I mean, if Don McEwen, who nobody's ever heard of, could raise $175 million, I figured I should be able to raise $50 zillion."

If that sounds immodest, it's because Shulman – whose speculative activities in a single year, 1982, netted him about $2 million after tax – is the least humble of men. He'd made his first stock purchase in 1949 when, as an impoverished young intern with a new wife to support, he scraped together $400 to buy a mining stock called Duvay. It was trading at 17 cents and Gloria Shulman had been assured by her uncle, a promoter named Sam Ciglin, that the stock would hit $1 before Christmas. Instead, the stock went to approximately zero. "I felt bad," Shulman recalls, "not just for me, but also for Gloria's uncle. I assumed he'd gone broke when Duvay collapsed. But then, a few weeks later, he started building a huge mansion in Forest Hill. It finally dawned on me that I'd helped pay for it. That's when I decided to learn everything I could about the stock market."*

His studies paid off swiftly. A few months later Shulman read in the papers that M.J. Boylen, a well-known mining promoter, was so fed up with paying commissions to underwriters that he was selling stock in his company, an established mining firm called Brunswick Copper, directly to the public for $12 per share, with a maximum of 100 shares per person. Then Shulman discovered something remarkable: The same shares that Boylen was selling for $12 were trading on the Toronto Stock Exchange for $15! "By the end of the day I had all my friends and relatives phoning Boylen, each buying 100 shares; I promised them half the profits when I resold. By the end of the day I'd made $14,000. I couldn't believe it! Here was I, a 24-year-old kid, working as an intern for $20 a month. And in *one day* I'd made myself $14,000. That's when I said to myself; 'This is a very interesting business.' "

Shulman's next coup came when he discovered that it was possible to buy an almost unlimited number of Canadian bonds, for delivery in six weeks, without putting up any money. He also had a hunch that interest rates would continue to fall, which would force up the price of the bonds. He gambled on

---

* The Duvay debacle also launched the fabulous stock-market career of Murray (the Pez) Pezim; see page 95.

159

his hunch and signed up to buy ludicrous amounts of bonds – $25 million, $50 million. His gamble paid off. Interest rates fell. When he resold the bonds after taking delivery of them six weeks later, his profit was $200,000. He was 25 years old.

Through the 1950s, a period of declining interest rates, he continued trading bonds, with spectacular results. "Every $100 I invested in convertible bonds turned into $4,100. The leverage was unbelievable. But by then I was making so much money I didn't need leverage any more."

In the 1960s, Shulman became a public figure – a crusading coroner whose battles with various entrenched Establishments made such great copy that the CBC produced a TV drama series based on his career. But his achievements as a speculator were less well known until an ambitious young book salesman named Ron Hume came to him with an idea: For a $10,000 advance from McGraw-Hill, would he write a book about how to succeed in the stock market? The opus that resulted, entitled *Anyone Can Make a Million*, made international publishing history; through successive editions it sold 400,000 copies in hardcover and another 2.5 million in paperback. "The crazy thing," says the author, "is that I hadn't really *been* a millionaire before I wrote the book. I'd made all sorts of money, but I'd spent it. But the book made me a million."

The book launched two careers – Shulman's as an author, Ron Hume's as an independent publisher. The success of Shulman's book convinced Hume that the world was hungering for financial information, written in plain English. In 1973 he quit McGraw-Hill, started his own company, and launched an advertising and direct-mail campaign to sell a home-study course on investment and money management. Hume's hunch was correct. Sales boomed and the company prospered. As an added inducement for subscribers to the investment course, Hume added an extra product in 1975 – an eight-page compendium of stock tips and financial advice called *The MoneyLetter*.

By the 1980s, *The MoneyLetter* was Canada's largest investment newsletter.* Although there was a large stable of contributing writers, its major star was Shulman himself. His column appeared in every second issue, and his name, face and inspiring track record were featured prominently in Hume's ubiquitous advertisements and sales brochures. As early as 1980, Shulman had proposed that Hume Publishing should get into the mutual funds business, with *The MoneyLetter*'s high-profile contributors as its portfolio managers. Hume had rejected the

---

* Since May 1983, Alexander Ross has been editor of *The MoneyLetter*.

idea, on the grounds that its involvement in a fund might impair the objectivity of the company's investment advice. But the idea was still alive in Shulman's mind. He wanted to start a fund, and he wanted the selling power of the Hume organization to be an integral part of the deal.

That is why, exactly three days after the Goldcorp issue was completed, Shulman started looking for an investment house that would be willing to underwrite his fund – a task which, in his innocence, he thought would be easy. He first approached Merrill Lynch, since they'd already underwritten Goldcorp. A covey of four junior bluesuits from that venerable firm wined him and dined him at Le Mascaron in the Royal Bank Plaza and expressed breathless interest in his proposal. But the next day, Merrill's man in charge of corporate finance, Phil White, phoned to say that his firm wasn't interested after all. An approach to McLeod Young Weir through a friend of Shulman's was equally unrewarding. Shulman himself approached a friend at Davidson Partners Ltd., one of the firms where he'd been trading for years, and received another brush-off. Finally, he approached Nesbitt Thomson Bongard Inc., another of the firms he'd used for trading – and this time got a serious hearing.

At a preliminary meeting, Nesbitt's director of Corporate Finance, Joe Oliver, told Shulman he was interested in underwriting a precious-metals fund but wanted a second person, besides Shulman, to manage the fund's assets. The person he suggested was Norman Short, one of Bay Street's canniest, best-respected investment counsellors, whose Guardian Capital Group manages $1 billion of other people's money. Oliver and Shulman scheduled a meeting for the following evening, starting at 6 p.m., in Nesbitt's boardroom. That meeting is worth describing in some detail, for it turned into a wonderfully unseemly haggling session that reveals the underwriting process in all its naked glory.

Dividing the Spoils

Shulman and his two lawyers, Bert Stitt and Peter McLaughlin, turned up at 6 p.m. sharp. Oliver wasn't there, but a colleague named Selwyn Kossuth ushered them into a boardroom with muted grey walls, seated them around a solid-oak table and invited them to help themselves to drinks from the adjoining kitchenette. Shulman and his lawyers sipped their drinks in uneasy silence, waiting for Joe Oliver to arrive. Shulman loathes wasting time, and the 20-minute wait clearly rattled him. "This is not an auspicious start," he muttered to his lawyer.

Finally, at 6:20, Oliver strode in and took a seat at the head of the table. He has a brisk, commanding manner and an air of horn-rimmed intensity that reminds you of the sort of fiendishly bright civil servants who employed Harvard Business School techniques to try to win the Vietnam war. With him came two redheads: Norman Short of Guardian Capital Group and Howard Beck, of the Bay Street law firm of Davies Ward and Beck, whom Nesbitt had retained for the occasion. Beck has attended hundreds of meetings like this. His technique is to keep his mouth shut, make notes on a lined, yellow pad and, at some crucial moment in the proceedings, earn his large fee by saying something incisive.

Oliver began the meeting briskly, plunging directly into one of the more contentious issues: the ownership of the management company of the proposed fund. This was nitty-gritty stuff, since the management company is the entity through which a fund's promoters are rewarded for their efforts. When someone sets up a fund and sells its shares to the public, the money so raised is used to buy shares in other companies – or, in the case of a precious-metals fund, to buy bullion or gold shares. The skill with which this money is invested is what any fund's promoters are really selling – their proven ability to make other people's money grow. In return for exercising this skill, the fund's management company charges the fund a percentage of the value of the assets it manages. Sometimes that management fee is a flat one or two per cent. Sometimes it's a smaller percentage, plus a performance bonus that the management company collects if the fund grows faster than expected. In the case of the company which would manage the money that Shulman proposed to raise through the Nesbitt underwriting, the fee was to be one per cent on the first $50 million, three-quarters of a per cent on the rest. If the Shulman fund managed to attract $200 million from the public, in other words, the management company stood to collect about $1.6 million every year, less expenses. The first question before the meeting, then, was how those spoils were to be divided.

"We don't think it's unreasonable," Oliver smoothly explained, "for Nesbitt Thomson to get 10 per cent and Guardian 30 per cent."

Shulman burst in before his own lawyer could frame a diplomatic reply. "We don't want to give the store away," he said. "There's too many people to cut into this deal already." Shulman thought Guardian and Nesbitt should split 25 per cent

162

between them, rather than own a cumulative total of 40 per cent of the management company. The rest of the table was silent. Howard Beck scribbled notes on his yellow pad. Bert Stitt pointed out, in an aggrieved tone, that Shulman's original offer, at the preliminary meeting, had been 15 per cent for Nesbitt and Guardian combined. As an act of sheer magnanimity, they were willing to consider 25 per cent. But *forty per cent*? Stitt shrugged eloquently.

"Look," said Oliver. "We're bringing in a partner who offers credibility and expertise."

"Well then," shot back Stitt, "It's between you and Guardian how you want to split it."

"I can't accept that," Oliver replied. "It's not just a problem of Nesbitt Thomson and Guardian. We're all involved."

"That's why we said we'd up your share by 10 per cent," said Morty.

The haggling see-sawed back and forth in this brisk vein for many minutes.

"I don't want to put anyone on the spot, but . . ." said Stitt.

"We don't want to stand in the way of a deal, but . . ." said Oliver.

"I might as well be frank," said Morty. "There's another broker who'll do it as an underwriter. I'd like to do the deal with Nesbitt Thomson, but you've got to be competitive." (This was pure bluff. Another brokerage firm had indeed been importuning Morty, but he hadn't bothered to talk to them because he thought they were too small to swing the deal.)

"I think we *are* competitive," said Oliver. "We're willing to take 10 per cent instead of 15 per cent."

"Look," said Morty. "Your underwriting commission on this deal is going to be $10 million. Perhaps we should talk about reducing *that* percentage."

Norman Short, who looks craggy and Scottish and sensible, finally entered the discussion. He'd driven down from the island he owns in Georgian Bay to attend this meeting, and he didn't want his holiday mood ruffled by a lot of acrimonious talk. Like a headmaster gently separating a gang of squabbling schoolboys, Short injected a note of sweetness into the proceedings. "It's a very interesting project," he said, looking at Morty, "and we at Guardian would like to be genuinely and meaningfully involved. But we'd want to feel sure that it would be a *good* experience, in terms of the temperament and philosophy of the people running the fund. It's no fun for partners to be fighting all the time."

163

"That's very nice," said Morty, sounding a little mollified in spite of himself.

Oliver had other problems with Shulman's proposal. "Can we get down to some real gut things now?" he asked. "Let's talk about the name. We think a terrific name would be 'Precious Metals Corp.' That would focus investor interest on the real purpose of the fund."

Shulman: "How about Guardian-Shulman Precious Metals Fund?"

Oliver: "I'm convinced we can get more mileage out of your name without its being in the title."

Oliver also had problems with Shulman's investment philosophy. Morty wanted to concentrate on precious metals, but to reserve the right, under certain circumstances, to invest in other inflation-resistant assets, such as resource stocks or real estate. Oliver disagreed with this approach. "We feel it's very important to confine the fund's objectives to gold and other precious metals. It would create a lot of smoke to include other investment vehicles. It would be perceived as dilutive of the purity of the concept."

Morty: "I think that's a mistake. At least one-third of the fund should be diversified."

Norman Short then intervened gently on the side of conceptual purity. "There seems to be a great hunger to buy bullion legally," he mused. "I don't think Merrill Lynch expected such brilliant results with their Goldcorp issue . . ."

Shulman: "Our people will be expecting brilliant results too. But with those limitations, it's going to be difficult to outperform the market."

Oliver: "I appreciate that. But is it an anti-inflation fund or is it a precious-metals fund?"

Shulman: "It's an anti-inflation fund specializing in precious metals."

Oliver: "I'll be frank. I have a serious problem with that."

Shulman: "I *live* in this town. Ten years from now, I want people to have made a profit. I've got my reputation to protect. Why don't we call it a precious-metals fund with 30 per cent of its assets diversified?"

Norman Short agreed with Shulman's diversified approach. But as a compromise he suggested that they start off as a precious-metals fund, then diversify later if it seemed advisable. "That's not totally immoral is it, Howard?" he asked the lawyer. Beck rifled through his fat copy of the Ontario Securities Act, mumbling to himself, and allowed as how there would be no legal

164

obstacle to a midstream change in the fund's investment objectives.

The meeting ran for nearly five hours, and the participants covered a lot of ground. They discussed the composition of the fund's management committee, and decided it would be a three-man group, so that Short and Shulman would be able to veto each other. They agreed that the expenses of the underwriting, estimated at $100,000, would be payable by the fund.

They also discussed the duration of the fund, and Shulman wanted it to wind up after 10 years. Nearly all funds trade at a slight discount from the per-share value of their underlying assets, but if this fund were given a fixed lifespan, Shulman suggested, its shareholders could be spared the built-in discount. The price of their shares would rise toward their net asset value as the winding-up deadline approached. In effect, Shulman was proposing a policy that would cost *him* money in foregone management fees, but would mean a better deal for the fund's shareholders.

Short, who had never met Shulman before, found himself pleasantly surprised. "I think that's wasteful, but very ethical," he remarked. He sounded impressed, and he was.

"Yeah," replied Morty. "Let's give them their money back. If we do well with it, we can always sell them another deal."

Around 9:30, when the haggling over the ownership issue was stalemated, with the opposing sides still at least 10 per cent apart, Oliver called a recess and retired with his colleagues to another room. Shulman and his two lawyers were left alone. Morty, who gets impatient when anyone takes longer than 30 seconds to decide anything, vented his frustration.

"Are you *used* to doing all this haggling?" he moaned to his lawyer. "Do you do this regularly? What a pain in the ass it must be! I've done a zillion deals in my life, and none of them took me longer than 10 minutes. I've never been through so much bullshit in my life." Bert Stitt puffed his pipe and looked philosophical.

"Come hell or high water," Shulman vowed to his lawyers, "I won't go over 30 per cent. Let's try for 27."

At 10:03 precisely, the Nesbitt delegation returned to the boardroom. It was the moment of ultimate confrontation. "I'm afraid," said Joe Oliver, settling into his chair, "that at this point it's just not possible for us to move off 35 per cent." Guardian must have at least 25 per cent of the management company, in other words, and Nesbitt wouldn't accept less than 10 per cent.

"Well, in that case," said Shulman, "I'm sorry we've wasted your time and ours."

Oliver pushed his chair back from the table in a gesture that communicated frustration and helplessness. "I don't know what to say. I could go back to my people, but . . ."

There was more desultory haggling and finally, after another hour, the two sides arrived at a formula which Oliver agreed to put before his partners the next day: a mixture of voting and non-voting shares giving Guardian and Nesbitt a combined total of 35 per cent of the management company. Shulman went home, feeling confident that he'd have a deal by morning.

He didn't. Late in the afternoon of the following day, Oliver phoned Shulman to report that his partners were unwilling to accept the terms they'd discussed the night before. "I'd been hammered into a corner and finally, in despair, I'd accepted all their conditions," says Shulman. "And then they didn't accept their own conditions – that was the crazy thing."

Shulman was crushed by the Nesbitt turndown. "I was at my wit's end. I'd blown between $50,000 and $100,000 in law-yers' fees, and I thought I'd done the whole damned thing for nothing. I was totally dejected and depressed – really upset. I thought the jig was up." But Nesbitt's involvement did have one positive result; it brought together Shulman and Short, who had never met before, and who discovered they liked and trusted each other. Within minutes of Oliver's phone call, they'd agreed to continue working as a team to find another underwriter.

Shulman then turned in desperation to Si Bramson, a stock salesman with Jones Heward & Company Ltd., a small, Mont-real-based investment house that was respected for its research capabilities but was ill-equipped to sell stock on an assembly-line basis to large numbers of people.* Bramson and Shulman occasionally played cards together at Toronto's St. Clair Bridge Club, and Bramson had been urging Morty for weeks to let Jones Heward have a crack at the deal. Morty hadn't responded, because he believed the firm was too small. Although he'd used Bramson's offer for bluffing purposes in his haggling session with Nesbitt Thomson, he'd never taken it seriously. But within half an hour of Oliver's phone call, he phoned Bramson: "Okay, you said you can deliver. Here's your chance. I've been turned down by Nesbitt Thomson and I'm ready to talk business." Bramson was at Shulman's house within half an hour.

---

* Jones Heward & Co. Ltd. merged with Burns Fry Ltd. in 1984.

One Share Plus One Warrant

The next morning, Bramson explained the deal to Harry Frost, Jones Heward's senior vice-president in charge of corporate finance. Frost in turn made a lunch date with his old friend Matthew Gaasenbeek, his counterpart at a much larger firm, Midland Doherty Ltd. Frost knew that his own firm didn't have enough salespeople to float an issue this large; but Midland Doherty, with a sales force of 550 and 160,000 customers across the country, would make an effective senior partner. Gaasenbeek liked the idea, and they shook hands on an agreement that, if the deal went through, their firms would split the underwriting fee 60-40 in Midland's favor.

By this time, Shulman knew exactly what he wanted to sell to the public, and his terms were clearly spelled out in a two-page memo which Frost and Gaasenbeek examined over lunch. The issue would consist of "units," priced at $10 each, and each unit would consist of one share in the fund plus one warrant.

A warrant is a piece of paper which entitles its owner to buy a certain number of shares in a particular company at a certain time and at a certain price, and the warrant that Shulman proposed to issue as part of his financial package would allow its owner to buy another share of the Shulman fund for $10, at any time up to three years from the date of the original issue. In addition, each share so purchased would come with *another* warrant attached – a so-called "piggyback warrant" – allowing its owner to buy *another* share of the Shulman fund for $12.50 within another three years.

What's the point of warrants? They're sweeteners. In the case of the Shulman fund, they gave investors an additional vehicle for betting on a long-term rise in the price of gold. If the price of shares in the Shulman fund were to rise to $15, for instance, the accompanying warrants, which allowed you to buy shares for $10, would therefore be worth $5. Warrants added excitement and flexibility to the game. Don McEwen's Goldcorp, in its dazzling $175 million issue, had used warrants and piggyback warrants. Shulman's package was exactly the same: a $10 unit, consisting of one share and one piggyback warrant.

Shulman's fund would not receive the entire $10, of course. The investment house would deduct 45 cents from each unit as its sales commission, part of which would be shared with the salesperson who actually made the sale. Another 12 cents on each $10 unit would be deducted as the underwriting fee. If Shulman's fund sold $200 million worth of units, in other

167

words, Midland Doherty and Jones Heward would together collect $2.4 million in underwriting fees; and the sales commissions would total another $9 million. Any investment house was free to sell as many units as it could; but Jones Heward and Midland Doherty, as the joint underwriters, could be expected to mount the strongest sales effort and thus to pocket most of the commissions.

Bay Street, Morty Shulman and his friends thus stood to make a pile of money if the fund really did sell $200 million worth of units. Bay Street dealers would collect more than $10 million in sales and underwriting fees. Shulman, Short and his fellow-shareholders in the management company, in return for skilfully investing the remaining $190 million, would receive an additional $1.625 million every year, from which would be deducted some not terribly onerous expenses.

But that wasn't all. If the world continued to unfold as Shulman predicted, bringing monetary chaos, renewed inflation and, consequently, a dramatic rise in the price of gold, Shulman's fund would become a veritable money-spinning machine. The fund's unit holders would be happy, as the value of their shares and warrants rose to dizzying heights. Then, in 1986, they would exercise their warrants, thus bringing another $200 million into the fund and doubling the management fees – which would already have risen in any event, because of the increase in the price of the gold shares and bullion in the fund's portfolio. And *then*, in 1989, if the fund's shares were still trading above $12.50, holders of the piggyback warrants would throw *another* $200-million-plus into the pot. If it all really happened that way, the management fees (before expenses) would total at least $4.6 million every year. On top of everything else, the investment houses which originally sold the shares would also collect a dime for each warrant exercised – an extra $4 million in return for filling out a few forms.

Gaasenbeek and Frost, at their friendly lunch, were mindful of this profit potential, so they didn't waste time. At 5:30 that same day, Shulman and his lawyers met with the corporate finance teams of Midland Doherty and Jones Heward. "In contrast to the weeks of agonizing negotiations with Nesbitt," says Shulman, "this meeting took 20 minutes. We shook hands and agreed on everything I'd presented in my two-page memo. They only requested one change – they wanted a big, international firm of accountants instead of the local firm we'd chosen. And they didn't even *ask* for shares in the management company! It never even arose as an issue. We were out of that

168

meeting by 6 p.m. and I had my deal. I just couldn't believe it."

From that point, once the broad outlines of the deal had been settled, lawyers began to dominate the proceedings, as they do at a certain stage in every underwriting. Their main job is to draft the prospectus, a legal document the size of a copy of *Time* magazine which minutely describes the terms under which the shares are being offered for sale, and which discloses considerable information about the company and the people who own and manage it. It is a painstaking process, involving consultations with dozens of people over hundreds of niggly details. Once it's complete, the prospectus is filed with the Ontario Securities Commission (and with securities commissions in other provinces, if the issue is to be sold across the country). The OSC's staff, armed with a Securities Act that is almost as detailed and complex as the federal Income Tax Act, then starts poring through the prospectus like a team of archaeologists, seeking potential violations or lapses in the level of disclosure. The process almost never goes smoothly, and the lawyers who specialize in underwritings (some of whom learned their trade as OSC staffers) are skilled at unravelling snags when they occur.

Theoretically, the securities cannot be sold to the public until the prospectus has been approved, which usually takes several weeks. In practice, the selling begins soon after the prospectus is filed. Salesmen ride their telephones, calling up one client after another, usually saying something like this: "Marty, there's something coming up in a few weeks that I really think you should be into. Now this is a new issue, and the shares are going to be scarce. But I *think* I can get you an allocation. Can I put you down for 200 units?" If an issue is hot, sometimes all the shares are spoken for before it actually hits the market. If not, the selling process continues, with the salesperson now asking for money, rather than verbal commitments, from his clients. Once the issue is sold, a chaste advertisement appears on the financial pages, known in the trade as a "tombstone." It gives the name of the issue, the amount raised, and the names of the investment firms that helped to underwrite and sell it. "These securities having been sold," the tombstones usually say, "this advertisement appears as a matter of record only."

What happens if the shares don't sell? Theoretically the underwriter is stuck with them. That's why underwriters must be cautious to the point of paranoia about the issues they take on, and they frequently agonize, right up to the moment when the prospectus is approved, over the exact offering price.

169

The company whose shares are being offered for sale usually pays most of the underwriting expenses, including legal fees, and also pays the out-of-pocket costs of selling the issue, including such things as brochures and travel expenses. In the case of Guardian-Morton Shulman Precious Metals Inc. – for that is the name that was finally agreed upon – the legal fees alone totalled nearly $400,000. It was not a painless birth.

The Rumors are Out

Shulman had already raised $200,000 to cover the initial expenses of the fund. He'd done it by selling 100,000 common shares in the management company, at $2 each, to various people associated with *The MoneyLetter*, including Ron Hume, Nick Steed, Andy Sarlos and Fred McCutcheon. Norman Short's company, Guardian Capital Group, had taken 25,000 shares, and Shulman had taken 30,700 shares himself. But once Midland Doherty had agreed to do the underwriting, he realized that he'd need more money. So he got on the telephone, talked to a few friends and, in a single day, sold 100,000 shares at $5 each. By this time, the rumors were out about Morty's fund, and it wasn't a question of begging people to buy shares in the management company. People were begging *him*. Among the lucky buyers, at $5 each, was a varied assortment of Shulman's relatives, friends and colleagues, including his long-time secretary, Ann Worobec; Sammy Kehela, a professional bridge player, and Pat Murphy, the producer of his TV show.

Now that Morty had an extra $500,000 in the kitty, the lawyers were about to consume it. On August 12, Guardian-Shulman discovered to their horror that Nesbitt Thomson, the firm that had turned down Shulman's fund, was bringing an almost identical precious-metals fund to market. It was another Goldcorp clone, complete with piggyback warrants, to be called BGR Precious Metals (after Beutel Goodman Ltd., the firm of investment counsellors that instigated the deal, and London's N.M. Rothschild Ltd., which was brought in to lend tone to the issue and handle European sales). It was crucial that Guardian-Shulman file its prospectus ahead of BGR. Teams of lawyers in several competing law firms worked around the clock, sometimes snatching catnaps on the couches in their offices, to get the rival prospectuses ready for presentation to the OSC. "These lawyers charge you an arm and a leg," says Shulman, "but, by God, they do work hard. They'll work 24 hours a day if necessary."

170

An Ugly Surprise

On August 30, at a final meeting of the underwriters, Shulman, Short and no fewer than seven lawyers, the deal that had occupied so many of their waking hours for so many weeks almost collapsed. Midland's lawyers sprang an ugly surprise: They asked Shulman and the Guardian representative at the meeting, Gurston Rosenfeld, to sign documents guaranteeing that they would be *personally* liable for any future lawsuits that might result in connection with the fund. Both men flatly refused, and the meeting broke up in confusion. Shulman, who'd been in a state of euphoria for days, was instantly plunged into the blackest despair. He took a sleeping pill and went to bed at 5:30 in the afternoon.

While he slept, lawyers for both sides held a haggling session of their own. By morning, they'd reached a saw-off. Luckily for Shulman, the document in which the fund agreed to pay the underwriter's expenses hadn't yet been signed. That omission turned out to be a useful bargaining lever; and Midland, fearing it might not be reimbursed for money it had already spent, agreed to defer its demand for personal guarantees. After clearing that final hurdle, the prospectus was presented to the OSC that same day – August 31 – a few days ahead of the BGR prospectus.

Salespeople across the country began "soliciting indications of interest" in the issue on September 12. (In other words they were selling as hard as they could.) A gold-and-black sales brochure had even been prepared weeks before the prospectus was approved, though as the law requires, it was marked "Confidential – for Internal Use Only," as if it were a suppository with dangerous side-effects. The wording, of course, only enhanced its appeal to eager customers who, if they happened to be visiting their broker, were not always discouraged from having a peek. By October 13, the day the prospectus was approved and the fund's units officially went on sale, some $19 million in "indications of interest" had already been received at Midland Doherty alone.

The Dog-and-Pony Show

But "indications of interest" are not money in the bank. And during September, several events conspired to make the sales task more difficult than anyone could have imagined. In the first place, the price of precious metals, after remaining more

171

or less static for more than a year, chose this moment to plunge precipitously. Gold dropped from $US413 to $US405 during a single week in September. Silver fell from $12 to $11. Platinum and palladium dropped too. Don McEwen's Goldcorp, which had traded as high as $13.05 per unit in September (including the price of the warrants), fell to $10.11. Another precious-metals fund, Central Fund of Canada Ltd., which had been underwritten several weeks earlier by Wood Gundy Ltd. and Walwyn Stodgell Cochran Murray Ltd., had pulled in a pleasing total of $104 million. But now its shares, for which thousands of eager investors had paid $10, were trading in the $7.50 range. The combined magic of Shulman's and Short's names prompted thousands of people to sign up; but hundreds of them, before they paid their money, thought better of it and cancelled their orders.

Institutional investors weren't biting either. On September 19, Short, Shulman, Fred McCutcheon, Phil Holtby and Ken Williamson of Midland Doherty flew across the Atlantic for a sales presentation to a roomful of brokers and pension-fund managers in the Plaisterers' Hall in the City of London. The presentation (they're known in the trade as dog-and-pony shows) was a flop. Two British pension funds bought only $1.5 million in units, the resultant sales commissions barely covering the costs of the trip.

In Canada, beginning September 23, the sales team staged similar dog-and-pony shows in Vancouver, Montreal, Calgary, Edmonton and Winnipeg. According to securities regulations, the public isn't supposed to be privy to these sales pitches, since they're usually held before a prospectus has been approved. They're for brokers only, though it isn't unheard of for a favored client to be invited along. Even reporters have been known to sneak in on occasion. Often attracting crowds large enough to fill a hotel auditorium, dog-and-pony shows tend to be fairly convivial gatherings.

All of which, in Shulman's case, led to near-disaster. According to complaints that originated in Winnipeg and landed on the desk of the Ontario Securities Commission, Shulman had made some statements he shouldn't have made. His family planned to invest heavily in Guardian-Shulman shares, the OSC claimed Shulman had said, for example. The first Shulman heard of this new threat to the fund's existence was on September 30, when a letter from OSC staffers Heather Main and Richard Wallace landed like a grenade on the desk of one of Shulman's lawyers. The letter listed a number of statements Shulman was alleged to have made in Winnipeg, and concluded: "It is the view of our staff that if these statements were made as alleged, they could constitute serious breaches of the statute and, in addition, could bear on Dr. Shulman's fitness for registration [as an investment counsellor licensed to manage other people's money]."

"When that letter arrived, there was panic in the ranks, let me tell you," Shulman says. "The lawyers thought that, at best, we had a 50-50 chance of salvaging the deal. I was numb." The letter arrived on a Friday. On Monday morning, almost everyone involved in the Guardian-Shulman issue assembled in a boardroom of the law firm of Tory Tory Des Lauriers & Binnington: Shulman, Short, Sarlos, Fred McCutcheon, senior people from Midland Doherty and Jones Heward and seven lawyers, none of them billing less than several hundred dollars per hour. No matter whom they represented, Shulman balefully realized, it was the management company that must pay their fees. And if the OSC really did kill the issue, Morty and the shareholders he'd brought into the management company would be on the hook for hundreds of thousands of dollars.

Everyone at the meeting seemed to have a different view of how the OSC should be approached. Collectively, they drafted a letter of explanation and abject apology, and debated how it should be presented. Should the whole gang physically grovel before OSC director Charles Salter Q.C.? Should Morty go in alone? Or should the peace delegation be led by Fred McCutcheon, a former chairman of the Toronto Stock Exchange? The seven lawyers batted the issue back and forth until Shulman hollered: "Quiet, everybody! I'm the client, and I'm the guy who's going to take it in the neck. So I'm making the decision. Tomorrow morning, if we can get the appointment, Bob Hamilton and I will go alone and make our pitch. That's the decision I've made."

They made an appointment with Salter for the following Wednesday, flew off to Halifax on Tuesday for the final dog-and-pony show, flew back to Toronto the same night and, at the appointed hour on Wednesday morning, were ushered into the office of the lawyer-bureaucrat who could decide whether the Guardian-Shulman Precious Metals Corp. would live or die. Bob Hamilton, a Tory Tory partner, did most of the talking. He explained that Shulman hadn't made several of the statements attributed to him. Others had been misinterpreted. Shulman had told the gathering, for instance, that the fund's managers would buy back as many shares in the fund as feasible, in the interests of maintaining a healthy market. But he had not, as alleged, promised to "maintain a market" in the shares, artificially propping up the price to shield investors from loss. And, yes, he *had* told the meeting, in response to a question from the floor, that he and his family planned to invest heavily in Guardian-Shulman shares. "I was as non-contentious as I could be with the OSC," says Shulman. "I told them I'd spoken honestly and correctly, that I hadn't known there were press people present, that I'd made a mistake and that all I could do was apologize." Salter listened impassively. But after the meeting, he accompanied his visitors to the elevator and shook their hands, a courtesy which the lawyer chose to regard as a favorable omen. Hamilton is a veteran of years of dealings with the OSC – in fact, he'd also acted for Don McEwen on the Goldcorp underwriting – and his reading of the situation turned out to be correct. That same afternoon, Salter phoned him: Apology accepted; the issue could go ahead. Shulman was too exhausted to celebrate. He simply went to bed, without a sleeping pill.

Then the sales campaign began in earnest. The main effort was mounted by Midland Doherty, whose sales force, scattered through branch offices in 48 Canadian cities, could beat the bushes for small investors with devastating effectiveness. Jones Heward, though much smaller, managed to sell a creditable total of $4.5 million worth of units by such imaginative measures as dropping brochures through the mailboxes of every luxury condominium building in downtown Toronto. Gerry McCardle, the firm's marketing manager, also sent sales brochures to hundreds of Toronto doctors – not at their offices, but *at their hospitals*, on the grounds that junk mail sent to a doctor's office gets tossed out by the receptionist.

When the order book was closed on October 31, 1983, sales totalled $77 million, about $20 million of which came from *MoneyLetter* subscribers. Sales to institutional investors, such as pension funds, totalled a disappointing $10 million. But Shulman, who'd known for months that his original sales goal of $200 million was unrealistic, was delighted. "I think we did very well, considering the market conditions, considering the Central Fund debacle, considering that Goldcorp was coming down steadily in price, and considering the fact that the precious-metals market collapsed in the middle of our sales effort."

How They All Fared

The collapsing market was, in a way, good news. At a congratulatory luncheon in the Midland Doherty boardroom on October 27, Holtby handed Shulman a cheque for $70 million.

That sum represented the fund's share of the proceeds, after deduction of sales and underwriting commissions. Midland Doherty also held back 600,000 shares, worth $6 million, which were used to support the market in Guardian-Shulman shares. Shulman and Short bought $5 million worth of gold bullion the same day, paying $387 per ounce – considerably less than rival gold funds had paid only a few weeks before.

It is instructive to note how the various participants fared in this underwriting. Shulman, who with his family owned 28 per cent of the management company's shares, expected to collect dividends of $140,000 annually in return for his skill in deploying $70 million of other people's money. Norman Short's Guardian Capital Group would receive $125,000 annually for doing the same thing. The salespeople who actually sold the units pocketed a total of $1.575 million in commissions. In addition, Jones Heward and Midland Doherty split $840,000 in underwriting fees – $504,000 for Midland, $336,000 for Jones Heward.

The people who actually bought Guardian-Shulman units fared less well, at least in the short term. Once the issue hit the market, the warrants and shares began trading separately. By the following June, the shares were worth $7.25, the warrants worth $2.25. A $10 investment, in other words, was now worth only $9.50. This lukewarm valuation reflected the market's general disenchantment with gold, not the specific performance of the Guardian-Shulman Fund. In fact, Shulman and Short had done rather well with their customers' money. On the day of issue, each share represented $9.33 worth of bullion and precious-metal shares. By June 1984, the fund's managers had increased the net asset value to $10.09, and had paid out a 21-cents-per-share dividend besides.

For Shulman, it had been a life-enhancing experience – perhaps even a life-prolonging one. "I'm happy about the economic success of the fund," he said in June 1984, "but disappointed that our people haven't made any money yet. But we've increased the dividend each quarter, and I'm still buying stock for myself.

"In terms of my personal life, starting the fund has opened up all sorts of new contacts. I now have promoters flying in to see me from places like Germany and Australia to show me deals. Most of them are lousy deals, but it's quite fascinating. In a way, it's made me younger. It keeps me running."

For its founder, that was probably the biggest dividend of Guardian-Morton Shulman Precious Metals Corp. Morty wasn't bored any more.

12
The Biggies

Practically the only thing a stockbroker has to sell is the abilities of his firm's people. And those people are notoriously skittish, job-hopping from firm to firm. Meanwhile, the firms themselves routinely change partners, merging and re-merging in an almost predictable pattern that usually coincides with downturns in the market. Most of the largest companies in the business contain the ghosts of several long-dead firms.

Many of the small firms are simply collections of people who found life uncongenial in large places, and now huddle together for mutual support and shared secretarial services. Some companies with seats on the major stock exchanges aren't really companies at all; they're simply individual traders, like Fred McCutcheon of Arachnae Securities Ltd. or mining financier John Allen, who find it convenient to carry on their personal investment activities under the guise of a brokerage house. Most of the country's investment firms are private corporations, with shareholders who are usually also employees. Three firms – Walwyn Inc., Midland Doherty Ltd. and First Marathon Securities Ltd. – are public companies, which have raised outside capital by selling shares in their firms to the public. To add a note of antiquarian charm, there is even one surviving partnership, structured exactly like a law firm: Pope & Co.

Most people think of "Bay Street" as an assortment of large and powerful firms. But it also consists, to a surprising extent, of clusters of individuals doing their own thing. Even in the largest firms, many salespeople are, in effect, quite independent. They ignore the firm's research department and pick the stocks *they* want to recommend to their clients; and in some cases, they even do their own little underwriting deals, bringing together a few of their best-heeled clients with a company that needs to raise money.

Bay Street, in other words, is still a competitive, enterprising place. There are very few other industries in which individual brains and gumption can be so swiftly and lavishly rewarded, where nothing can be taken for granted. No firm's position of dominance can ever be regarded as thoroughly secure. The largest, seemingly most impregnable firms can vanish suddenly, and new firms can rise to positions of importance in only a few years.

What makes the difference is usually the abilities and, to a lesser extent, the luck of the people at the top. Individual excellence is still crucial, and that's why the following profiles of some of the country's largest investment houses tend to focus on the people who dominate them. IBM will always be IBM, no matter who occupies the presidential suite. But in the Bay Street Village, the right management can quickly strengthen or transform even the largest of firms, and the wrong management can sometimes kill it. What follows, then, is a series of profiles of some of Canada's largest investment houses – which means, inevitably, a series of profiles of some extraordinary individuals.

Wood Gundy Limited:
The West Point of Bay Street

Running a large investment firm must feel a bit like playing a large cathedral organ. If the firm is to aspire to greatness, its various departments can't simply do their thing in splendid isolation from one another.

If large corporate clients are to be kept happy, they must receive sympathetic attention from seven or eight different areas within the firm. Corporate Finance must know when the time is auspicious for the client company to go to the public for more capital; Marketing must know what kind of bells and whistles to add to the issue to ensure that it will sell; the money-market traders must ensure that the client gets the best possible mileage from its spare cash; the skill of the firm's fixed-income traders can keep the client's bonds liquid and sought after; Retail Sales must know how to sell the client's stock issues.

The collective performance of these and other departments is what persuades the treasurers of the nation's largest companies to place their business – which can be worth millions of dollars a year – with one investment firm instead of another.

No investment dealer can expect to be strong in all areas all the time. If you're running such a firm, the best you can hope for is a strong *presence*: an almost regimental feeling of shared excellences, an unspoken commitment to doing and being the best, a certain elitist elan that extends from the CEO's suite to the lowliest mail clerk.

The strength of Wood Gundy, and the achievement of successive generations of its managers, is that it has always possessed this feeling in abundance. The firm has often been

177

criticized for the buttoned-down, blue-suited, ever-so-earnest style that Wood Gundy's clever young men apparently imbibe with their mother's milk. But that's only the external manifestation of a corporate culture that has proven to be ferociously effective. Wood Gundy's strongest asset is that its people, from top to bottom, *know* that they're damned good. "There's a real belief that we're doing things right," says Jim Pattillo, vice-president of the firm's Money Market department. "We have a belief in one another, and a real faith in one another. What's behind that belief is accountability. Everyone is accountable. No one can duck the issue, and if they do, they're tagged immediately. That's got a lot to do with it. Our corporate style is very open and direct. Some people say we're arrogant, that we're cocky little bastards. But I believe in my colleagues – I really do."

Joining the firm is like pledging a particularly exclusive fraternity. Most years, Wood Gundy hires more Harvard Business School graduates than does any other Canadian company. Resumes of prospective employees are widely circulated throughout the firm. Comments are invited, and heeded. Says one Wood Gundy executive: "I've seen the top people really like somebody and the people lower down say, 'No, we don't feel comfortable with him.' "

Wood Gundy is one of the very few firms on Bay Street – Dominion Securities Pitfield is probably the only other one – whose corporate identity is stronger than that of its current chief executive. One assumes that IBM will always be IBM, no matter who's nominally running the place; the same can be said of Wood Gundy. As a result, the firm's dominance of the Canadian underwriting market seems almost effortless. In 1983, Wood Gundy, as lead underwriter in some 51 stock and bond issues, helped raise more than $3.2 billion for Canadian companies, plus another $1.5 billion for provincial governments. Its nearest competitor, McLeod Young Weir, which raised $1.57 billion for companies and $1.2 billion for provincial governments, didn't even come close. According to *The Financial Post*, which tracks the underwriting performance of Canadian investment dealers, Wood Gundy has scored first for eight consecutive years. With 1,500 employees in 32 offices across Canada and in such exotic foreign capitals as Tokyo and Bridgetown, Barbados, Wood Gundy is the closest thing on Bay Street to a multinational corporation.

The firm was founded in 1905 by two ambitious young men from Dominion Securities, G. H. Wood and J. H. Gundy. They quickly established the firm as a major force on Bay Street –

thanks, in no small part, to Gundy's friendship with Sir Herbert Holt, then chairman of the Royal Bank of Canada and the nation's most powerful financier. Holt and Gundy even owned a company that originated underwriting deals, which were then sold to Wood Gundy, which in turn distributed them to the public – in effect, a personal vehicle for skimming a little extra off the top. A retired executive recalls how it worked: "They'd buy a company, recapitalize it, then say to Wood Gundy, 'Okay, you sell the bond issue and the preferred share issue, and we'll keep the common shares.' " Was there a conflict of interest? Probably. Would it be allowed today? Probably not. But the world was a different place in the 1920s.

The firm was almost wiped out by the Great Crash, and it was only through the forebearance of the Royal Bank that its doors remained open during the 1930s. J. H. Gundy, a brash, gregarious man with a temper that intimidated some of his colleagues, was succeeded in 1948 by his son Charles. And it was Charles, a milder, quieter man than his father, who set the firm on the unruffled course it pursues to this day. He guided the firm through the 1950s, when it ran a distinct third behind A.E. Ames and Dominion Securities. But in 1961, Charles Gundy made a decisive commitment to the firm's future: Instead of appointing his successor on the basis of seniority, he reached well down into the management ranks and elevated William Wilder, then 38, as executive vice-president and heir apparent.

For Wilder, the firm was Family. His own father, who died in 1929, had joined Wood Gundy shortly after its founding and had been J.H. Gundy's right-hand man. Wilder was a graduate of Upper Canada College, Royal Roads naval college, McGill University and Harvard Business School; and, not counting universities and the war, he'd spent 26 years with the firm, from messenger boy to executive assistant to director then Executive Vice-President. But it was a departure for the firm to appoint a president who didn't have white hair. "They told me: 'If you make a mistake and don't live up to our expectations, you're out,' " Wilder recalls.

With Charlie Gundy looking on approvingly as President, Wilder set out to modernize the firm. He hired McKinsey & Co., a management-consulting company, to study how to reorganize the firm, then spent the next five years remaking it in the image of Morgan Stanley and the Harvard Business School. To make room for younger men, he persuaded a number of senior people to retire early – so many, in fact, that a separate suite was rented in the Toronto Dominion Centre for retired directors, and is in regular use to this day. Among those who

179

moved up the ladder during Wilder's regime were Ian Steers, who ran the firm's large London office; C. E. (Ted) Medland, an institutional salesman whom Wilder placed in charge of trading, sales and money-market operations; John Abell, whom Wilder sent to run the New York office; and Ross LeMesurier, a law graduate and Harvard MBA who'd joined the firm from Dominion Securities in 1964. Wilder, who became president in 1967, used the latest in strategic-planning techniques to predict the shape of the company's business years ahead, and to hire and train people accordingly. "So when the big wave of financings came in the late 1960s and early 1970s," says Wilder, "we were well positioned, because we had the trained people to handle the business." That was the period when Gundy began wrestling formerly exclusive underwriting accounts away from Dominion Securities and A.E. Ames.

Wilder left the firm in 1972 to head the Canadian Arctic Gas Consortium, which was organized to move Canadian gas from the Mackenzie Delta and U.S. gas from Alaska southward across the tundra to markets in the United States. "When Bill told us he was thinking of leaving," says Medland, "we tried to talk him out of it. But Bill had always wanted to do something for Canada. He's the kind of guy who would have tried to build the CPR."

That was on a Thursday in July. On Friday, once his partners realized that Wilder was determined to leave, the succession occurred with the swiftness and smoothness that Bay Street has come to associate with Wood Gundy. "That Friday," says Medland, "a few people met. No one wanted a vacuum. Then Ross LeMesurier came to me and said, 'I've canvassed the senior partners, who are prepared to support your appointment as CEO if you will accept it.' "

Medland, in spite of a full head of silver hair, appears youthful and deceptively casual. In fact, he's very well organized, which allows him to appear as if he has all the time in the world. In spite of his administrative responsibilities, he's still known around the firm for his exquisite feel for the market. As Wilder's successor, he's piloted the firm into a position of dominance as a corporate underwriter – an area which accounts for about 40 per cent of Wood Gundy's revenues. "The trick," he says, "is to know you're in a service business. What does the client want? How do you package it for him? How do you provide him with the best advice?"

Everything about Medland is unruffled. When someone mentions the lucrative Royal Bank preferred-share issue that Daly Gordon Securities snatched from a syndicate led by Wood Gundy in the spring of 1984, he seems totally nonchalant. When you mention the bank reconciliation clerk who stole more than $750,000 from the firm before being caught, he shrugs; the loss was insured. And it's ancient history that Wood Gundy directors and the firm itself invested $500,000 in John DeLorean's disastrous scheme to build sports cars in Ireland, and got the firm to do the same. You take risks; you win some, you lose some.

The firm's most recent exercise in risk-taking is a major thrust into the United States. To survive the chilly 1980s, some Bay Street firms hope to merge with foreign partners, or sell their stock to the public to beef up their capital position. Wood Gundy's game plan, however, is to grow through expansion south of the border. The firm has had an office in New York since 1916, has been in Tokyo for more than a decade, and in 1973, just a few months before the Arab oil embargo, Ian Steers made a fortuitous prospecting trip through the Middle East. But the current U.S. thrust is far more ambitious. There are only 37 investment firms authorized as dealers in federal U.S. treasuries by the U.S. Treasury; those firms, which sell U.S. Treasury bonds and bills to the public, constitute the inner circle of American finance. "Our objective," says Medland, "is to become one of those firms." Medland plans to open bond-trading offices in eight key U.S. cities and has invested $10 million in the campaign to conquer the U.S. Expanding geographically happens to suit Medland. "I have a great personal affinity for international business," he says. "I like travelling, meeting people in different countries. I'm comfortable in that environment."

Medland was 56 in 1984 but he'd already arranged what appeared to be a smooth succession. After Charles Gundy died in 1978, Medland became chairman as well as president. In 1980, when two key directors retired, he named Gordon Homer ("I think he's got the best brain in the company") as chief financial officer and Donald Bean, who'd joined the firm in 1969 from the Mercantile Bank of Canada, as general manager. Bean is 11 years Medland's junior. "We put him on the firing line and had a look at him for a couple of years," says Medland. "By 1982 it was logical that he should become president and chief operating officer."

Bean is a planner, the kind of executive who's obsessed by the question of where the industry, and his firm within it, will be five or 10 years down the road. He even asks that question about individual employees. "He lets people know they're being thought of," says one of his colleagues. "He tells them: 'We're thinking about where *you're* going to be in five years.' In a firm

181

that's so dependent on the performance of individuals, that kind of attention is appropriate. "One bad apple in the organization can really screw you in this business," says Medland. "One dishonest bond trader who cooks the books, or a foreign exchange trader can cause enormous financial harm which can hurt your reputation for quality and integrity. Anyone who does anything to even *scratch* that reputation better go looking for another job."

Dominion Securities Pitfield: Onward And Upward From The Old-Boy Network

The nation's largest, richest investment dealer got that way mainly by swallowing smaller, compliant competitors. That's half of the explanation for the success of Dominion Securities Pitfield Ltd. The other half is what made those competitors willing to be swallowed by DS.

The answer has something to do with the ineffably Old-Boy quality of Dominion Securities. One firm, A.E. Ames, agreed to merge with DS in 1982 because Ames was in deep financial trouble and, frankly, had damned little choice in the matter. Another firm, Pitfield Mackay Ross Ltd., sold out to DS in 1984 largely because the firm's autocratic chairman, Ward Pitfield, was getting close to retirement age and wanted to cash in his chips. Scores of employees of the merged firms, some of them quite senior, lost their jobs immediately. Others hung on, hoping to continue their careers inside this unfamiliar new environment – but then parted within a few weeks or months, leaving trails of bitterness behind them. From this, you would be entitled to wonder why DS is regarded as such an attractive merger partner. It's simple: DS people know what they're doing, and they know everybody who's anybody. No other investment firm so perfectly embodies the verities of the Canadian financial Establishment: its integrity, its good manners, its damnable caution, its occasional ruthlessness and, above all, its ability to survive.

Survival, of course, was an additional motive for the DS-Pitfield merger. It happened at a time when, because of a wave of rate-cutting and rapacious competition, the industry was feeling particularly queasy about its own future. Bigness is always regarded as an acceptable defence against the storms of competition, and the merger made DS-Pitfield one of North America's larger investment dealers. With $100 million in capital, with more than 2,000 employees (including 550 retail sa-lespeople), with 65 offices in 59 Canadian cities, the newly merged firm seemed well-positioned to dominate Canada's financial markets, and perhaps to have some impact in New York and London as well.

The Pitfield merger was in large part a tribute to the persuasive powers of the firm's two guiding spirits: Anthony Smithson (Tony) Fell, DS's president and chief executive officer; and dep-uty-chairman Jim Pitblado. Fell is quiet, cautious and bankerly. He is open and accessible to his staff, but much less so to outsiders. His desk is always clean, his mind always orderly. By background and inclination, he stands somewhere close to the absolute dead-centre of the tight little cabal that has dom-inated Canada's financial markets for much of this century. His grandfather was a lieutenant-governor of Ontario. His father Percy joined DS in 1917 and left the firm only after he'd bought control of Empire Life Insurance Co. His uncle is Major-General A. Bruce Matthews, who was executive vice-president of Argus Corp. Ltd. His brother Fraser is chairman of Dome Mines Ltd. So foreordained was his path in life that Fell didn't even bother attending university; he simply joined Dominion Securities in 1959, after graduation from St. Andrew's College, and he's worked there ever since.

Fell and Pitblado are the firm's main dealmakers, while day-to-day operations are supervised by executive vice-president Robin Younger. Pitblado, according to an admiring rival at Wood Gundy, is "probably one of the most valuable assets they've got. He's simply the best corporate finance man in the country, bar none. I've been in meetings with senior bankers and some very senior people on the Street – and, believe, me when Jim Pitblado talks, everybody listens." It was Pitblado who stage-managed one of the largest corporate marriages in Canadian history: the merger of The Consumers' Gas Co. and Hiram Walker-Gooderham & Worts Ltd. into the conglomerate now known as Hiram Walker Resources Ltd.

Like A.E. Ames, the firm that it absorbed in 1982, Dominion Securities was founded (in 1901, twelve years after Ames) by Senator George Albertus Cox, the resourceful Edwardian fin-ancier who also fathered Imperial Life Assurance Co. of Canada and National Trust Co. Ltd. For most of its history, DS spec-ialized in underwriting and selling government and municipal bonds. Until the early 1960s, in fact, stocks were regarded around DS as a new-fangled and faintly disreputable investment ve-hicle. The firm's driving force for much of this period was the late Douglas Ward, whose dedication to the firm was so complete that he didn't take a vacation until the age of 75. Ward's only other interest in life, apart from the firm, was the antique buggies and horse-drawn carriages he collected on his gentleman's farm near Caledon, Ontario. He was close to the Eaton department-store clan and to John Angus (Bud) McDougald who, as chairman and president of Argus Corp. Ltd., was the doyen of the Canadian Establishment.

Under Ward, the firm's true power-base was the Toronto Club, where, in that much less competitive era, mergers, bond issues and underwritings could be quietly arranged over a friendly lunch between like-minded gentlemen. The 1973 merger with Harris & Partners Ltd. was a key step away from this old-boy approach to the securities business. The merger combined DS's strengths as a distributor of securities with Harris's skills as a corporate underwriter. Harris had some important underwriting clients, including General Motors Acceptance Corp. of Canada Ltd., Ford Motor Co. of Canada Ltd. and International Harvester Co. of Canada Ltd. It also employed some excellent people, including Jim Pitblado, Robin Younger and Michael Wilson, a specialist in government finance who later became a Tory MP and an unsuccessful contender for the leadership of his party. Through various eccentric unions with actresses, chambermaids and American heiresses, the British aristocracy has managed to avoid the worst effects of inbreeding; the Harris merger had the same effect on Dominion Securities. "If we hadn't done the deal with Harris," says one DS veteran, "we could have gone the way of Ames. Until the merger, the firm just wasn't changing fast enough."

In 1977, with the active encouragement of Bud McDougald, DS also absorbed Draper Dobie Ltd., a medium-sized firm controlled by Montegu and Conrad Black. The Black brothers had offices at DS until 1978, when they gained control of Argus Corp. Ltd. and moved on to larger concerns.

Like the Harris merger, the marriage with Draper Dobie brought new people and new strengths to the firm, and the combination was reflected in the composition of DS's 11-member executive committee. Just before the Pitfield merger, this committee consisted of three people who'd always been with DS, three from Harris, two from Ames, two from Draper Dobie and only one member, Gary Ball, who'd joined DS from another firm.

The Pitfield merger, which took effect on June 1, 1984, brought in some excellent people and about $38 million in new capital. Of the 11 members of the merged firm's executive committee, four – Ward Pitfield, Mario Caceres, D.L. Torrey and Doug

Mackay – are from Pitfield Mackay Ross. But the manner in which Ward Pitfield consummated the merger underlined the weaknesses of the firm he led – weaknesses which, without the DS connection, might have proved fatal.

The trouble was that Pitfield, although he owned only 6 per cent of his firm's shares, always acted as if he owned all of them. Some of his partners were so alarmed at the secretive way he conducted the merger negotiations that they demanded his resignation so they could do the haggling with DS themselves. (In response, Pitfield actually did hand in his resignation one day before the merger was announced; but his fellow-directors then refused to accept it.) Over the years, his autocratic management style had driven away some of the firm's most promising employees; and some of them went on to become vigorous competitors. "There's no question about it," says a former Pitfield executive. "The place was slipping. I think the problem is that you need a participatory management style these days, and I'm not sure Ward ever understood that."

Pitfield's father founded the firm in Montreal in the 1920s. Ward Pitfield joined the firm after his father's death, and became president in 1965. In the 19 years of his presidency, the firm never suffered an unprofitable year – an almost unheard-of achievement on Bay Street. He was sometimes accused of excessive conservatism, but in fact he pioneered some significant innovations. His was the first Canadian securities firm, for instance, to advertise on television. But during the 1970s, Pitfield Mackay Ross began to lose ground to leaner, hungrier, faster-moving firms, some of which were started by Pitfield refugees. Loewen, Ondaatje McCutcheon, for instance, one of Bay Street's more aggressive and successful investment boutiques, is the creation of three former Pitfield employees who thought they could do better on their own. An up-and-coming firm called First Marathon Securities Ltd. was founded by Larry Bloomberg, a marathon runner and yet another Pitfield alumnus. The president of McLeod Young Weir, Tom Kierans, left Pitfield when it became clear to him that he'd never succeed Ward Pitfield as boss. At McLeod, running in tandem with chairman Austin Taylor, he's muscled in on some of Pitfield's most cherished underwriting accounts. "We've always tried to attract high-calibre people," Pitfield vice-chairman Doug Mackay once explained. "The trouble is, the higher the calibre, the greater the ambition and therefore they want to do their own thing."

Tony Fell's style is light-years away from Ward Pitfield's. He is very choosy about who becomes DS directors; but once they're inside, those directors are treated as genuine partners, not employees. There are more than 250 of these director-shareholders; and under Fell's quiet, self-effacing leadership, membership in that charmed circle has never been more prized or more valuable. Thanks in large part to his skilful management and all those mergers, Dominion Securities Pitfield has emerged as perhaps the fittest firm in the Bay Street Jungle.

Midland Doherty Limited:
No Illusions

When the market is running in Vancouver, when the speculative stocks are chasing each other uphill, when pensioners and electricians and housewives start crowding into the stockbrokers' reception rooms to watch the magic figures on the electronic tote board, when people start phoning their brokers because they've heard about a fabulous gold prospect from their neighbor's brother-in-law, the chances are excellent that they'll phone one of the hundreds of accommodating fellows who man the telephones at Midland Doherty Limited. With more than 160,000 clients, Midland Doherty is one of Canada's largest retail investment houses. Some firms specialize in bonds, others in peddling stocks to pension funds. Under the relentless leadership of a horn-rimmed super-salesman named Phil Holtby, Midland Doherty has learned to specialize in people.

Holtby doesn't look remotely like the public's idea of a senior Toronto stockbroker. With his nondescript suits, his close-cropped hair, his laconic manner, his utter lack of small talk, he could be mistaken for the cost accountant in a medium-sized button factory, the guy who sends back the salesman's expense accounts with a scribbled notation questioning the $13.68 item for client entertainment. He works in what is probably the least ostentatious presidential office on Bay Street, refuses to join clubs ("I don't like them. I think they're anachronisms where people go for lunch every day to see the same people.") * and tends to grow impatient with any conversation lasting longer than 90 seconds. He runs Midland Doherty like the captain of a high-speed destroyer: instant decisions, clear commands, unquestioned obedience. Some Bay Street firms pride themselves on a collegial style of management, in which decisions emerge from a process of partnership and consensus. That's not Holtby's

---

* Holtby is, however, a member of Toronto's exclusive Badminton and Racquet Club. "It's for the kids," he growls.

186

style. "Of the 10 top people in this firm," says one underling, "about eight of them are Phil Holtby."

Holtby's father owned a Toronto company that manufactured kitchen equipment and he sent his son to Ridley College, but that's where Holtby's Establishment credentials end. He attended the Ontario College of Art because he liked to draw, but dropped out after two years because he'd run out of money. In 1951, an uncle helped him get a $25-a-week job as a runner in Matthews & Co., but delivering stock certificates around Bay Street had nothing to do with boyhood ambition. "I didn't know anything about the business," he says. "It was just someplace to get off the street and make some money." In 1958 he joined Doherty Roadhouse McCuaig, then one of Toronto's leading specialists in mine financing, as a salesman. He started out by making cold calls, culling his prospect list from the City Directory. "You'd start at the top of a high office building and work your way to the bottom. The next day you'd start at the next building. I spent a certain amount of my time each week doing exactly that – building a prospect list, building a clientele."

By 1970 he'd assembled a lot of clients and won a place on the firm's eight-member management committee. As other members left or retired, Holtby came to dominate the committee, and thus the firm. Doherty Roadhouse's fortunes had been declining since the mid-1960s, when the Ontario government clamped down on free-wheeling mining promotions, which were the firm's bread and butter. Holtby's hands-on management style and merciless cost controls saved the firm from serious financial difficulties, but it was obvious that the company needed to add new strengths if it were to survive. And so, in 1974, Holtby helped engineer a merger with Midland Osler Ltd., itself the product of a 1962 merger of Osler, Hammond & Nanton (founded in Winnipeg in 1883) and Midland Securities (founded in London, Ontario in 1925).

At the time, it seemed an improbable alliance. Midland, with its old-money connections, was the corporate equivalent of a millionaire's steam yacht. Doherty McCuaig Ltd. (it dropped Roadhouse from its name in 1972) was more like a rum-runner's speedboat. "Holtby took what was essentially a bucket shop and turned it into the best-managed, most profitable retail firm in the country," says an admiring competitor.

Holtby did it mainly by thinking like a salesman instead of a stockbroker. Of all the Bay Street CEOs, Holtby is one of the very few who talks knowledgeably about demographics and market share – indeed, the only one who seems to evince a lively interest in what his customers are actually *like*. Earlier than most, he also spotted one of the trends that is making Bay Street a more powerful force than ever before: the investing public's increasing concern with protecting its savings from the ravages of inflation. "We felt that the two-income family and the whole demographics of the inflationary era were moving toward more people having disposable income," he says. "And they weren't looking for guaranteed investments. They were looking for investments that resisted inflation. We felt the whole movement of the securities industry was in our favor, and that if we had more salesmen covering the market, we'd get a bigger market share. And that's what happened."

Holtby has no illusions about the lofty mission of his calling. The name of the game, as he sees it, is to get people to trade stocks. He refers to various investment vehicles, such as life-insurance policies or mutual funds, as "product" and "merchandise." "Churn 'em and burn 'em," he's been known to remark, only half in jest. "It's a business of fear, greed, hope and excitement. That's what we're selling – as compared to the insurance companies, which are just selling fear and need."

Holtby reaches heights of scornful eloquence on the subject of insurance companies. "They're selling guaranteed products and they've been eroded by inflation and people have had their asses whipped, eh?"

Holtby's own market research tells him that people with savings to protect are now willing to accept *some* risk, in return for being sheltered from the erosive effects of inflation. That's why he's convinced the stock market is a growing popular phenomenon. Midland Doherty, significantly, was one of the few large investment firms that did *not* oppose the Toronto Dominion Bank's 1983 bid to dip its toe into the securities business. "It will expand the market," says Holtby. "It will create more liquidity, which is good for the capital markets. And in a country like this, when you expand the capital markets you have more companies being formed – and that's good for the country."

It goes without saying that it would also be good for Midland Doherty. Under Holtby's leadership, the firm has already expanded significantly. Its capital base – meaning, roughly, the money the firm has in its own kitty – has expanded from about $6 million at the time of the 1974 merger to about $40 million in 1983. Some $9.6 million of this was chipped in by the public; in 1983, the firm, which has taken dozens of firms public, decided to go public itself. The prospectus which accompanied the share offering constituted a rare, detailed glimpse into the financial operations of a Bay Street securities firm.

For one thing, it showed how vulnerable such firms are to swings in the stock market. In each of the palmy years of 1980 and 1981, when everyone thought the world was running out of energy and Midland's salespeople were merrily flogging Alberta-based oil and gas stocks, the firm earned more than $16 million before taxes. In 1982, the year the energy boom collapsed, it earned only $74,000.

Most of Midland's employees – including its 550 salespeople (at Midland they're called "investment executives") and no fewer than 53 vice-presidents – are heavily dependent on a buoyant market to support their lifestyles. In the recession year of 1982, they collected about $9 million less, in salaries, commissions and benefits, than they did the year before. That works out to an *average* pay cut of about $7,000 per employee, or about $17,000 per salesperson.

But the great years tend to make up for the bad ones. Midland's six top investment executives each grossed close to $600,000 in 1983, and the firm's 30 senior people, including Chairman David Weldon, President Phil Holtby, Executive Vice-Presidents John Eliot and Donald Page, and Senior Vice-President Ian Falconer, who runs Midland's operation in Vancouver – were paid a total of $1,630,995, and collected hundreds of thousands more in the form of dividends and, one presumes, personal trading profits.

If the firm has a weakness, it's related to its principal strength. No one can sell stocks to the multitudes with as much skill as Midland Doherty, but that's about the only thing the firm does supremely well. It is not a leading factor in selling securities to financial institutions, and it is not a strong force in underwriting. The stock issues it underwrites tend to be those of junior companies, and Holtby is probably less interested in their intrinsic value than in how well they'll sell. According to one competitor, Phil Holtby once told a gathering of brokers: "If the public wants oranges, we'll sell 'em oranges. If they want apples, we'll sell 'em apples. And if we don't have any apples, we'll paint the goddam oranges red."

Burns Fry Limited
The Art Of Trading Bonds

On September 1, 1983, Jack Lawrence, the president of Burns Fry Limited, hosted a quiet little reception at the Toronto Club to commemorate an event which practically no one, outside a tiny but very powerful circle of men, would have even understood, let alone remembered. The date was the twenty-fifth anniversary of what was probably the largest single financial transaction in Canadian history: the conversion of more than $6 billion worth of Victory Bonds, issued by the Canadian government during World War II, into four new series of peacetime bonds. In effect, in 1958 the government was reorganizing its wartime debts, and giving itself more time to pay, by swapping the short-term victory bonds for four series of bonds with longer maturities.

This huge and intricate deal was masterminded by a group of financial technicians on Bay Street, in the Bank of Canada and in the federal Department of Finance – members of perhaps the most exclusive club on Bay Street or in Ottawa: the Bond Establishment. Their names are practically unknown to the general public, but the collective judgment and day-to-day decisions of them and their successors exercise a profound influence on the direction of interest rates, and therefore on the economy as a whole.

The bond conversion deal went through on September 1, 1958. Twenty-five years later, the last of the four series of bonds matured – that is, was repaid by the government. To mark the occasion, Jack Lawrence gathered together about 50 of the country's most senior bankers, government financiers and bond traders for a quiet little celebration. An elder statesman named Howard Hunter was the main guest of honor. In the late 1950s, as president of a firm called Equitable Securities Ltd. (which was later absorbed by Levesque, Beaubien Inc.), Hunter was a commanding figure in the Canadian Bond Establishment, and had played a leading role in engineering the conversion deal. Other guests included Alan Hockin, who now runs the investment department of the Toronto Dominion Bank, and was a senior Finance Department official when the deal went through; Douglas Humphries, a retired deputy governor of the Bank of Canada and perhaps the most senior of the group of civil servants that managed the federal government's $150-billion debt; Joe Baxter, a recently retired official of the Bank of Canada; Denton Lewis, a former vice-president of the Bank of Montreal; and Gordon Jones, who learned the bond business at the Bank of Canada and went on to become head of the Canadian branch of Merrill Lynch.

But these days, the single most influential member of the Bond Establishment is probably Jack Lawrence himself. No other firm is as large a factor in the Canadian bond market. Burns Fry does about 18 per cent of the total bond business in Canada; only one other firm, Dominion Securities Pitfield, even comes close. Other companies, notably McLeod Young Weir and Wood Gundy, are powerful forces in the provincial bond market; but Burns Fry is the unchallenged leader in Canadian government bonds, and it achieved this eminence almost wholly through Lawrence's efforts.

Because Jack Lawrence has guessed right so consistently about the future direction of interest rates, Burns Fry is probably the most profitable investment firm of its size in the country. From a trading desk not much larger than a delicatessen counter, the firm annually trades bonds with a total face value of more than a *trillion* dollars. And since at least half of this vast mountain of debt is owed by various governments, Lawrence's influence is far greater than he likes to acknowledge. Governments can dream up endless ways of spending money, but unless they can raise it through taxes, they must borrow it by issuing bonds and treasury bills. If they want to borrow, they will almost certainly have to deal with someone like Jack Lawrence.

Governments have needed bankers since the days when monarchs financed their pleasures or their wars by going hat in hand to the Medicis or the Rothschilds. The relationship today is far more complex, and the amounts borrowed are vastly larger; but the relationship between borrowers and lenders is as symbiotic as it ever was. Although Lawrence is as eloquent as any businessman on the evils of excessive government spending, the assistance that the Bond Establishment renders daily to the federal and provincial governments and their quasi-independent agencies, such as Ontario Hydro, is what makes such over-spending possible.

In 1983 alone, Ottawa borrowed more than $26 billion: about $6 billion through the medium of Canada Savings Bonds, another $8 billion through the sale of "marketable securities" (which, unlike CSBs, are bought and sold just like stocks) and another $13.3 billion through the sale of treasury bills, which are short-term instruments – the national equivalent of borrowing 10 dollars from a friend until payday. In the same year, Canadian corporations also borrowed more than $5 billion by issuing bonds, plus billions more through bank loans. In terms of the sheer volume of money deployed, the Canadian bond market is thus about 10 times the size of the stock market. For skilled practitioners, the arcane art of trading bonds can be vastly more profitable than stocks.

Lawrence's great insight, when he was a young man starting out in the business, was that in spite of the bond market's importance and potential profitability, practically everyone on Bay Street was ignoring it. "Most people coming into the business tend to gravitate toward the equity areas – underwriting and retail sales," he says, "so a very large proportion of the industry's total business ends up being neglected. There are too many institutions which don't take their bond holdings as seriously as they should. They have all kinds of analysts looking after the 30 per cent of their money that's invested in stocks, and they leave less experienced people to look after the bond end, which represents 70 per cent of their holdings."

Lawrence is pushing 50, but doesn't look it. He's a small, compact, coiled spring of man who ran the 1981 Ottawa Marathon in three hours and 22 minutes, plays a fiercely competitive game of squash and commands the sort of personal loyalty around Burns Fry that you'd expect from a winning football coach. When he's not running the bond market, he dabbles in the fitness business; he was one of the Cambridge Club's original backers (he later sold his stake) and still owns 25 per cent of the Adelaide Club, another downtown Toronto squash emporium. At the University of Western Ontario, he was revered around the Zeta Psi fraternity house because he never lost a poker game. After graduation he went to work for Howard Hunter at Equitable Securities, learning the bond business at the feet of a master. Five years later he was hired away by Fry & Co., a small and exclusive Bay Street firm that wanted to set up its own bond department. "We gradually built up the department, made some money and became a significant factor in the bond market," he says. In 1971, Fry & Co. merged with a larger firm called Mills Spence, which was strong in underwriting and retail sales, but was losing money. As the merged firm grew, so did its profits – and so did Lawrence's influence. In 1976 the company merged with Burns Bros. & Denton, which had been founded in 1932 by Latham and Charles Burns. This time, the merger was a marriage of strengths: Lawrence's bond expertise fitted nicely with the stock-market skills of Burns Bros.

Today, with 1,100 employees and 13 offices across the country, Burns Fry has almost outgrown its original reliance on the bond business. Its 1984 acquisition of Jones Heward Ltd. gave it added strength in the institutional equities side of the business. Lawrence runs the store as president, but shares power and ownership with the three Burns Bros. executives who helped engineer the 1976 merger: Chairman Latham Burns, son of the co-founder of Burns Bros.; Vice-chairman Peter Eby; and Executive Vice-President Don Johnston, who runs the trading and administrative end of the business. There's also a strong corporate underwriting department.

But about one-third of the firm's profits – and, in a good year, as much as half – still comes from the bond department, run by Bob Dacks. That's largely because Lawrence and his traders, for the past decade or so, have consistently and profitably bet on inflation. When inflation increases, interest rates rise; and when interest rates rise, bond prices fall.*. For most of the 1970s, Lawrence accurately predicted the trend of inflation and the consequent rise in interest rates to their dizzying peak of more than 20 per cent in 1981. Since bond prices were falling in consequence for most of this period, Lawrence's traders made most of their money by shorting bonds – that is, selling bonds they didn't own, paying for them later at lower prices, and then pocketing the difference.

Since these transactions can involve tens of millions of dollars, it's not a game for triflers. But Lawrence's bond traders are emphatically not amateurs, and there's very little new competition on the horizon. "Every once in a while, some firm will decide that it's time to get aggressive in the bond business," he says. "So they go out and hire a few people, give them some money to play around with and lose a couple of million dollars in the next few months. Then they suddenly lose interest in the bond business. That happens with regularity to two or three firms every year." But not to a man who runs the Marathon in 3:22 and never loses at poker.

Levesque, Beaubien Inc.:
Brokers to the New Quebec

Quebec used to be known as a province of under-the-mattress savers; it may soon be known as a province of stock-market players. One of the main beneficiaries of this shift is Levesque, Beaubien Inc., the largest Quebec-owned investment house. Founded in 1902 by two young stockbrokers, Louis-de-Gaspé Beaubien and Charles-Henri Branchaud, the firm grew by underwriting new stock and bond issues, and by opening a string of branch offices throughout Quebec. In 1963, the firm was bought out by Credit Interprovincial Inc., one of the links in the interconnected financial conglomerate created by Quebec

---

* Why do bonds go down when interest rates rise? It's simple, when you stop to think about it. Suppose you've bought a $1,000 bond paying 8 per cent. Now suppose interest rates rise to 10 per cent. That means you can get a better return on your money somewhere else. Therefore, the price of your bond *must* fall until its yield approximates what everybody else is earning on their money. In this admittedly crude example, your $1,000 bond would have to drop to around $800.

financier Jean-Louis Levesque. In 1970, to reflect the realities of its ownership, it was renamed Levesque, Beaubien Inc. Levesque, who retired in 1972, was a scaled-down French-Canadian version of E.P. Taylor: a visionary financier who shuffled and reshuffled companies like a riverboat gambler with a deck of cards; a passionately devoted racehorse owner; and the personal owner of a $1-million, eight-passenger Jet Commander/Westwind 1123.

Born in Quebec's Gaspé region, Levesque worked in a bank before launching Credit Interprovincial in 1941, and began acquiring other companies. By the late 1950s he controlled about 15 medium-sized firms. In 1960 he backed a hustling young entrepreneur from Sudbury named Paul Desmarais, who wanted to borrow money to buy control of a bus company called Provincial Transport. A few years later, in 1965, Levesque sold his conglomerate, Trans-Canada Fund, to Desmarais, in a $32-million reverse takeover that created the core of what is now the legendary Power Corporation.

By 1972, Levesque, Beaubien was an important presence in Quebec; but it was still a regional firm, little known outside the province. In 1972, Levesque sold most of his shares to André Charron, the firm's president. Charron and Pierre Brunet, an accountant who'd been hired as managing director, decided to take the firm national. They did it slowly, by buying six smaller brokerage houses across the country, and by beefing up the firm's research and underwriting departments. "We asked ourselves many times, should we keep our name?" Brunet recalls. "If you're dealing in Calgary and Vancouver, is there going to be an adverse reaction to a French name? We finally decided that we had to stick with the name, and it's worked perfectly."

By 1984, Levesque, Beaubien was among Canada's 10 largest securities firms, with 650 employees across the country, 27 offices, 100,000 retail clients and revenues of $50 million. Its Toronto office had grown from a two-man operation in 1969 to 125 people by 1984 – including more floor traders on the TSE than any other firm. In 1983, the Toronto operation generated as much revenue as the entire firm was generating in 1975. "If you believe in excellence," says Brunet, "the best test is to go outside your own bailiwick to see if you can compete."

The firm's importance can be measured in symbolic as well as in financial terms. Levesque, Beaubien now occupies the former Montreal head-office building of the Royal Bank of Canada. The building is a St. James Street classic – an immense banking hall on the ground floor; huge, sculptured doors of beaten brass; mahogany panelling and brass chandeliers, adorned by unobtrusive nineteenth-century landscapes hanging above wide, log-burning fireplaces. Charron and Brunet, wheeling and dealing all day in French, occupy offices that were once the innermost sanctums of the city's Anglo-Celtic Establishment. One of their boardrooms was once the office of Sir Herbert Holt, one of Canada's richest men and, as chairman of the Royal Bank of Canada, the most widely feared banker in the country.* Now it's a symbol of the new confidence of French-Canadian business.

---

* The Royal Bank's head office since the 1960s has been located a few blocks west, in Place Ville Marie. But the bank, although it maintains this nominal head office, is really run out of Toronto.

13
The Boutiques

The firms profiled in the previous chapter include the giants of the industry, and they tend to present a monolithic, unchanging face to the world. It's the apparent solidity of these large firms that has given Bay Street its image of pin-striped impregnability, but beneath the unruffled surface there are hidden undertows: sudden financial crunches which can threaten to bring down even the largest, most venerable of firms; mass migrations of talent, which can swiftly boost one firm's status at the expense of another's; and the forces of entrepreneurial competition, through which the dominance of the older firms is constantly being attacked by new competitors.

Bigness still matters, of course. In 1971, according to a study by the Ontario Securities Commission, the industry's 12 largest firms controlled 84 per cent of its assets, leaving another 61 firms to fight over the remainder. The five largest Canadian-owned firms earned more than one-third of the industry's gross income, and the 10 largest earned about half of it. By 1984, with the surprise merger of Dominion Securities Ames and Pitfield Mackay Ross, the trend toward bigness seemed more firmly established than ever. But despite the apparent trend toward concentration, there has been an encouraging counter-trend: the rise, in the past decade or so, of the so-called investment boutiques.

Although they call themselves investment dealers, the boutiques are usually nothing more than investment think-tanks, sometimes consisting of only one or two people, which specialize in selling market advice to large financial institutions. They seldom employ armies of retail salespeople. They seldom underwrite issues of securities for sale to the public. Instead, in transactions known as "private placements," they help large companies sell millions of dollars' worth of stock to a few large institutional buyers. Their customers are the most sophisticated and demanding investors in the country. And what the boutiques are selling them is their own expertise and credibility.

The people who run the boutiques tend to represent the cream of the industry; they're among the smartest, the richest, the fastest-moving, the most entrepreneurial people on the Street.

They also represent an extraordinary diversity of styles and approaches. There are one-man firms – such as Ivan X. De-Souza's Investcan Ltd., whose offices are conveniently located above Winston's Restaurant. There are voracious upstarts like Jimmy Connacher's Daly Gordon Securities which, in the 1980s, emerged as one of the industry's most powerful firms, and certainly its most secretive. There are boutiques, such as Loewen, Ondaatje McCutcheon & Co. Ltd., which have outgrown their entrepreneurial origins and are beginning to resemble the larger firms. And there is even one boutique, Lafferty, Harwood & Partners Ltd., which makes a specialty of baiting the rest of the financial industry.

I've singled out two firms – Lafferty Harwood and Partners, and Daly Gordon Securities – for detailed attention because they present such a wide contrast of approaches, and because their principals struck me as especially interesting people. But there are many other firms I wish I'd had space to describe, including Toronto's Brown Baldwin Nisker Ltd., Alfred Bunting & Co. Ltd., Gardiner, Watson Ltd., and Loewen, Ondaatje McCutcheon & Co. Ltd.; Calgary's Charlton Securities Ltd. and Peters & Co. Ltd.; Vancouver's Pemberton, Houston Willoughby Ltd. (which isn't really a boutique at all, but a heavy-weight, full-service investment house); and Montreal's Maison Placements Canada Inc., run by the ebullient Dominick Dlouhy. Most of these firms are the creations of a few remarkable individuals, and reflect their individual styles. And because most of them are striving for their place in the sun, rather than defending an already established position, they also reflect the industry's future.

Richard Lafferty:
The House Radical

"Are you writing about that idiot Lafferty? Is he still peddling the same old crap?" That's one of the more charitable responses you hear on Bay Street when you mention the co-proprietor of Lafferty, Harwood & Partners Ltd., a Montreal-based investment boutique which has made a profitable specialty out of selling the sort of advice that no one wants to hear.

Because he deliberately places himself outside the Canadian financial Establishment, and because he publicly criticizes that Establishment as a greedy, self-serving monopoly, Lafferty has been called everything from a maverick to a Marxist to a mental case. He seems to love it when people call him names.

"Canada is a conformist society dominated by the banking system," he says. "Wall Street is crass and noisy and vulgar, but you get a quality of excellence there which is unsurpassed. Here in Canada we have an elite, but it has no quality. They're all a bunch of paper-shufflers. There's no creativity and there's no contribution. The reason for this is the big banks and their power-base." That is Richard Lafferty speaking in a mild tone of voice.

The investment industry can tolerate this sort of talk as long as it comes from people whom Bay Street regards as uninformed, and therefore beneath notice: pinko professors, NDP politicians, malcontent journalists and the like. But when it comes from a *stockbroker*, a member in good standing of exchanges in Montreal, Calgary, Chicago and Philadelphia, a person whose birth and upbringing amply qualify him for Establishment status – well, if you can't actually prevent him from earning a living, the only gentlemanly thing to do is ignore the fellow.

The financial Establishment has been trying to ignore Richard Lafferty for more than 30 years. It hasn't always succeeded. His attacks are too strident – on occasion he's taken full-page newspaper advertisements to broadcast his views – and his investment recommendations, unfortunately, are often too good to pass up.

Lafferty is the financial equivalent of I.F. Stone, the gadfly journalist who for decades terrorized official Washington by piecing together from public documents the various machinations of the U.S. political Establishment, and trumpeting his discoveries aloud in his own newsletter. Lafferty has the same rumpled quality of an old newshound, and works in a cluttered office on Montreal's St. James Street that looks like the receiving bin of a waste-paper recycling depot. He reads *everything*, including a lot of material that most analysts haven't even heard of. One of his sources of information on international politics, for instance, is the *Executive Intelligence Review*, a New York-based Marxist organization with an extremely well-developed sense of paranoia. One nonsensical publication that Lafferty showed me, a pamphlet on the international drug trade, accused Walter Gordon, the former Liberal finance minister, of laundering money for international drug traffickers. It also identified Stephen Clarkson, a University of Toronto professor who once ran for mayor of Toronto, as the co-founder with Gordon of Clarkson Gordon Ltd., the accounting and management consulting firm. Stephen Clarkson, in fact, has no connection with Clarkson Gordon; and to accuse the gentle Walter

Gordon of being a drug-dealers' banker is about as plausible as accusing Mother Theresa of running an international white-slavery cartel. But Lafferty pays for this kind of sloppy, wild-eyed paranoiac research, and – without vouching for its accuracy – sometimes distributes it to his firm's institutional clients.

The firm's main research product, however, is a series of bulky, spiral-bound volumes, issued monthly, which track Canadian and U.S. political and economic conditions, and recommend, in consequence, which stocks to buy and sell. The recommendations tend to be conservative, favoring sound, debt-free, well-managed companies that manufacture such mundane products as chequebooks or tampons. Between 1963 and 1983, Lafferty Harwood's recommendations for purchase of Canadian stocks would have produced a compounded return of better than 1,000 per cent. These recommendations are accompanied by Lafferty's wide-ranging, and often quirky, commentaries on the perfidy of politicians and bankers, the trend of geopolitical events and, on at least one occasion, by a documented account of the firm's run-in with a federal tax auditor.

Whether these reports are bought for their recommendations or for their entertainment value is a matter of debate on Bay Street. But the firm has 165 institutional clients in Canada, the U.S. and Europe, including some of the largest pension funds and financial institutions in the country; and it's built up a capital base of more than $1.3 million – not counting its investment-counsel affiliate, which keeps another $500,000 or so in the bank.*

The firm is a brokerage house in name only; it does no underwritings, and prides itself on not buying and selling securities for its own account on the grounds that such trading constitutes a conflict of interest. All it does, really, is sell research to institutional clients. But instead of being paid through regular retainers, like an investment counsellor, the firm charges commissions on the trades it executes for its clients. This is probably prudent. Lafferty's research is so controversial that most portfolio managers would be hard-pressed to justify a retainer arrangement to their superiors; but by paying the same amount in the form of brokerage commissions, such awkwardness can be avoided.

Professional outsiders are, by definition, homeless people; and Lafferty's early wanderings may have contributed to his jaundiced view of the way his native land's affairs are managed.

---

* Lafferty does his day-to-day banking with the Toronto Dominion, and also patronizes the Swiss Bank Corp. of Canada.

His grandfather, a physician, settled in Calgary about the time the CPR came through; he later founded a bank and became mayor of the infant city. Lafferty was born in Calgary, but was raised in England after his parents separated and his English mother returned home. He attended an English public school, joined the Middlesex Regiment when war broke out, was seconded to the Indian army and officered Indian battalions through the Italian campaign and in Japan. He remained with the Indian army until independence in 1947, then returned to Canada with a fluent command of Hindustani and Urdu, but no job qualifications to speak of. Three years as an executive trainee with Ford Motor Co. of Canada Ltd. convinced him that he wasn't a team player. "I decided," he says, "that the luxury of life was to be master of one's own soul. So I chose the investment business, where you make your own decisions and live or fall by them."

He spent 12 years on St. James Street, most of them with a firm called C.J. Hodgson Ltd., and was fired, he says, for issuing a research report that inconvenienced the banking Establishment. The report concerned Ivanhoe Corp., a subsidiary of Steinberg's and was very critical of the wisdom of its real estate purchases. "It's only hearsay, but I heard that Steinberg's was displeased, and complained to Earle McLaughlin at the Royal Bank. Archie Hodgson, my boss, was a close friend of McLaughlin's; their offices were in the same building. So they decided that Lafferty had to go. They changed the locks on the door and kicked me out the same day. I was a partner, too."

And so, with a colleague from Hodgson's named Robert Harwood, and with the financial backing of Harwood's father, they founded their own firm in 1962. By this time Lafferty's views on the iniquities of the banks were well known, and he was persona non grata on St. James Street. When his firm applied for membership in the Montreal Stock Exchange, he says, he was blackballed by many of the major firms, some of which had intimate and long-standing links to the big chartered banks. It is his understanding that he got in only because Eric Kierans, then the exchange's president, threatened to resign if the firm's membership application weren't approved.

Getting a seat on the Toronto Stock Exchange was even harder. Between 1969 and 1972, the firm's application for membership was repeatedly rejected under various pretexts. It wasn't until Lafferty bought full-page ads in newspapers across the country, accusing the Toronto Establishment of trying to shut him out, that the firm was finally admitted to membership. Even then,

200

the TSE accepted the firm only on condition that another partner, not Lafferty, put his name on the application.

The ad was not calculated to endear him to Bay Street. "The financial world is a great 'con game,' " Lafferty wrote. "It is the informed who sell to the uninformed and buy from them before they are aware of change. If the marketplace is kept informed, the con game is more difficult to play. Our research reports therefore spoil the game."

In a hearing before the TSE board of governors in May 1972, Lafferty complained that the exchange's counsel, Alex MacIntosh, was also an influential director of the Canadian Imperial Bank of Commerce, an institution that had no reason to welcome Lafferty's presence in Toronto. "We have contended for years . . . that the chartered banks in Canada have exploited the public," he told the nonplussed governors. "None of the chartered banks or directors thereof have ever to my knowledge publicly refuted our statements. In my opinion they have engaged in activities intended deliberately to frustrate our business and at times to drive us out of business."

Many of Lafferty's critics assume, on the basis of statements like these, that the man must be a raving Marxist. They couldn't be more wrong. He is a disciple of Ludwig von Mises, a little-known, and practically unreadable, Austrian economist who believed passionately in the efficacy of free markets and the beneficial effects of entrepreneurship. "I'm not a capitalist," says Lafferty. "I'm a free-enterpriser."

The irresistible tendency of capitalism – which the Canadian banks, in Lafferty's view, perfectly exemplify – is to swallow smaller competitors, to form cartels, to shut out new competition. The banks, the five largest of which control about 90 per cent of the country's banking business, constitute one such cartel; so does the Investment Dealers Association of Canada which, until recently, set the commission rates its members could charge their customers. Lafferty also argues that the intimate, yet informal, links between the big banks and the largest Bay Street investment houses have strengthened this monopoly. A.E. Ames, until its merger with Dominion Securities, was allied with the Bank of Montreal. Dominion Securities Pitfield enjoys a long-standing alliance with the Canadian Imperial Bank of Commerce; Wood Gundy was and is allied with the Royal Bank of Canada. Although banks by law cannot control brokerage firms, these alliances allow them to act as if they did. Each firm tries to steer banking business to its banking ally, and each bank tends to steer underwriting and merchant banking business to its pet investment house.

The effect, Lafferty argues, is a tight little circle of privilege which has encouraged foreign control of the economy, discouraged creative entrepreneurship and shut out minorities from participation in Canada's financial markets. It is no accident, he says, that ethnic groups are under-represented on Bay Street. "There are no Jewish member houses of the Montreal Stock Exchange, and the last such applicant was blackballed," he told Parliament's committee on finance, trade and economic affairs in 1965. "There is now one Jewish member firm in Toronto . . . It is a restrictive measure based on fear of competition that would disturb the status quo of the dominant interests."

Lafferty has been saying the same things for 30 years, even though a process of evolution has altered the tight little world that so distresses him. Larry Bloomberg, a Jew who founded First Marathon Securities Ltd., one of Bay Street's fastest-growing firms, thinks the suggestion of anti-Jewish bias is nonsense, and so does every other Jewish financier I've questioned on the subject.

Wood Gundy took extraordinary risks in the early 1970s to underwrite the initial stock issue of the Unity Bank of Canada, whose declared purpose was to inject an ethnic component into Canadian banking.

Because of negotiated commission rates, the Investment Dealers Association of Canada is no longer a true cartel. Because of an influx of foreign banks, the power and market-share of the big Canadian banks is beginning to erode.

But the core of his complaint is still intact. The banks *are* too powerful, the Bay Street village is still too cosy and homogenous. The fact that Richard Lafferty has prospered mightily in this environment is a testament to his integrity and energy. It may also indicate that the forces of entrenched privilege are not quite so intolerant of diversity as he supposes.

Jimmy Connacher:
The New Goliath Of Bay Street

There's a persistent story about Jimmy Connacher that's been circulating on Bay Street for several years. Although it comes in various versions, it goes something like this:

Connacher, the president and driving force behind Daly Gordon Securities, strides into the office of the chairman (or perhaps it's the president) of one of Canada's major chartered banks. He reaches into his briefcase, pulls out a certified cheque for $250 million, made out to the bank in question, and lays it on the desk. "Now that I've got your attention," Connacher tells the nonplussed banker, "let me explain why I'm here."

Connacher gives his pitch to the banker. He thinks it's time for the bank to issue some more preferred shares – say, $250 million worth. As they both know, banks must regularly sell new shares, since the law requires that their capital base must expand in proportion to the growth in their assets. Every time a bank's loan portfolio increases by $25, in other words, it's obligated to sell a dollar's worth of additional stock. Normally, banks sell their shares through underwritings by Bay Street investment houses, which compete hotly for the business. But Connacher has a better idea: Why not short-circuit the whole tedious, costly, complex business of an underwriting? "There's the money," he says, pointing at the cheque on the table. "Just give us the shares."

The banker, who is practically hypnotized by the spectacle of all that money staring up at him, says he'll have to think about it; he must consult his executive committee and perhaps his board of directors. Connacher presses him for a reply; the bank chairman says he'll be in touch the following day. The next day, as promised, he phones Connacher and congratulates him on his prescience in divining that the bank needs to issue more preferred shares. Partly as a result of Connacher's visit, the bank has decided to do exactly that, thank you very much. But instead of accepting Daly Gordon's offer, it will raise the $250 million through a conventional underwriting.

That story, regrettably, is uncheckable. Canadian bank chairmen seldom confide their innermost financial secrets to journalists; and Connacher is famous for refusing to talk to any reporter, any time, for any reason, and for his alleged threat to fire any Gordon employee who does. But the fact that this story floated around the Street for several years tells a great deal about the way Connacher operates, and how he's regarded on Bay Street: with a mixture of admiration for his chutzpah, puzzlement about how he gets away with it, and a certain amount of naked fear. "Jimmy has had more impact on the structure of the industry than any other individual in the past 10 years," says one of his competitors. "And the whole Gordon mystique really pisses me off."

The mystique, and the fear, reached the panic level in April 1984, when that apocryphal story about Connacher and the banker suddenly came to life – with a happier ending for the broker. In a dazzling coup that stunned the Street, Daly Gordon stole a $228-million preferred-share issue by the Royal Bank of Canada from beneath the noses of five large investment dealers.

It was what Bay Street calls a "bought" deal – that is, Daly Gordon handed the bank a cheque for its shares, and took its own chances about reselling them. Not only that, but it charged a one-per cent commission, instead of the usual 2 or 3 per cent, thus saving the bank about $3 million in underwriting costs.

In all Bay Street's chequered history, there has never been a firm like Daly Gordon. Few firms have achieved a position of such strength in so short a time. No other firm takes such large risks with so much of its own (and its creditors') money. No other firm has snatched away so much business, and snatched it away so rudely, from the traditional investment houses. And no other firm has caused such consternation among its competitors. In the space of 15 years, Connacher and his hyper-aggressive henchmen have shoved and bullied and elbowed their way into the front ranks of the Canadian securities industry, like a gang of street-smart ghetto punks marching in and terrorizing the schoolyard at Upper Canada College. On the Toronto Stock Exchange, Gordon's floor traders buy and sell blocks of shares in awesome quantities; and, most awesome of all, they're often trading for the house account, gambling their own money, not their clients'. Since 1981, Gordon's trades have accounted for about 9 per cent of the dollar value of the TSE's trading. And on one memorable day, February 10, 1983, Gordon's block trades of huge parcels of shares of Trimac Ltd., Denison Mines Ltd., Cadillac Fairview Corp. Ltd. and the Royal Bank were worth $133 million – more than 70 per cent of the TSE's trading value that day.

What is it that Gordon does, exactly, which so alarms the competition? To understand the concept, think of Bay Street as a pack of used-car dealers, strung out along an ugly suburban thoroughfare. Instead of buying and selling cars, these dealers trade pieces of companies. Most of the dealers on this strip will accept your rusting Toyota only on consignment, and they've all agreed to charge roughly the same commission. But Gordon offers to pay hard cash instantly, the minute you walk onto the lot – and to pay you considerably more than the dealer next door. How can they afford to do it? For one thing, they eschew fancy offices and a lot of salaried salesmen; for another, they're so attuned to the market that they sometimes find a buyer for your Toyota before you've even decided to sell it. And because their overheads are so low, they can afford to take gambles that other dealers wouldn't touch.

A major investment firm such as Wood Gundy Ltd. or McLeod Young Weir operates from a capital base of between $40 and $60 million. The largest Canadian firm, Dominion Securities

Pitfield, has capital of about $100 million. The way these firms make their livings, in addition to charging commissions, is by playing the markets with their own money. They must keep some capital in reserve to run the business, and there are stringent rules on this imposed by the securities commissions; but, in general, the more money they have available for playing the markets, the better off they are – not only because of the opportunities for trading profits, but because of the flexibility these activities afford to the firm's clients. (When a pension fund buys several million dollars' worth of bonds, for instance, it likes to deal with a firm that's willing to buy them back on short notice.)

One of Daly Gordon's strengths is that it deals only in stocks, instead of tying up part of its money in bonds, options, treasury bills, foreign exchange or any of the other markets in which the larger firms are forced – by their clients' needs – to participate. McLeod Young Weir, for instance, with capital of about $42 million, has about $9 million invested in various markets. Gordon, with $32 million in capital, invests only in stocks – and, because of low overheads, can invest more in stocks than McLeod invests in everything. "Sure we have more capital," says a McLeod executive. "But you have to wonder: who's the David here, and who's the Goliath?"

"He's got no people, no branch offices," complains one of Connacher's competitors. "All he's got is dollars. And what does he do with them? He does one thing. He concentrates on dealing in big liability positions as an underwriter or as a participant in the market."

Actually, Connacher has all the people he needs – about 130 employees, including some of the brightest people on the Street – and a suite of offices, modest by Bay Street standards, at the top of a tower in the Toronto Dominion Centre. From there, on the fifty-fifth floor, he can peer down into the offices of most of his competitors and plot further raids against their established positions.

From the moment of its founding in Montreal in 1968 as Gordon Eberts Securities Ltd., the firm has been a haven for mavericks, for boat-rockers, for people too quirky or too competitive to fit in anywhere else. "Most of us were too ornery to be welcomed into the sedate world of Bay Street," says a former partner named Michael Gilbert. "Even today, they won't play by the old school tie, and have alienated brokerage firms run by arteriosclerotic upper-crust British."

Monte Gordon, one of the co-founders, was an imaginative promoter and financier who, in his spare time, was a hot-air balloonist and member of the bobsled team that won the gold medal at the 1964 Olympics. Gordon Eberts was an underwriting specialist. Connacher joined the firm from Wood Gundy in 1970; that he might have been a trifle flamboyant for that august institution may be judged from the fact that, at a New Year's Eve party in Montreal in the late 1960s, Connacher turned up dressed *only* in a string of Christmas-tree lights.

Under Monte Gordon, the firm hired some of Montreal's best research talent and, through the early 1970s, built a reputation as a very bright, very aggressive institutional boutique. But the late 1970s were characterized by a series of power struggles which led to the departure of Monte Gordon, of Eberts and of most of the research talent, and the emergence of Connacher as the firm's leader. At one point, Connacher even resigned briefly, to force the firm to choose between him and his Montreal-based rival, Peter Miller. Miller left after the entire Toronto office threatened to quit unless Connacher returned.

Once he'd seized control, and owned 20 per cent of the firm's shares, Connacher set about rebuilding it in his own image. He hired new people, including a team of analysts as strong as those who had departed. And he enhanced the firm's dominance as a block trader, arranging transfers of huge blocks of shares between buyers and sellers. In 1981, for instance, Gordon handled the largest block trade in Canadian history: the purchase by Brascan Ltd. of 4.9 million shares of Noranda Mines Ltd. for $177.6 million. He also refined the technique of using the firm's own money, plus short-term borrowed funds, to buy large blocks of shares, and then reselling them at a profit.

A 1983 merger with R.A. Daly & Co. Ltd. bought Gordon the formidable trading skills of Don Bainbridge, Daly's president and commonly regarded as the TSE's smartest, richest floor trader. And in 1984, the merged firm of Daly Gordon Securities terrified Bay Street even more by proposing an alliance with a Belgian holding company, Lambert Brussels Corp., which would have given Connacher a capital base of $100 million. The TSE refused – on fairly flimsy pretexts – to approve the deal; the last thing they wanted was to see Connacher's bully-boys armed with larger slingshots. But thanks to an alliance with a secret backer, Connacher, with a capital base of about $40 million, had already been able to buy, for subsequent resale, share issues worth hundreds of millions.

Who was his secret backer? Connacher, needless to say, wasn't talking. But the loans were believed to have come from Edward and Charles Bronfman, the Toronto-based billionaires whose holding company, Edper Investments, is one of Canada's largest pools of corporate power.

At this writing, in mid-1984, no one can predict how powerful Daly Gordon might become, or how lasting will be its impact on Bay Street. Bay Street was fervently hoping Jimmy Connacher would go away; and Bay Street's corporate customers were happy he'd arrived.

14

McLeod Young Weir: Steering Through The Icebergs

Whoever books the meeting-rooms in Toronto's Harbour Castle Hilton Hotel must have a mordant sense of humor. How else can you explain the fact that, on the hotel's convention floor on a grey spring morning in 1984, a roomful of socialists was assembled in one room, discussing the demise of capitalism; while just down the hall, almost within earshot, a roomful of stockbrokers was uneasily discussing its renewal?

In one room, the federal council of the New Democratic Party was reliving the pieties of the Old Left, singing happy birthday to a 79-year-old Tommy Douglas and rededicating themselves to a vision of social democracy that hasn't much changed since the 1930s. In the meeting room next door, the 60 members of the board of directors of McLeod Young Weir, one of Canada's largest investment dealers, spent the day discussing their own performance and the blizzard of changes that were overtaking their industry.

The surprising thing wasn't the difference between the two groups, but their similarities. Outside of office hours, stockbrokers like to dress with a studied, preppy casualness. And since this was a Saturday meeting, they'd left their three-piece suits and Turnbull & Asser shirts at home, and worn their Bermuda golfing togs: open-necked shirts, coral-pink pullovers, Harris-tweed blazers, Lacoste T-shirts, corduroys and grey flannels. Austin Taylor, the firm's 365-pound chairman, a man with the physical presence of a grizzly bear on its hind legs, affected grey cords and a forest-green pullover the size of a pup tent; he wouldn't have dressed much differently if he'd been mucking out the stables on his gentleman's farm in the Caledon hills.

Eerily, the NDPers were almost indistinguishable from the stockbrokers. In their jeans and tweed jackets, most of them looked pleasant and prosperous, the kind of people who drive

Volvo station wagons and affix save-the-whales posters to their refrigerator doors with little magnetic bugs. Bob Rae, the angelic ambassador's son who leads the NDP in Ontario, could have passed for an up-and-coming securities analyst in McLeod's research department. Some of the younger trade-union honchos even looked as if they might play a decent game of squash.

The similarities didn't stop there. Both groups, the socialists and the stockbrokers, were there to discuss the delicate matter of their own survival. After coming through the worst recession in 50 years, the NDP's share of the popular vote, as measured by the Gallup poll, had dropped to the lowest level since the party's founding in 1960. The directors of McLeod Young Weir were facing a similar challenge to their continued existence. The financial environment in which these men had grown up, an environment which had always been characterized by clear boundaries, by a gentlemanly avoidance of competition and by a certain *cosiness* – it all seemed to be shattering before their eyes, and no one knew what new patterns were about to emerge.

How do we compete and, yes, survive in this harsh new environment? That's what the NDPers, with only 11 per cent of the popular vote, were asking themselves. Exactly the same question obsessed McLeod Young Weir's board of directors that Saturday morning in April 1984. It seemed clear to them that their firm must undergo profound changes – either that, or disappear as A.E. Ames had done, one more corporate dinosaur in the Bay Street boneyard. Was the firm strong enough, and smart enough, to muster the flexibility that the times required? That depended very much on the man sitting at the head of the table in the forest-green pullover.

The Rich Man's Son

When Austin Taylor was elected president of McLeod Young Weir in 1978, no one in Toronto could believe the announcement. Austin *who*? It wasn't merely Taylor's falstaffian girth which made him a figure of merriment or wonderment; it was also the fact that he'd been plucked from the obscurity of a Vancouver branch office and brought to Toronto to head the entire organization; and the fact that, until he was into his middle years, Taylor was an under-achiever, a rich man's son who'd never made his own mark. "Austin Taylor is the only man I know who started to succeed at 40," says Peter Brown, president of Vancouver's Canarim Investment Corp. "Prior to

209

that it seemed that business was very much a secondary concern."

Perhaps it was too easy, growing up as the only son of one of Vancouver's richest men. Austin Taylor senior first came to Vancouver during World War I, as a dollar-a-year man sent out from Ottawa to organize the harvesting of Sitka Spruce from the Queen Charlotte Islands, for aircraft production. His chief forester on the project, another easterner visiting Vancouver for the first time, was one H.R. Macmillan. Taylor married a Winnipeg girl in 1919 and decided to make his home in Vancouver, and by the late 1920s he was one of an elite handful of local businessmen who virtually ran the raw young city. He owned a piece of a fish cannery and a string of service stations; he became shareholder in the company that H.R. Macmillan set up to export his lumber around the world; and he owned a large piece of Macmillan's company, which was destined to become the province's largest forestry firm.

If you wanted to do any kind of business in Vancouver in the 1920s and 1930s, Austin Taylor was one of the people you had to see. Around 1928 two prospectors came to his office looking for a grubstake. Taylor loaned them money and, three years later, found himself the major shareholder in Bralorne Mines Ltd., a major new gold producer. For Taylor, it meant a transition from rich to super-rich. He bought a vast Georgian mansion on south Granville Street, its manicured acres of ornamental gardens separated from the outside world by brick walls and tall trees.

It was here that Austin Taylor junior grew up, behind an impenetrable wall of brick and foliage. The servants who occupied the gatehouse at the front entrance kept out unwanted visitors. Other servants lived above the coach house, whose ground floor was a five-car garage. The elder Taylor favored Cadillacs and, at one point, owned two identical black 16-cylinder limousines – one for him, one for his wife. When World War II came, Taylor sold his 90 thoroughbred racehorses and went back to work for Ottawa as a dollar-a-year man. One of his duties was to arrange for the resettlement of Japanese-Canadians in internment camps in the B.C. interior. "Internment of the Japanese was regarded as necessary at the time," says his son, "but my father had nothing to do with the subsequent confiscation of their property." The young Taylor spent his childhood years shuttling between Vancouver and the family's rented cottage near Pasadena, riding and playing tennis in the mornings and passing his afternoons with a private tutor. When the family was in Vancouver he attended St. George's School, where he usually came near the top of the class. University was less successful. He was asked to leave Princeton after a semester of congenial idleness. He spent a second, equally idle year at University of B.C., playing bridge in the mornings mostly with his friend Peter Bentley, who later became president of his family's firm, Canadian Forest Products Ltd. Taylor dropped out after Bentley was asked to leave at Christmas; he concluded that the university authorities were weeding out the drones in alphabetical order, and that it would be only a matter of time until they reached the Ts.

A dropout from two universities, he became a clerk in his father's office, until he was rescued by a colleague of his father's, a partner in the New York investment banking house of Morgan Stanley & Co., who offered him a three-month job trial. Taylor passed, and spent the next five years glorying in the sophistication of New York and Wall Street. He married briefly, divorced, then married again, a Manhattan socialite named Betsey Newbold. His sister Pat, meanwhile, had married William F. Buckley Jr., the conservative commentator, and Taylor was persuaded to leave Morgan Stanley to help develop the petroleum interests of the wealthy Buckley clan. The job took him to the Philippines, where the Buckleys were active in the free-wheeling Manila Stock Exchange. Taylor, impatient at the strictures of working for a family company, decided to resign. Using his own money, he tried to start a distillery in Manila. The venture was a failure and in 1964 Taylor, with a wife and four children, returned to Vancouver.

The Prodigal Returns

He was in his mid-thirties, and without money or prospects; but he was not without cards. For one thing, being Austin Taylor's son still counted in Vancouver, even though the son was virtually disinherited. For another, the son knew how to make and keep friends, something the father had never learned. The old man was known for his habit of sitting alone at the Vancouver Club, his haughty manner discouraging familiarity. The son, by contrast, was generous, humorous and fiercely loyal to his old friends, who by now were moving into commanding positions in the Vancouver Establishment. That's why McLeod Young Weir hired him to develop underwriting in Vancouver. "They were gambling a small salary" says one insider, "on the proposition that Austin had enough friends in the Vancouver Establishment to pay his way."

211

It proved to be a sound gamble. Taylor's connections helped McLeod to charm its way into important underwriting relationships with several large Vancouver-based firms. Westcoast Transmission Co. Ltd., Woodwards Stores, Finning Tractor and Cornat were among the companies that Taylor brought in to the McLeod fold. "He has a very personal style of business, which engenders tremendous loyalty in his clients," says Mike McKibbin, who used to compete with him from Wood Gundy's Vancouver office. "But he must click with them. His one failing is his difficulty in dealing with someone who keeps things strictly business. But because he was a product of the Vancouver community and had strong ties, his approach was very effective."

Taylor's major breakthrough came when Bill Bennett, son of B.C.'s former Social Credit premier, decided to run for premier and named Taylor as his chief bagman. "B.C. has never had a more successful fund-raiser," says Ed Phillips, a Taylor friend who was CEO of Westcoast Transmission when it became a McLeod underwriting client. McLeod later became the province's fiscal agent, selling hundreds of millions of dollars worth of bonds issued by the B.C. government and various provincial agencies.

Taylor did so well, in fact, that by 1978, in spite of the fact that he knew practically no one in Toronto, he was able to take over the firm – a seizure of power so improbable that it continues to astound Bay Street. The firm was then undergoing a leadership crisis. Its two most senior executives, Chairman George MacDonald and Vice-Chairman Alistair Fraser, were both close to retirement. Bryce Farrill, the firm's president, hadn't managed to convince the other partners that he was a logical heir-apparent. And below Farrill, there seemed to be no one with enough clout, and with few enough enemies, to be regarded as a plausible candidate.

That left Taylor, whom almost no one knew, and therefore no one despised. He was named president at a remarkable board meeting which a former partner, Pete Sutton, describes as "the stupidest meeting I ever attended. Bryce and Austin both stood up and had to make a little speech as to why each should be president. Then they left the room and we all voted." Taylor won, unanimously. "Austin wasn't a compromise candidate," says Tom Kierans, whom Taylor hired away from Pitfield Mackay Ross in 1979 and installed as president. "He was really the only option the firm had." Bryce Farrill, by way of consolation, was named vice-chairman and sent to head up the New York office.

What Taylor found, when he moved into the big corner office on the thirty-second floor, was a firm that had been doing well enough, but not as well as some of its major competitors. For the previous decade or so, McLeod had stayed aloof from toe-to-toe competition with firms such as Wood Gundy and Dominion Securities, and became known instead for innovative financing strategies. When Air Canada wanted to buy new airplanes, for instance, it was McLeod which came up with a fresh wrinkle: It found well-heeled investors to buy the aircraft, who then leased them to the airline – in effect, a complex fiddle which secured attractive tax writeoffs for the investors and reduced the airline's borrowing costs. The B.C. government, with McLeod as its agent, used the same ingenious technique to buy a new fleet of ferries. It was McLeod which developed the first Canadian real-estate investment trusts, the first oil and gas tax shelters, the first Canadian issue of retractable preferred shares. Some of the younger partners, such as David Wilson, Mark Harris and Dan Sullivan, became expert at using computers as financial wind-tunnels, to test how these fiendishly complex financing strategies would work in the real world. "We became niche players," says Kierans. "Whatever was complicated, and tax-based and new – and people hadn't done it before – our people got into that and developed a good reputation."

Toe-To-Toe Competition

Taylor's achievement was to transform the firm from a moderately successful peripheral player into a centre-stage contender. Instead of looking for new specialties, under Taylor's leadership the firm concentrated on direct competition with the largest investment dealers. McLeod did it by pitching harder than ever before for underwriting business, and by hiring and training hundreds of new salespeople, so that the firm would be better able to sell the stock and bond issues it was underwriting. The firm had fewer than 100 retail salespeople when Taylor became president and CEO in 1978. Six years later there were 350. Under Taylor, McLeod also developed one of Bay Street's most rigorous sales-training programs for new employees, installed a costly new computer system and improved the firm's performance as a trader of bonds and other fixed-income securities, which meant the firm began making a lot of money, instead of just a little, from playing the markets with its own capital. The bottom-line result: McLeod, which had about $6 million in equity capital when Taylor took over in

213

1978, had about $45 million by 1984. Those figures represented a five-fold increase in the wealth and importance of the firm, and – not at all incidentally – of the executives who owned its shares.

But all of this was not achieved through a process of sweet consensus. Taylor's surprising assumption of power, and the manner in which he exercised it, resulted in a mass defection of senior management. No fewer than seven McLeod directors moved to other firms or into other lines of work. Some of them cited Taylor's high-handed ways as a major reason for their departure. Others were unceremoniously fired. "Austin has an autocratic management style, which is singularly inappropriate in the operation of what is essentially a partnership," said the late Ed Darroch, who, along with ex-director Bob Borden, joined ex-director Ivan X. De Souza in his newly formed investment boutique, Investcan Securities Ltd.

The Taylor style must certainly have seemed autocratic to the people whom he decided had no future with the firm. But to those he'd hired or promoted, and to those who won his confidence – which is to say, nearly every senior executive who survived the initial bloodbath – Taylor was like the Pope among his cardinals: *primus inter pares*, first among equals. "Austin expects you to be absolutely on top of your area," says Mike Edwards, whom Taylor plucked from the Vancouver office to manage the explosive growth of the retail sales force. "When my phone rings and it's Austin with a question, he expects an immediate answer. The greater your ability to respond to his direct questioning, the greater the amount of freedom you have in running your own operation. So if you're not on top of your situation, Austin's management style would probably strike you as fairly autocratic and close to the chest. But if you're coping, if you're managing your department in a way that inspires confidence, then he tends to give you a high degree of freedom."*

The Taylor Mystique

In spite of the failures of his early years, Taylor, by the time he moved to Toronto, had acquired an air of massive personal authority. Although his manner is shy, almost evasive, he can be very convincing. "Taylor's strength is, first and foremost,

---

* In mid-1984, Edwards resigned from McLeod to become president of Gardiner Watson Ltd.

his self-confidence, which is immense," says Kierans. "It's not overweening, it doesn't lean on you – but it's there." In the mid-1970s, for instance, McLeod had all but completed a deal to merge with a smaller firm, Bongard Leslie Inc., which had developed a large retail network. Taylor flew in from Vancouver and, almost single-handedly, convinced his partners that the merger would be against McLeod's traditions and its best interests. That performance is what persuaded some partners to start thinking of him as leadership material.

Some Taylor-watchers attribute his persuasive powers mainly to his size (six-foot-four) and bulk, and to his amazing eyebrows, which reminded one awed journalist, Mike Macbeth, of "gigantic whisk brooms." At the weekly meetings of McLeod's executive committee, Taylor's bear-like presence dominates the gathering the way Dr. Samuel Johnson's girth and wit once commanded the coffee-houses and literary salons of eighteenth-century London. He sits at the head of the boardroom table, sipping tea from an oversized mug, throwing out questions for discussion, listening patiently while the partners kick the subject around. When he speaks, it's usually close to the final word on the subject. It may sound as if he's summing up the sense of the meeting, but in fact he's usually stating his own view of the issue at hand; and that is the view that usually prevails.

So it was at the Saturday-morning board meeting at the Harbour Castle Hilton. The 60-odd directors spent the morning listening to canned presentations from various department heads on how well or how badly the firm was doing. Then, in the afternoon, it broadened into a rambling discussion of what was on everybody's mind: the changes that were overtaking their industry, and how McLeod Young Weir might manage to survive them. From around the table, one after another, came little intimations of corporate mortality:

"Wood Gundy hired a guy from Chase-Manhattan and paid him half a million a year to give them a leg up in London . . ."

"What about the mortgage business? The banks are doing 40 per cent of the market now, from a standing start in 1967 . . ."

"We lost our utilities analyst to Burns Fry . . ."

"There's an ugly aspect to our business. Some of our competitors are giving their clients furniture or TV sets or trips to China as sweeteners in underwriting deals . . ."

"That's fine as long as you don't go broke doing it . . ."

"Well, I say we've got to play the same game. I'm not going to be the most ethical guy in the poorhouse . . ."

215

"These long-distance charges are *killing* us. Our phone bill is $4.5 million a month, and 60 per cent of it is long-distance . . ."

"What are our thoughts on partnership? Do we want to associate with a domestic financial institution, or a foreign investment bank? What do we really want to *be*? . . ."

"Personally, I don't want to sell out. I don't want to become a paid employee . . ."

Taylor, sounding almost self-effacing, listened patiently as the debate rambled on for much of the afternoon. Then, with an air of finality, he summed it all up. The age of computerization, he said, had made the world into a single, seamless financial marketplace. The big Canadian banks, a decade before, had transformed themselves into multinational corporations. Canadian investment dealers would inevitably be forced to do the same: "We're no longer living in the little, protected, tribal market of Canada," Taylor told his fellow-directors. "The local capital market is a thing of the past. To survive, we must become an international player. Unfortunately, there's a rule which says that aggregate foreigners can't own more than 25 per cent of a Canadian securities firm."

"In other words," added Tom Kierans, "if government policy doesn't change soon, there won't be much of our business left to fight over."

Everybody looked glum. Most of them were experts at analyzing other people's businesses, and they could be merciless at analyzing their own.

What Investment Firms Really Do

McLeod Young Weir is a "full-service" brokerage firm. In an age of increasing specialization, it tries to do and be everything for everybody. As with every other large investment house, the way the firm is structured reflects the range of clients it's trying to serve. It is therefore useful for an outsider to walk through the firm's various departments; a guided tour helps define the firm's strengths and weaknesses, and shows what investment firms actually do.

McLeod Young Weir makes its living by purchasing bonds from various governments and then reselling them, hopefully at a profit; by trading stocks, bonds, options, futures and other securities for a commission, on behalf of individual or institutional clients; by underwriting the stock and bond issues of client companies; and by trading stocks, bonds and other types of securities for its own account. Most of these activities reinforce one another. It helps to have a strong bond-trading department, for instance, if you're trying to convince Bell Canada's chief financial officer, or B.C.'s deputy finance minister, that you're qualified to underwrite their latest bond issue. Similarly, if you want to underwrite corporate stock issues, it helps to have hundreds of retail salespeople who can sell the issue to individual clients across the country.

What McLeod is really selling, in all these departments, is the quality of its market information and the skill and judgment with which it's interpreted. The chiropractor's widow in Red Deer and the president of Bell Canada Enterprises both want to feel confident about their broker's ability to handle their money responsibly; and that confidence is generally based on how well-informed the customer believes the broker to be. It is far more plausible, in fact, to think of an investment firm as an information clearing-house, rather than as a trading agency. The organization chart makes more sense if you look at it that way.

Ian Delaney, for instance, is listed on McLeod's organization chart as vice-president for marketing, but it's hard to see what, exactly, he markets – except his own superb sense of what the stock and bond markets are likely to do next. Kierans explains the marketing function this way: "Every day we're accepting liabilities – buying bonds, stocks or something or other. And we have to know whether we can sell them and whether we can price them; we have to know who we can sell them to and who wants to buy them." Delaney makes it his business to know. He spent most of his career as a senior executive at Merrill Lynch Canada and in 1980, after hearing what Taylor was up to at McLeod, decided it was time to move. "I knew that Austin gets in to the office very early," says Delaney, "so I phoned him up one morning at 7:30 and asked if I could drop around for a chat. We drank some coffee and, around nine he said to me: 'You'd better come to work here. What would you like to do?' "

What Delaney does is make deals, which means he spends long hours riding the telephone, staying in touch with potential underwriting clients, talking to financial people all over Bay Street – as well as McLeod's own people in Calgary, Vancouver, New York, Montreal and London – swapping gossip and market insights, striving to achieve that slight but crucial informational edge.

217

The Kierans Connection

This is also how Tom Kierans spends most of his time as president. But while Delaney focuses on the stock market and the firm's corporate clients, Kierans tends to concentrate on the intricacies of government finance. A glibly articulate over-achiever in his early forties, Kierans spent most of his career with Nesbitt Thomson and Pitfield Mackay Ross, two middle-of-the-pack investment houses, where he gravitated toward government finance. He's a seasoned member of the coterie of advisors whom Ontario Premier Bill Davis always consults. Because the firm acts as fiscal agents for B.C., Alberta, New Brunswick, Nova Scotia and Newfoundland, and also helps Ottawa borrow another few hundred million dollars every few weeks, Kierans is plugged into an informal intelligence network that spans the nation. He knows what the big U.S. insurance companies are thinking this morning about B.C. Hydro bonds. He talked to Bill Davis or lawyer Eddie Goodman an hour ago. He knows who in which provincial cabinets drinks too much. And if the newspapers splash a political scandal all over their front pages tomorrow morning, it's a safe bet that Kierans has known for weeks that it was coming.

It was Kierans, operating as a private consultant, who stage-managed the 1975 deal whereby the Ontario government bought a 5 per cent interest in the Syncrude heavy-oil project in Alberta, to save the project from cancellation. And it was Kierans, operating as McLeod's president, who guided Ontario's policy-makers toward their controversial decision in 1981 to buy a 25 per cent interest in Suncor Ltd. It's probably not surprising that he should gravitate to the world where business and government overlap; his father is Eric Kierans, a McGill University economist who, in the 1960s, ran the Montreal Stock Exchange and later served in the Trudeau cabinet. "I'm an economist and I've followed my father all my life," he says, "so I have a natural and reasonably sophisticated sense of public policy." He sharpened that sense in the mid-1970s as an advisor to D'Arcy McKeough, who was then the most influential minister in the Ontario cabinet, and as chairman of the Ontario Economic Council. "I was totally involved in that network that overlaps bureaucrats and academics in Ottawa, in Queens Park, in Nova Scotia, everywhere."

Much of this formidable expertise is directed toward persuading governments and corporations to allow McLeod to handle their bond issues – to get product onto the shelf, so to speak. McLeod *buys* these bonds for resale, as surely as Eaton's

218

buys the socks it sells. Once Eaton's sells a pair of socks, however, that's usually the end of it. But when McLeod sells a bond, the transaction usually marks the beginning of a long and intricate relationship. "Selling someone a bond is only part of the bargain," says Gordon Cheesbrough, the whiz kid who runs McLeod's fixed-income department. "The other part of the bargain is giving them the opportunity to sell it back whenever they want." McLeod, like most other major investment dealers, buys and sells interest-bearing securities literally around the clock. Trying to do so profitably is Cheesbrough's awesome responsibility.

The Wunderkind of the Bond Desk

Cheesbrough, a graduate of Upper Canada College with a 1974 philosophy degree from the University of Toronto, was only 30 when Taylor placed him at the head of the firm's fixed-income department. He is an authentic *wunderkind* – the youngest head of any Bay Street bond-trading operation – who manages about 80 traders and support staff the way a football coach runs a winning team: lots of encouragement, plenty of attention to detail, and no lasting regrets about the games you lose. The trading desk, with its blinking green VDTs and the dozens of shirtsleeved, stress-ridden traders barking urgently into telephones, resembles an air-traffic control tower.

"The main reason we trade all this stuff," says Cheesbrough, "is to not only service our clients but to make money. We're using part of the firm's capital to make as much money as we can. Most trading firms – and we're no exception – try to at least double the capital that they employ in trading every year. But of course it's risky. You're making judgments on the market all the time. Which direction will interest rates go? Am I positioned in the right sort of stuff? It's a lot harder than just sticking your money in the bank."

Cheesbrough's department trades a whole spectrum of interest-bearing instruments – everything from "overnight money" to government treasury bills, bearer discount notes, and long-term bonds issued by corporations and governments. When interest rates rise, the price of these instruments falls, and vice versa. Bond trading is therefore an endless crap game, with the players betting minute-by-minute on the future cost of money. The other players are hunched around similar trading desks in the world's financial capitals, from London to Hong Kong and points between. It's an auction market, just like a stock ex-

219

change – except that the traders, scattered around the planet, exchange their bids and offers on video-display terminals and dedicated long-distance phone lines.

A wrong guess in this game can cost the firm tens of thousands of dollars, perhaps hundreds of thousands. Cheesbrough's worst trade cost the firm about $50,000. He outbid several other firms for several million dollars' worth of bonds being offered by an insurance company, betting that interest rates would remain stable for a few days, and that he'd be able to resell them at a profit. "As it turned out," he says, "I'd bought them at the absolute high on the market, and it took several weeks to sell them to another client at the absolute low." The pressure is heavy and unrelenting, and traders tend to burn out early. Cheesbrough's oldest trader is 35. The youngest is 22. No school can equip a person for the job; you have to be born with the smarts. "When I'm hiring," says Cheesbrough, "I have a bias toward people who have played sports competitively. People who know what it is to win and lose. They probably like winning a hell of a lot better than losing, and they probably like to see their results fairly quickly. They're used to team playing, and they tend to have a fairly thick skin." Cheesbrough plays squash, tennis and hockey. He used to play in a Sunday-night hockey league that included teams from various investment houses. "The league had to be disbanded," he says, "because the games got so dirty."

The Best Game in Town

Underwriting and bond-trading are important activities for an investment house, but they're activities that the public never sees – private poker games played by members of highly sophisticated elites. But the best game in town is still the retail business – buying and selling stocks, bonds and other investment vehicles on behalf of individuals. For McLeod Young Weir, it's the side of their business that employs the most people and, in a good year, generates the most profit. When Austin Taylor assumed the presidency in 1978, one of his earliest decisions was to expand the sales staff. He knew that to compete with Wood Gundy and Dominion Securities, McLeod would have to match their manpower.

He brought Mike Edwards, a trusted colleague from the Vancouver office, to find, train and manage all these new troops. "When Austin took over," Edwards says, "the big three were Ames, Gundy and Dominion Securities. They were big because

220

they were important underwriters, plus they had large sales staffs, *and* the ability to distribute the issues they underwrote. You had to have one or the other to differentiate yourself, and McLeod had neither. Well, when you review the logic of the thing, it's impossible to develop one without developing the other. To get underwriting clout, you've got to have distribution, and vice versa."

In six years, McLeod went from 15 offices to 35, and from 80 salespeople to 350. It was a painstaking process. McLeod puts new sales employees through a rigorous, six-month training program, which includes classroom training, week-long apprenticeships in various departments and a touchie-feelie weekend seminar at a secluded holiday resort. Some emerge from the course so well-trained that they're immediately offered jobs by other firms.

McLeod Amid the Icebergs

It's a proud and seemingly impregnable institution. But Taylor and his fellow-directors knew how swiftly a firm the size of McLeod Young Weir can disappear. In the spring of 1984, with the stock market in the doldrums and commission revenues sinking, the firm was losing money – as much as $500,000 in a single week. All those bodies, all those offices, all those clever machines, all those overheads. It's difficult to maintain them if people and institutions aren't trading, and in the spring of 1984 it was especially difficult because the underwriting business, one of the firm's major sources of revenue, was being subjected to an unaccustomed bout of price-cutting competition. Tom Kierans sat immobilized in his office one afternoon, overseeing haggling session with a major Canadian corporation that wanted to raise a few hundred million dollars in new capital. In the good old days, the investment dealers would have competed on the grounds of service and performance – but would have charged a uniform 2 or 3 per cent of the sum raised. Now Kierans found himself battling with several other firms for a commission of less than one per cent. At that level, McLeod wouldn't even make money on the deal. But what can you do? Refuse to play at all?

As far as Taylor and his colleagues were concerned, salvation lay in an alliance with a foreign partner. A few years earlier, McLeod had sold 10 per cent of its treasury shares – the maximum allowed by law – to a foreign owner, Shearson American Express, in return for taking over Shearson's Canadian branch offices. Shearson/Amex is the product of a merger of a large Wall Street brokerage firm and the company famous for its traveller's cheques; by combining, they created an early model of the so-called "financial supermarket" – an all-purpose financial services organization which could trade your stocks, sell you traveller's cheques, pay you interest on your cash deposits and even sell you insurance, all from a single convenient account. For Shearson/Amex, owning 10 per cent of McLeod represented a toehold in Canada. For McLeod, the affiliation gave the Canadian firm direct access to Shearson/Amex's vast and knowledgable commodities-trading network.

But Taylor wanted a closer affiliation, even though it wasn't currently permitted under Canadian law. McLeod's best chance for long-term survival, he believed, was as a multinational corporation, competing on equal terms with the world's largest brokerage houses in London, New York, Tokyo – wherever in the world money is raised and people's savings are deployed.

Down the White-Water Canyon

And there the story stops. We leave one of Bay Street's older and more venerable firms plunging downhill through a white-water canyon, struggling to stay afloat; its present stormy, its future impossible to predict. Under Austin Taylor, McLeod Young Weir had already demonstrated its ability to transform itself in response to changing conditions.

If brains and determination and shrewdness were all it took to survive on Bay Street, the firm's future would be secure. But it also takes luck, and a continual supply of the right people at the right time. The directors of McLeod Young Weir, as they contemplated their firm's future one Saturday morning in spring, needed to look back only three years, back to the collapse of a venerable old firm called A.E. Ames, for a reminder of the perils that Bay Street reserves for the unwary and the unlucky.

15
A.E. Ames:
The Fall of a Mighty House

The remarkable thing about the investment firm of A.E. Ames & Co., now that it's gone, is the warmth and affection with which its former employees regard it. When they speak of the old firm, which began its corporate existence in 1889, it's as if they were recalling a great old ocean liner: huge and antiquated, probably unfit for service in the jet age; but a vessel with proud and lovely lines and mahogany cabins and art-deco dining rooms and gleaming brasswork and a crew which – until the power struggles began – worked together like brothers until the moment the ship went down.

Ames went down on August 1, 1981 when, after 92 years in business, it merged with Dominion Securities Ltd. Mergers between brokerage firms are almost as common on Bay Street as job-swaps in the advertising trade, but this merger was something special. It was as if Ford and Chrysler had joined forces to gang up on General Motors.

The merger created the largest firm in the Canadian securities industry, with $50 million in capital, 1,800 employees, and offices across the country and in financial capitals around the world. With as much underwriting firepower as the mighty Wood Gundy Ltd., and with 20 per cent more capital (which would allow it to participate in even bigger underwriting deals), DS-Ames seemed well equipped for the role of giant-killer. "This merger," said Tony Fell, the new firm's chairman, "is an aggressive move by two of the largest and most diversified firms . . . to combine their strengths and to capitalize on future opportunities."

Dissension and Desperation

Fell's confident words concealed the holes beneath the water-line. In fact, the merger was the product of division and desperation. If DS hadn't rescued the firm by absorbing it, Ames would have had to shut its doors within a matter of months. Its disappearance was the culmination of decades of mismanagement – or, more precisely, a peculiar species of anti-management. Its downfall cannot be attributed to any one individual so much as to the process by which its leaders were chosen.

Ames, like most firms on Bay Street, was owned by the senior people who worked there. No partner owned more than 5 per cent of the shares of the company, and most partners owned less than that. When a partner died or retired, his shares were sold back to the remaining partners, or resold to younger employees on their way up. This system was supposed to guarantee continuity of management and control, and it has worked well for many securities firms. It works especially well if there is a single dominant partner, or if there is a broad consensus among the partners about how the firm should be run and who should run it.

But at Ames, since the 1950s at least, the succession had been the subject of intrigue and dissension worthy of a Balkan dictatorship. The in-fighting weakened the company. So did the fact that, like every other securities firm, Ames suffered from a 20-year gap in its management ranks. Between 1929 and the end of World War II, running an investment firm was mostly a question of keeping the doors open and selling Victory bonds. The men who found themselves at the head of the firm in the 1950s had spent most of their careers merely surviving the Depression and the war. By the late 1950s and mid-1960s they were approaching retirement age, and – because of the management gap – there were few partners in their forties and fifties ready to succeed them.

Some Bay Street firms, confronted with the same management vacuum, responded appropriately. Charlie Gundy, when he was still young enough to be a decisive influence in Wood Gundy Ltd., appointed Bill Wilder as president of Wood Gundy in 1967, gave him a broad mandate to modernize the firm – and stayed around as chairman for 11 years to help him do it.

But at Ames during the 1960s and 1970s, there was never much pressure to change anything. In those days the firm was one of the country's most powerful and best respected financial institutions, and for the 20-odd senior partners who owned about 80 per cent of the firm, it was a seemingly inexhaustible money machine. Its trading operations spanned two continents. Governments and huge corporations sought its counsel and expertise to raise the money they needed for expansion. Some of those relationships – between Ames and the government of Quebec, between Ames and Bell Canada, between Ames and Moore Corp. – encompassed several generations of intimate and honorable dealings. The senior partners who handled those major accounts regarded them almost as their personal property. In good years, their share of the firm's profits might total more than $150,000, in addition to their salaries and the money they made by trading for their own accounts in stocks and bonds.

"That's where the blame lies," says one close observer of the company. "I think those guys should have said, 'Okay, we're going to retire; we've got to spend some money and build up the firm, not take it all out in dividends. And secondly, we've got to bring younger people up – we've got to set our own egos aside.' But those guys got to the point where their main strength was their connection with company A, B or C. And they felt that, so long as I've got that connection, I'm so important they can't do anything to me."

There had been indications for years that the firm was slipping. Successive management teams – and there were at least four of them in the firm's final decade – attempted to arrest the decline. But it wasn't until the last months that the bitterness and sense of failure spilled out of the boardroom to permeate the entire company. Until almost the very end, Ames continued to be a wonderful place to work, an enclave of kindness and fair dealing and good manners. "The atmosphere was one of anything but competence in terms of planning, organizing, reviewing, motivating," says one Ames veteran. "But the people were open and decent and good to you. Many of them had never worked anywhere else. And, you know, they really loved each other." Years of inflation and rising markets had insulated this band of brothers from a sense of its own vulnerability; the money was still rolling in, and only a few malcontents insisted on pointing out that the firm was being overtaken by its competitors.

The Only Acceptable Solution

And so, when the end came, it seemed to come suddenly. Late in 1980, the latest management team was grappling, in its amiable way, with the problems in the back office and the bond department – problems that were bleeding the company of the cash it needed to survive. If the stock market had continued to soar, the team members might eventually have solved the problems and Ames might have continued to roll on as before. But the market stalled, the firm's revenues shrank and, almost before anyone realized it, extinction was staring them in the face. The only acceptable alternative to bankruptcy was a gentlemanly merger with Ames's ancient and respected rival, Dominion Securities.

A Huge And Venerable Firm

In its 92 years of doing business, Ames had reflected and, to a large extent, participated in and influenced the economic development of the country. Although Ames had prospered for generations as an advisor, money-raiser and handmaiden to large Canadian businesses, it refused to behave like a modern business itself. Its management style, even as late as the 1970s, was essentially Victorian. In an era when the Canadian banks were transforming themselves into powerful multinational corporations and invading the traditional territory of the large investment houses, when capital markets around the world were attracting the fiercest and brightest minds from the business schools, when the competition for underwriting accounts grew more savage and sophisticated than ever before, when the large competitors were running their firms as aggressive outposts of the Harvard Business School – in such a perilous era, Ames saw nothing incongruous about maintaining one of the country's last surviving executive washrooms, with special keys that were issued to the senior partners. "There were fresh bars of Pears soap in little trays, there were bottles of mouthwash on the shelf in front of the mirror, and little cloth towels that you'd throw into a bin when you'd finished drying your hands," says a former Ames executive, marvelling at the recollection. "It was just like the Toronto Club – except that, for some reason nobody could understand, there were no urinals."

Perhaps the most telling epitaph for Ames was pronounced by Peter Harris, the firm's second-to-last president, a man who looks like a duke, lives like a country squire, rides like a prince and made himself unpopular among many of his colleagues at Ames. Trotting out some of the Latin he learned at Upper Canada College, Harris quotes Cicero's remark about an unfortunate friend: "Idem manabat neque idem decebat" – "He remained the same, but the same was no longer fitting."

But the fall of the House of Ames is more than the story of a single firm failing to change with the times. Its disappearance

226

signified a decisive shift in the way Bay Street goes about its business. It marked the final triumph of professionalism in the securities industry. Today, Bay Street's large investment houses are run like large companies selling a specialized range of services, which is exactly what they are. In such a merciless environment, performance is everything.

For many members of the brotherhood, the downfall of Ames was a personal tragedy from which some will never fully recover. For others it was merely a financial disaster. They'd borrowed heavily to buy Ames shares and the status which such ownership conferred; suddenly, their shares were worth almost nothing and their status consisted only of their skills and contacts and reputations. Some Ames old boys have done quite nicely since the merger. Others find themselves sitting at metal desks in lonely little offices where the phone seldom rings, calling themselves consultants and wondering what to do with the rest of their lives. And for Peter Harris, a principal actor in the drama, it meant simply that the ordered progress of his life – everything he'd planned and hoped for since his days at Upper Canada – was blasted apart.

But for the system as a whole, the downfall of Ames meant only that capitalism was still working as it will: rewarding the bold, remorselessly penalizing the less efficient, elevating some contestants, tossing others on the scrapheap and, in the process, constantly regenerating itself. That is the league in which Ames always played, the ethic in which it professed to believe. The tragedy is that all those years of successful dealing had made the firm a self-contained vessel of prosperity and human warmth – an environment so comforting that it was easy to forget about the icebergs that were always out there somewhere, looming up in menace and majesty beyond the rolling banks of fog.

Family Ties

It is striking, when one contemplates the long history of A.E. Ames & Co., to note how often the firm seems to have been dominated by men who married money. Ames himself started his business in 1889, just after marrying the daughter of one of Canada's reigning financiers, George Albertus Cox. F.J. Coombs, who started with the firm in 1895, typing letters and cleaning inkwells for $16.60 a month, married Ames's daughter and was a dominant figure in the firm until his retirement in 1951. Roy L. Warren, who joined the firm in 1916 and was chairman when he died in 1965, married an oil heiress named Jessie Rogers. Peter Harris's rise to the presidency was not impeded by the fact that he married Taddy, the daughter of Brig.-Gen. Bruce Matthews, an Argus Corporation director and a leading figure in the Toronto Establishment. Even today, although they are no substitute for performance, family capital and family connections still count in the securities business. But in the 1890s, when Canada's financial community consisted of a handful of closely held banks, brokerage houses and insurance companies, family ties were almost everything.

Ames, the son of a Methodist minister, grew up in a parson's manse in the village of Lambeth, near London, Ontario, and, at the age of 15, went to work for the Merchants Bank of Canada in Owen Sound. He joined the Ontario Bank in Mount Forest, Ontario, soon afterward and, by 1889, was running a branch of the Imperial Bank in Lindsay. That same year he married Mary Cox, whose family came from nearby Peterborough. There is nothing like having several million dollars in the family to encourage entrepreneurship; and so, at the age of 23, Ames quit the bank, moved to Toronto, settled into a house on Sherbourne Street next door to his new in-laws and, on December 1, 1889, with an office boy as his only employee, opened his own business in a storefront office on King Street West.

His first partner, F.W. Scott, died at the age of 37 in 1898. The following year, Ames made partners of two young employees, E.D. Fraser and R.H. Tudhope. Before the century ended, the firm arranged its first private placements of shares, raising $1 million for the newly formed Imperial Life Assurance Company and $1 million for the National Trust Company. Both companies were controlled by Senator Cox, who by this time was also president of the Canadian Bank of Commerce, president of Canada Life Assurance Company, a director of about 50 other companies and one of Canada's richest and most powerful men.

Senator Cox's money and influence came in handy in 1903, when a stock market plunge left the 14-year-old firm on the brink of insolvency. The senator and his companies stepped in to bail out Ames with a carefully concealed loan from Canada Life for $389,500, though it wasn't enough to save the firm from temporary failure. A.E. Ames closed its doors on June 2, 1903, the victim, according to one newspaper account, of "an overload of securities carried in a declining market." This stock market plunge was known as the "rich man's panic" because it was not accompanied by a general business depression. But it must have felt like a depression to Ames. There were six weeks of frantic behind-the-scenes efforts to re-establish the firm, and on July 13 it reopened for business, its creditors mollified and its future once again guaranteed by large infusions of Cox money. By 1905 the creditors had all been repaid in full.

Propelled by Cox's money, a booming economy and the founder's growing influence, the firm once again prospered, moving several times to successively larger quarters in the environs of King and Bay Streets. There was a selling panic in 1907 that was even worse than the one in 1903, but Ames, tempered by the adversities of four years before, weathered it handily. When Bay Street went to war in 1914, the situation was regarded as regrettable but not, on the whole, devoid of positive aspects. The bloodshed in the trenches was undeniably good for business. Ames's son-in-law, F.J. Coombs, in a 1938 speech, recalled those years on the home front with what almost sounded like fondness: "All the essentials of a bull market were present and there were recurrent outbreaks of fierce buying. This was little wonder, in the face of reports by many companies of profits three to six times the normal figure."

For the securities industry, there was an added benefit: Canadians by the millions learned about buying bonds. Until 1914, British lenders had financed more than 70 per cent of the public works and railway construction that were the underpinnings of the great prewar boom. After 1914, the government turned to Wall Street for money to finance the war – and to patriotic Canadians, who delighted Bay Street and the government by buying undreamed-of quantities of bonds. Between 1915 and 1919, they loaned their government nearly $2.5 billion – an astonishing amount from a nation of under 10 million people. Before 1914, there were fewer than 5,000 Canadian bondholders; by the end of the war, more than a million Canadians had discovered the joys of compound interest. If you're a bond dealer, that's a lot of potential customers. It is not surprising that one of Ames's best-remembered acts of public service was his chairmanship of the Dominion executive committee for the 1917 Victory Bond campaign.

After a deflationary pause in 1920 and 1921, the greatest boom of all began. Ames, with branch offices in London, New York, Montreal and Victoria, participated fully in the prosperity of the jazz age.

When Ames died in 1934, at the bottom of the Depression, the obituaries were fulsome. *The Financial Post*, recalling how the firm had gone broke in 1903, observed: "Most bankruptcies would have cancelled the debts which this firm then assumed. The obligations were moral, not legal. That is why the name of A.E. Ames has become a tradition for honor in business and why it will remain an inspiration to new generations of financial men." The funeral service was held at Ames's vast estate in east-end Toronto (it had its own nine-hole golf course), with most of Toronto's financial Establishment in attendance, and floral tributes arriving from the likes of the Granite and National Clubs, the Royal Bank of Canada, the Toronto Stock Exchange and someone called Princess Jennie Chikhmatoff. At Ames's request, there was no eulogy. But the presence of high officials from the United Church of Canada and Victoria College testified to his many benefactions. Both his children had died before him; his son only a few weeks before.

H.R. Tudhope, who had been an Ames partner since 1902, became president after Ames's death. Tudhope and Ames, with the memories of 1903 still fresh, had steered a conservative investment course through the 1920s. When the crash came, Tudhope swiftly and ruthlessly sold out the firm's margined clients – people who had borrowed money from the firm to buy stock. Thus, at a time when dozens of brokers and investment firms were closing their doors, and when even Wood Gundy was being run by its bankers, Ames sailed through the 1930s in a state of enviable solvency.

Tudhope piloted the firm through 10 years of depression and six years of war, when 61 Ames staffers served in the armed forces and those who remained at home sold Victory Bonds. "All you see, right from my desk, is girls and more girls," wrote one Ames staffer in 1944 to a colleague serving in Italy. Tudhope retired as president in 1949, to be replaced for two years by another partner, C.E. Abbs.

The Best Years

The firm didn't really enter the postwar era until 1951, when Roy Warren, who had been with the firm since 1916, became president. He'd begun his career with the Metropolitan Bank, which later merged with the Bank of Nova Scotia, and started out at Ames as a bond salesman. He became an Ames director in 1928, and when H.R. Tudhope retired in 1957, Warren succeeded him as chairman. Warren was cautious, shrewd and powerful. "He was a dealmaker," says his son Roger, who spent 19 years with Ames. "He just had that sixth instinct for market values. And he knew how to use his connections." He was a close friend of Ontario Premier Leslie Frost and, it was said, could get C.D. Howe on the phone any time he wanted.

"In those days," says one Ames veteran, "the industry was dominated by a handful of men who had capital. Warren had capital, partly because his wife was one of the Rogers, and he was smart enough not to lose it in 1929."

Warren's counterpart in Montreal – and his bitter rival – was F.D. (Doug) Chapman, a financier who ran Ames's Montreal office as his personal fief. Chapman was one of the legends of the industry. His contacts, his forbidding manner, his seemingly effortless ability to raise large amounts of money for his clients, made him at least as powerful in the firm as Warren himself. "He was a guru, a giant of the industry," says one of his former colleagues. In the 1950s, Montreal was still at least as important a financial community as Toronto, and Chapman, who didn't speak French, was one of its leading members. One of his major clients was the government of Quebec, for which Chapman routinely floated bond issues worth hundreds of millions of dollars. His best-remembered coup came in 1962, when Premier Jean Lesage and his Natural Resources Minister, René Lévesque, bought out 11 Quebec power companies, including the haughty Shawinigan Water and Power Co. Ltd. Wall Street, naturally, cried socialism when the deal was announced, but Chapman effectively silenced the province's critics by raising $300 million for Hydro-Quebec to finance the takeover. He did it in a matter of days – and he raised it on Wall Street.

These were the firm's best years. Ames, Wood Gundy and Dominion Securities were the holy trinity that dominated Canadian finance. In that pre-inflationary period, large companies used the banks only for their short-term financing needs. The larger, long-term projects were paid for by issuing stocks or bonds. The investment houses which sold those issues to the public, or to large financial institutions such as insurance companies and pension funds, were central to the growth of the economy. And the men in the investment houses who controlled those corporate accounts, the men who settled the terms of a bond issue over lunch with a corporate treasurer at the Toronto or St. James Club – well, those men were mighty financial powers in their own right. The accounts they controlled through their charm, their contacts and their expertise were the basis of their power and status and self-assurance.

Chapman's clients included the CPR, the Bank of Montreal, Bell Canada, CIL and the Aluminium Company of Canada. His clients were his cronies. Once a year he'd go on a salmon-fishing trip down the Ste. Marguerite's River, a waterway that was virtually owned by his client, Alcan. The party usually included several high Alcan officials, a few priests from Arvida (the town's name was a contraction of the name of Alcan's founder, Arthur Vining Davis), a troupe of guides and, more than once, a premier of Quebec. On one such trip, Jean Lesage dismayed his hosts by telling the guides he'd see to it that their wages were doubled; Alcan's vice-president, Edmond Eberts, got his revenge by depriving Lesage of several hundred dollars in a poker game at Alcan's riverside lodge.

School Ties

In Toronto, each of the Ames senior partners had similar corporate accounts which they seemed to regard almost as their personal property. Warren himself managed the Union Gas account. (Utilities and banks were always especially coveted as clients, since they had to raise new capital continually.) Other partners handled such plums as Moore Corp., Stelco, Dominion Foundries and Consumers Gas, some of which were shared with other investment houses. "It was a club atmosphere," recalls Don Foyston, a former partner. "The school tie meant a lot. Connections and loyalty were what mattered. That's how business was done – connections, more than the abilities that became required as the business and competition developed."

By the late 1950s, the weaknesses of this old-boy system were becoming apparent. As older partners reached retirement age, their prized underwriting accounts tended to depart with them, or be divided with other investment houses. Worse still, some of the corporate treasurers with whom Ames partners had been lunching for decades started retiring too; and the men who took their places had no stake in the chummy relationships that had prevailed among their elders. Also, as companies tried to raise larger and larger sums of money, it became more common to divide the business between two or more firms, since none was large enough to handle the entire issue alone. The old patterns of exclusivity were breaking down.

So were the old patterns of brotherhood and loyalty. The intercity cold war between Warren and Chapman intensified. "That was one of the unfortunate things that happened," says Don Foyston. "It caused senior people to have to take sides." When Warren stepped up from president to chairman in 1957, the partners attempted to heal the rift by bringing Chapman to Toronto as president, and naming another contender for the president's job, Jack Ridley, to the newly created post of executive vice-president. Recalls Peter Harris: "It was said at the time, 'Poor Warren. If he chooses Ridley as president he'll lose

232

all his clients; and if he appoints Chapman he'll lose all his staff." This uneasy troika lasted for less than a year. Chapman disliked Toronto almost as much as he disliked Roy Warren. He spent his entire term as president living in a suite at the Royal York Hotel and commuting back to his Montreal home on the weekends. Then, in the late 1950s and early 1960s, a number of key partners retired, including Ridley, James Fullerton, Douglas Wood, Mac Stewart and Howard Leeming. The generation that had run Ames since the 1930s was finally departing. Behind them they left a divided firm, with no dominant figure available to reconcile the factions that were developing.

During the 1960s, which saw the greatest bull market since the war, Ames was led by a succession of less than memorable partners. But these were the go-go years, and Ames was making too much money to worry about the deepening problems of succession. Bill Spragge, Bruce West and Jim Hughes attempted to provide leadership, but were troubled by ill-health. Spragge had a heart attack; West was ill during much of his tenure as chairman and chief executive officer. "None of these guys was out chasing business," says one veteran of this period. "The place was in a state of suspended animation."

A Shattering Decision

The extent of the divisions within the firm became apparent to outsiders in 1972, the year of what is still remembered as The Kaiser Episode. In 1969, Ames had done an underwriting for a new company, Kaiser Resources Ltd., a U.S.-controlled firm which planned to develop its extensive coal properties in southeastern British Columbia. Some of Kaiser's American executives had set up their own private company, KRL Investments Ltd., to hold shares in the new Canadian entity. Bill Macdonald, who'd become president of Ames in 1967 and had worked for months to bring the Kaiser deal together, had been assured by Kaiser's lawyer that there could be no legal objection to the private company. Unfortunately, there was; the Ames prospectus stated – not quite correctly – that Ames would not sell Kaiser shares to U.S. residents, since the issue had not been cleared by the U.S. Securities and Exchange Commission.

The stock, which came onto the market at $12, climbed as high as $22.25 and, after the company encountered technical problems in developing its coal mine, fell below $4 by 1971. Before the stock collapsed, however, some of the Kaiser insiders sold their shares and reaped large profits. *The Wall Street Journal* broke the story, the SEC started investigating and the Ontario Securities Commission held hearings to discipline those responsible.

The OSC's final decision, in 1972, was to suspend Bill Macdonald's trading privileges for a week and to reprimand another Ames partner, Ron Gunn. It was only a slap on the wrist. Macdonald's transgression was narrowly technical, and he hadn't profited personally from the Kaiser deal – in fact, he'd lost money because he and his wife had bought Kaiser shares and hung on to them. Macdonald's only motive had been to avoid the expense of getting the issue approved by the American regulatory authorities. If he could be criticized for anything, it was for failing to consult Ames's own lawyers about the deal. But for a firm like Ames, which prided itself on a long and unblemished record of integrity, the effect of the OSC decision was shattering.

A few weeks later, Jim Hughes, the firm's chairman, scheduled a meeting of the partners one morning to discuss "communications." Macdonald came to the meeting in the innocent belief that they were going to discuss telephone switchboards or something. Instead, he discovered that the meeting was about communication among the partners. Macdonald looked on aghast as Hughes, sitting at the head of the boardroom table, asked each partner in turn whether he thought Macdonald should remain as president of the firm. One by one, with various qualifications, each partner said no. Peter Harris was the last to be asked. "I remember the terrible dilemma I found myself in," recalls Harris. "I'd always been pretty close to Macdonald, and now the trigger was being pulled at my head. So I replied that if four partners didn't think the relationship was going to work – well, then, it wasn't going to work." That was the end of Macdonald's presidency. A few weeks later he announced his "retirement" at the age of 61. Instead of shielding and supporting him, his partners threw him out.

The Kaiser incident illustrated the weaknesses of the system by which Ames selected, and occasionally rejected, its leaders. The system was supposed to operate by consensus; since most senior partners each owned between 3 and 7 per cent of the firm's shares, their powers were theoretically equal. In practice, however, the outgoing partners had a major say in choosing their successors. It was natural, of course, for a departing chairman or president to want to leave the firm in good hands, but since retiring directors customarily sold their shares to the remaining partners – who in turn resold them to new people rising in the firm – it meant that the firm's future was, to a disproportionate extent, influenced by people who no longer had a stake in it.

In order for such a system to function securely, a firm must be consistently profitable. The profits ensure that the retiring partners can sell their shares for more than they paid for them. The profits also create dividends, with which the younger partners can pay off the money they must borrow to buy into the company. The strength of the system is the sense of commitment it generates. Dozens, or even hundreds, of employees-partners have a direct financial stake in the company's profitability. The weakness, in the case of Ames, was the power this system gave to departing directors – men who, by and large, had demonstrated a greater interest in protecting the capital they'd built up than in ensuring the company's future. The system also bred an unhealthy tolerance of partners who weren't pulling their weight. If you fired a partner, it meant you had to buy his shares – a purchase which, in some years, the remaining partners could ill-afford. In the view of some Ames partners, the system's weakness was vividly demonstrated by the rapid rise of Peter Harris.

Everything about Peter Harris proclaimed the presence of quiet, old money. He has a long, aristocratic face – the kind of face you'd see at a hunt breakfast at a country house in Suffolk or in the member's lobby at the House of Lords, or looking out at you from the pages of *Country Life*. His impeccable manners, his impeccable shirts, the impeccable silk handkerchief in his breast pocket – they were all impeccably, impossibly English. He had an air of effortless assurance that made one think of proud racehorses, of wide lawns dappled by the shade of fine old elms.

But Peter Harris was not what he seemed. The languid manner disguised a furious ambition. The chain-smoking, the nervous mannerisms, suggested unconquered inner furies. The smell of old money was acquired, not inborn.

Peter Harris's father, a Toronto insurance man of modest but comfortable means, deserted his family when Harris was 16. The son didn't hear from him again – "not so much as a postcard" – until he was 41. His mother, a law graduate of the University of Toronto who never practised, scrimped to keep her son at Upper Canada College. But even before he went to school, when he was five or six years old, Peter Harris fell in love with riding. By the time he was a teenager he was one of Toronto's better young equestrians. Through the sport he met the sons and daughters of the monied old Toronto families who kept horses at estates in Caledon and King City. Without ever attending university, he joined Ames in 1954 at the age of 19, the master plan of his life already beginning to form in his mind. "From almost the beginning of my career," he says, "I was attracted by the prospect of being a partner in a small, high-quality securities firm. And if I chose to go that route, I knew that my seniority at Ames would have been a good jumping-off point."

In 1972, Bill Macdonald named Harris as executive vice-president, an appointment that surprised and dismayed some of their colleagues. Harris was in his mid-thirties when he was plucked from his job as head of the stock department and placed firmly on the fast track. But there seemed to be plenty of other, equally well-qualified people of about the same age. So why was Harris chosen? Everyone knew that he was the son-in-law of a director of Argus Corp., and the scuttlebutt around Ames was that he'd been chosen because the senior partners hoped to attract some Argus business. Harris indignantly rejects the suggestion: "I think that is atrociously unfair. The General was a mentor and a great civilizing influence in my life. Undoubtedly, because of who he was, I knew some people I might not otherwise have known. But to suggest that he would direct business to a son-in-law is to misunderstand completely the ethics of that man." Ames did, in fact, become co-manager of the underwritings of one or two Argus-controlled companies.

He and his wife, Taddy, lived in a magnificent restored farmhouse in Uxbridge, northeast of Toronto, on a property where their horses and dogs and children – the three main interests in Taddy's life – could live graciously and expansively. They were members of the local hunt club – foxhounds, scarlet tunics, silver stirrup cups – and, in 1968, Harris was chairman of the Canadian equestrian team which won a gold medal at the Mexico City Olympics.

Like his father-in-law, Harris was a member of the Toronto Club, and he used it frequently for business lunches. And although he mentioned it to no one at Ames, Harris had a dream. The General's uncle had founded a well-regarded brokerage house called Matthews & Co. It was small but exclusive, and its list of clients included some of Toronto's oldest and wealthiest families. Harris felt justified in hoping that some day, after he'd proved himself as president of Ames, he could step into the top spot at Matthews & Co., whose management wasn't getting any younger.

Harris's lifestyle was in marked contrast to that of most of his Ames colleagues. In spite of its historical roots and venerable reputation, Ames was *not* a blue-blooded firm. There were no Oslers or Masseys or Gooderhams or Strathys in its ranks. Ames staffers, typically, tended to be hard-working men who'd grown up in small towns, with no social credentials to speak of. Unlike Harris and Roy Warren, few of them had access to family money. If they were chosen as partners, they had to borrow to buy their shares. Those shares became their pension plan; and few Ames partners, after they retired, lived grandly. Ames people, by and large, were comfortable but not rich. They tended to live in houses that were respectable but seldom stately. Their children usually attended public schools, as had their fathers. They were nice, normal, middle-class people. Says one former Ames executive: "When it came to being well-connected, either to the grand old families of Toronto or to the *Harvard Business Review* types that Bill Wilder [of Wood Gundy] knew – no! I was really surprised by the lack of – I hate to use the term – of well-connected people in the firm."

Whatever Peter Harris was, he was not middle-class; and "nice" is not a word his former partners often choose to describe him. "To characterize Peter," says a former colleague, "I would have to use a word I hate using, but I've heard Peter use it himself. The man was a thruster. He wanted to get ahead. He could be charming and attentive if he wanted something from you. But once a person had outlived his usefulness to Peter, he kind of moved on. I don't know if he even realized he was doing this."

Once Harris had been named EVP, his elevation to the presidency was only a question of time. Jim Hughes remained as chairman for two years after Macdonald's departure, then retired himself in 1975. Macdonald's replacement as president was E. Cameron Lipsit, who had been Chapman's understudy in the Montreal office. Everybody loved Cam Lipsit, which is one way of saying he wasn't a tough administrator. Like Chapman, he remained in Montreal during his first months as president. At the same time, he also took on the chairmanship of the Investment Dealers Association of Canada – a demanding double assignment which, his friends say, helped to break his health. Almost incapacitated and deeply depressed by a serious stomach ailment, Lipsit in 1975 stepped up to the less demanding post of chairman. His replacement as president and chief executive officer was Peter Harris.

On Harris's first day as president, as he settled into his big office on the third floor of 320 Bay Street, Jim Hughes, the retired chairman, walked in to greet the new boy: "Good morning, Mr. Personnel Manager," is what Hughes said. Notes Harris: "He was very prescient about the problems I was going to face." The management ranks were thin and getting thinner. There were too many grey heads and too many drop-outs among promising younger executives. Two men who had been regarded as presidential material, Ken Murton and Ron Gunn, had left the firm soon after Harris was made executive vice-president. And their departure, along with the firm's other problems, amounted to a personnel crisis.

Meanwhile, the firm's business reverses were becoming the subject of comment on Bay Street. The Quebec government, in an attempt to inject a less Anglified flavor into its financial dealings, in 1976 fired Ames as its fiscal agents. It appointed several Francophone firms as replacements – but Wood Gundy, Ames's arch-rival, also muscled its way into the syndicate which had once been an exclusive Ames preserve. The new Tory government of Newfoundland, in 1972, had also fired Ames as its chief money-raiser. Worst of all, Wood Gundy had been named joint underwriter with Ames on the coveted Bell Canada account, which formerly had been an exclusive Ames client. Harris had to play catch-up ball, and he needed help to do it.

He plunged into the task of modernizing the company, even though a riding accident soon after his appointment left him with a broken arm and shoulder. One facet of his strategy was to rebuild the firm's strength as a distributor of stocks and bonds, in order to increase its power as an underwriter. In other words, Harris needed more retail customers to buy the issues he wanted to sell. That's why Ames bought an old-line brokerage house in London, Ontario, and another in Halifax. That's also why Ames bought Matthews & Co. soon after Harris became president. This was the firm founded by his father-in-law's uncle, the firm that Harris had for years dreamed of leading some day. But when its aging partners approached him to suggest a merger as an alternative to winding up the business, Harris had to swallow his ambition, and his tongue, and tell his partners he thought the merger would be a wonderful idea. He'd given Jim Hughes a commitment that he'd stay as president of Ames for at least five years; he couldn't jump ship early, even for so tempting a prize as the chairmanship of Matthews & Co. "For me," says Harris, "that was a heartbreak. I had to let on to my partners that [absorbing Matthews] was a source of satisfaction. But it shattered a dream."

Harris's game-plan was showing flaws in other areas. He was working frantically to modernize the firm, but the stuffy old organization was not responding as quickly as he'd hoped.

He hired a firm of management consultants to advise the company on updating its computer system. He built up Ames's money-market business, buying and selling currencies on behalf of clients and of the firm itself. He fought harder for underwriting accounts, and managed to get Ames included in some syndicates which formerly had been the exclusive territory of rival firms. The Wood Gundy accounts which Ames came to share included Texaco, Dupont, the Royal Bank of Canada, Massey Ferguson and the Thomson interests.

But two mundane problems, the ones that were crippling the firm most directly, resisted solution. The first was the bond department, the second the back office. The main difficulty with the bond department was that it wasn't very good at trading bonds. The company had had a successful track record as a bond house for most of the century; but in the inflationary 1970s, when interest rates rose and bond prices correspondingly declined, Ames's traders couldn't seem to get the hang of the volatile new trading style that the times demanded. The firm's bond-trading profits were declining steadily. "We had two generations of bond traders brought up to trade our way," says Harris, "and it was difficult to change."

The "back office" – the department which is supposed to keep track of clients' accounts, and of the disposition of the millions of dollars' worth of securities that are bought and sold every day – was an even worse mess. The firm's business had expanded greatly during the 1970s: more salesmen, more customers, more trades, more transactions. But this enlarged operation was still served, increasingly inadequately, by a back-office operation which hadn't changed fundamentally for a generation. Quite simply, Ames did not know at any given moment where a lot of its money was. The firm's patrimony was out on the street somewhere, in the form of bills unpaid, in share certificates being shuffled between Bay Street offices by aged messengers, in uncleared transactions awaiting processing on people's overloaded desks.

It was the sort of problem that the banks and trust companies solved during the 1970s by massive investments in skilled personnel and new technology, but there was virtually no one at Ames who understood such matters, or much wanted to. Says one former Ames director: "I think Peter tried in his own way, in a very sincere fashion, to impose modern-day management techniques on the firm. But he didn't know the first goddam thing about it." Even Harris concurs in part in this assessment. "Administratively, we were like 14-year-olds. The administrative structure hadn't changed since Tudhope's time. The firm was still being run as it had been when it was one-quarter its size. I made a very bad mistake in judgment in underestimating the importance of the operational side of the business. I had a sense of the back-office problems, but I didn't act forcefully enough to correct them. I had no background that would have prepared me for dealing with those kind of problems – and I should have had."

Between 1974 and 1977, when the stock market was in the doldrums and no one on the street was making any money to speak of, Ames had managed to maintain its profitability. But in later years, the firm's weaknesses began to be reflected on the bottom line. More than one ex-partner has compared these years to what happens when you brake a freight train. At first, nothing happens; and then the train shudders suddenly to a halt. By 1979, the shuddering was apparent to anyone who owned shares in the firm. "The Street was out there making money," says Bob Bellamy, who was to become Ames's last president, "and we were doing a pile of business – and *not* making money." In the fiscal year ending March 31, 1980, Ames earned only $196,000 after taxes; the year before it had earned more than three times as much. Midland Doherty, a firm of roughly the same size, earned about $8 million in the same period. There was nothing abstract about these figures. Many of Ames's 240-odd employee-shareholders needed large dividends to pay off their bank loans; and suddenly, at a time when all their friends in rival firms were rolling in wealth, those large dividends were not forthcoming.

Something clearly was wrong. The triumvirate that was running the firm – Harris as president, Lipsit as chairman and Paul Fisher as executive vice-president – wasn't producing the profits the partners needed. And so, through that mysterious process of consensus and compromise that no one at Ames could adequately explain, it was decided in 1979 to appoint Lipsit vice-chairman, elevate Harris from president to chairman and appoint Bob Bellamy, who'd been running the corporate finance department, as president. The three-man executive committee was also enlarged to seven. Bellamy, a large, friendly man, had no illusions about the magnitude of the firm's problems. "The perception was abroad internally that the existing leadership of the firm wasn't functioning effectively," says Bellamy. "I was chosen as president because I had rapport with the different factions. Also, my background was not unimportant. It's not unusual to pick a president who's used to dealing with your major accounts."

Suddenly, as the freight train slowed down, the men responsible for running the company began to feel a sense of urgency. The back-office problems caught up with them in the spring of 1980. When the auditors totalled up the firm's assets and liabilities for the fiscal year, they discovered what no one else at Ames had noticed – the firm was dangerously close to a capital deficiency; so much Ames money was out floating on the street that the firm had come close to dropping below the minimum capital requirements set by the Investment Dealers Association. Don Foyston, who had been appointed EVP along with Paul Fisher when Bellamy became president, was responsible for the back office; after the capital shortage was discovered, he was swiftly made to understand that his performance was deemed inadequate. "I wouldn't say he was fired," says Bellamy, "but his position became untenable." Foyston had been with Ames for 26 years. The time was past for nice-guy management.

In the summer of 1980, Ames hired George Currie, a management consultant, as an administrative psychoanalyst. Currie had resigned as president of FP Publications when the newspaper chain was bought by the Thomson interests, and he had time on his hands. Harris, meanwhile, was feeling increasingly unhappy and increasingly isolated as chairman. He'd begun confiding to some partners that he didn't want or expect to be around Ames forever. He was overworked and miserable. "I was increasingly unhappy. I was doing nothing but work. My relationship with Taddy was slipping away. Life had taken twists that I hadn't planned or counted on."

His relationships with his partners also deteriorated. In August 1980, when Ottawa developer Robert Campeau launched a takeover bid for one of the country's most powerful financial institutions, Royal Trustco, he asked Ames to act as his financial advisor. Bellamy and Lipsit wanted to accept, but Harris fiercely opposed the connection; Royal Trustco was at the core of a financial elite which regarded Campeau as an outsider and an upstart. Says Harris: "We were in no position to start tackling one of the high temples of the Establishment. There was no sense in alienating them." The disagreement ended one weekend in an acrimonious session in Bob Bellamy's living room. Harris says he was accused of "lacking the necessary instinct for the jugular." Campeau proceeded with his takeover bid, using another firm as financial advisor. As Harris had predicted, the Establishment, including the Toronto Dominion Bank and Olympia & York Developments, closed ranks to shut out Campeau, by buying enough Royal Trustco shares to defeat his bid.

241

After the confrontation in Bellamy's living room, Harris took a week's holiday. When he returned in September, Currie came to him to report on his investigation into the firm's problems. The main problem, it seemed, was Peter Harris. Currie told him that the partners were increasingly unhappy with his leadership, that they found him aloof and autocratic. Harris replied: "George, that makes it very easy. It's better that I go now." He began making arrangements for a graceful year-end departure. Then, with his marriage collapsing, Harris phoned his old friend Chris Barron and was offered another job, as managing partner of Cassels Blaikie – a small, high-quality, old-line investment firm, founded in 1877, with an exclusive list of wealthy clients; a firm very much like the one he'd always wanted to lead. Harris sold his stock in Ames to the remaining partners, according to the then-prevailing formula, for about $33 per share and, at the end of the year, walked out the door for the last time. He'd spent 27 years at Ames; the shares and debentures he'd sold back to the firm fetched about $700,000.

The remaining partners named Currie as president and Bellamy as chairman. Paul Fisher remained as EVP. By now, in the opening weeks of 1981, the firm's deepening problems were common knowledge on the street. The stock market was still soaring, the firm's commission's revenues were still rolling in, but Ames was barely breaking even. It was obvious to Bellamy and Lipsit that the buoyant stock market was due for a correction. And if that happened, and the firm's revenues declined before the senior people had a chance to perform corrective surgery, the company would be in deep, perhaps terminal, trouble. But the partners had a plan, including installation of an improved computer system, which they hoped would correct the back-office problems by the end of March. Barbara MacDougall, one of the few women with executive status at Ames, recalls being asked by Bellamy how long she thought it would take to turn the firm around. MacDougall thought it might take a couple of years. "No, you're not even close," replied Bellamy. "If we can't do it in six months, we aren't going to do it at all."

Bay Street runs on rumor, gossip and, occasionally, hard fact. It thus came as no surprise when, one day in January 1981, Tony Fell, the president of Dominion Securities, phoned Bellamy and asked to drop around for a chat. Fell came to the point quickly: Would Ames possibly be interested in a merger? DS had had a couple of fat years and was in an expansionist mood. "We had a good, frank chat," says Bellamy, "and it was left that we'd think about it. I didn't think we were ready to make a move, but it was certainly on our minds."

In mid-March, the senior shareholders – Bellamy, Lipsit, Fisher and Mel Binnington, but not George Currie – met to consider their position. They knew that Ames was running out of time and money. To buy more time, the firm needed a fast infusion of capital. The partners believed they could find people willing to buy either a minority or a majority interest in the firm, but at distress-sale prices. The only other alternative, short of closing the doors, was an honorable, face-saving merger. The best marriage partner, they agreed, was Dominion Securities, which was roughly equal in size, and was strong in the areas where Ames was weak. And so the courtship dance began.

DS shared Ames's ethical approach to the business, and even shared the same historical roots. It had been founded in 1901 as a bond house by the same Senator Cox whose son-in-law had founded Ames. At the time of the proposed merger it was Canada's second largest investment house. Ames was third. Together, they calculated, they would constitute, with Wood Gundy, the industry's two kingpins.

Mergers are part of Bay Street's tradition. They are not regarded as cataclysmic events, but as part of the normal process of evolution and growth. Historically, the securities industry has developed like a colony of cells in a petrie dish: Some organisms enlarge themselves by swallowing their neighbors; or a new organism may split off from its parent and grow by initiating the swallowing process itself. Dominion Securities was the product of several mergers. In the 1970s alone it had absorbed two old-line Bay Street firms, Draper Dobie Ltd. and Harris and Partners.

The negotiations lasted through April and May, and were conducted in great secrecy in Paul Fisher's apartment and in a series of hotel rooms. There was little haggling over money; most of the negotiations consisted of what one of the participants delicately called "people problems" – figuring out, that is, who at Ames would be let go and who would be allowed to remain. Ames had about 800 employees, DS about 900. Both sides knew that the merged firm could operate effectively with about 1,350 to 1,400 people, after the closure of duplicate offices in various cities. That meant laying off at least 300 people, including about 50 professionals: traders, securities analysts and salespeople. "That was considered to be quite manageable," says Bellamy.

The people problems were painful and protracted, and the negotiations over price were simple by comparison. The two sides agreed to conduct the merger on the basis of the relative strength of each firm's balance sheet on July 31, 1981. Shares would be exchanged, in other words, on the basis of how much capital each firm had in the kitty at mid-year, as determined by their auditors. Both sides assumed that, by mid-year, DS would have about twice as much capital as Ames. Thus, it was assumed, the Ames partners who remained with the merged company would end up owning about one-third of it. That was the way the deal was presented to the press when it was finally announced in June; DS would contribute $27 million worth of capital, Ames about $13 million.

But between the time the merger was announced and the time it was consummated in August, the Ames capital practically disappeared. As DS accountants combed through the Ames books, and as the stock market plunged, Ames's capital dropped with it. There had been no deliberate concealment of the firm's financial condition; the Ames partners had honestly underestimated the seriousness of its condition, and how swiftly it would deteriorate if the revenues slowed down. It has also been rumored that the auditors took a severe view of the firm's inventory of unsold stocks and bonds, in some cases writing off assets that had been carried on the books for hundreds of thousands of dollars. By August, the relative strength of the two firms had dwindled from two-to-one to four-to-one. Putting it on a more human level, the people who owned Ames shares discovered they were much poorer than they'd assumed. The shares which Peter Harris had sold less than a year earlier for $33 were now worth less than $20. One partner, John Milne, had joined DS-Ames with what he thought was $275,000 worth of shares. A few months later they were worth $55,000.

For the Ames partners settling into their new quarters, this shrinkage in their capital meant a corresponding reduction in their personal bargaining power. They'd gone into the deal in the spring with their dignity intact, as roughly equal partners. By summer, they were being regarded as very junior partners – and beginning to feel like employees. "After being an insider for so long, you find yourself being treated as an outsider – and in your own house, as it were," says Bellamy, "It creates feelings of bitterness and acrimony and frustration."

By September, with the stock market slump in full swing, the DS directors decided they had to cut staff. Not surprisingly, considering their reduced bargaining power, the first to go were people from Ames. DS summarily fired eight men who'd been senior Ames directors: Paul Fisher, John Milne, Bill Andrews, Brook Angus, Ted Thomson, Colin Oates in Montreal, Rod

Ireland and David Currie in the Calgary office. Bob Bellamy left a few months later. Two of these men had been vice-presidents; all had been with the firm for more than 20 years. All of them had been shareholders, and some of them had borrowed heavily to buy shares that were now virtually worthless. Bob Bellamy, John Milne and Bill Andrews had been part of an informal club which used to gather in the downstairs room at Winston's every lunch hour and, very frequently, after work as well. Andrews was one of the shareholders of that famous restaurant, and there had been people at Ames who had grumbled that he was enriching Winston's partly at his own firm's expense. Now, on their final day at the firm which had sustained them for more than two decades, around the same tables where so many stories had been told, so many deals conceived, the old friends gathered for a farewell wake. Late in the evening, as the company grew sadder and sadder, John Milne, a man in his fifties who had once been the firm's sales manager, a gregarious man who loved to be first-named by headwaiters, wept openly as he contemplated all the money that had vanished and all the years that had passed. More than a year later, still without salaried employment, he talked about how it felt: "It still seems like a crazy dream. I never thought it could happen. It's not so much losing your job – it's losing all your capital too."

Bellamy lost more than anyone else – more than two-thirds of his substantial investment in Ames. But with a new and congenial job at Burns Fry, and in a rising stock market which promised eventually to repay his past losses, he felt bitterness toward no one. Indeed, he took a perverse pride, like a captain going down with his ship, in the fact that he'd suffered worse than anyone else. "If I hadn't taken my full share of the loss, then I'd feel there was something wrong with me. It may be the wrong thing for a shrewd trader or a hard-nosed capitalist to say, but I feel more whole in myself, knowing that I took my full share. Ultimately we're responsible for our own conduct. That's the definition of maturity."

For all of its 92 years, A.E. Ames was never anything but a collection of highly skilled people, brilliantly led in its early years and badly managed in the latter ones. Considering the divided nature of its leadership and the toughness of the times, the firm probably should have foundered long before it did. A vivid tradition of honor and integrity, a sense of shared decencies, is what kept the firm going for so long. And those qualities were present to the very end.

Conclusion

The Canadian securities industry, as I've tried to show in this book, is a lovable, and still quite serviceable, anachronism. But it's not so much an industry as it is a collection of fiercely independent-minded individuals. Most industries consist of an assortment of organizations with at least some claim to permanence. But with more than 300 mergers, closures or bankruptcies in the past 20 years, it's scarcely meaningful to describe this shifting population of financial bedouins as an industry at all.

But what a likable bunch of bedouins they are! After more than two years of interviews, I can't recall a single unpleasant encounter. Businessmen, especially when confronted by the press, tend to be stuffy, bland and overprotective of their reputations. People who make their livings around the stock market, even those with the largest offices and the most exalted titles, tend to be unpretentious and surprisingly frank – very similar, come to think of it, to the inhabitants of a small, pleasant village.

That village may be in the process of transformation into a large city; or it may be in the process of absorption by larger neighbors, such as the domestic banks. By the early 1980s, the Canadian financial community was beginning to outgrow its cosy, small-town origins, but there was little certainty about what sort of financial structure would arise to take its place. Would the industry ossify into a few large firms at the top, and a few struggling little ones at the bottom? Would the chartered banks muscle their way into the stock market and hammer the brokers into the pavement with their awesome financial clout? The debate on the industry's future was conducted, in suitably polite tones, in boardrooms, in hearings before the Ontario Securities Commission and in various government offices. It boiled down to a quarrel about who should be doing what.

For more than a century, Canada's capital markets – the institutional machinery by which savings are transferred to spenders – have been managed by four separate "pillars," four different types of financial institutions performing separate, specialized functions. Banks take in deposits and loan money to individuals and businesses; trust companies manage portfolios and take deposits, and invest most of the proceeds in mortgages; insurance companies collect premiums instead of deposits, and invest most of the proceeds in bonds and mortgages; and investment dealers underwrite stock and bond issues and trade securities on behalf of themselves and their clients.

The trouble with these four neat categories is that they're no longer relevant. As times and conditions change, the functions of the four separate pillars have begun to overlap. Banks are now heavily involved in mortgage lending, formerly a preserve of the trust companies. Investment dealers now accept cash deposits from their clients, and pay better interest on these accounts than most banks. In mid-1984, Midland Doherty Ltd. even introduced its own chequing account – an innovation for Canada, but old stuff in the United States. The introduction of computerized technology has enabled all financial institutions to offer a wider range of services to their customers. The financial requirements of those customers, in turn, are becoming more varied and sophisticated.

Until 1983, it was possible to maintain the fiction of the four separate pillars. That was the year the securities industry, after years of agonizing, finally authorized the introduction of negotiated commission rates. Until then, nearly all Canadian brokerage firms had charged their retail customers a fixed rate for buying or selling securities. For an industry which loves to preach the virtues of free enterprise, it was a flagrantly anti-competitive arrangement. The industry's large, institutional customers had been complaining for years about this cosy little monopoly. In the mid-1970s, accordingly, the brokers introduced lower rates for institutional customers. They gave quantity discounts, in effect, to the clients with the most money and the most clout.

In 1983, yielding to pressure from the Ontario Securities Commission and from some of the more restless elements among its own membership, the industry also introduced negotiated rates for both small and large clients. That gave any customer, no matter how small his account, the theoretical right to haggle with his broker over the commission to be charged.

In practice, not much changed. Most retail customers continued to pay whatever their broker chose to charge. Because their accounts were small, their bargaining power was not large. In fact, most firms *increased* the rates they charged their retail customers, and reduced the rates they charged their large, institutional clients. But the deregulation of brokers' rates prompted several firms to set up discount brokerage houses, which charged lower commissions in return for a "no-frills" brokerage service. Customers who dealt with these discount houses were entitled

247

to no conversation, no advice, no hand-holding, from their broker. They were expected to make up their own minds on what to buy and sell, and to communicate their wishes to their discount broker as briefly as possible. Trading stocks with a conventional broker is like conferring with an interior decorator; he is willing to spend time listening to you, pampering you, figuring out your needs and then trying to satisfy them. Dealing with a discount broker, by contrast, is like ordering goods out of the Sears catalogue; you're supposed to know in advance what you want, and your discount broker is simply there to execute the order.

The new era of negotiated rates came into effect – appropriately enough, some brokers noted – on April Fool's Day, 1983. Within a matter of days several discount brokers opened for business. But then a far more powerful entrant appeared on the scene: the Toronto Dominion Bank. Canadian banks have been empowered since Confederation to trade stocks, bonds and other securities. It was a power they seldom exercised, except as a convenience to bank customers living in out-of-the-way places. In 1980, nevertheless, Ottawa amended the Bank Act to limit this power. The banks would continue to be allowed to execute their own customers' stock-market orders through a broker, but they couldn't solicit business, they couldn't offer investment advice and they couldn't manage portfolios.

Undeterred by these provisions, the TD Bank was now proposing to set up special stock-trading accounts for its customers, to relay their orders through a discount broker, and to advertise this new service as "the TD Green Line Investor Service." For much of the securities industry, the implications were terrifying: Did this mean that the big banks, by muscling in on the brokers' traditional territory, were about to drive them out of business?

A year or so later, the fears seemed premature. Discount brokers hadn't made much of an impact. But by that time, the traditional investment dealers were facing a challenge that was far more compelling, and long overdue: savage price competition in the underwriting side of their business.

Although firms such as Wood Gundy and McLeod Young Weir have always competed vigorously to attract underwriting clients, they have seldom competed on the basis of price. The firm that upset that cosy little tradition was Daly Gordon Securities, which stunned the Street in 1984 by doing "bought" underwriting deals – that is, using their own and their backers' cash to buy a company's share issue outright, then taking its own chances on reselling it later. What's more, Daly Gordon

248

was willing to pay a wholesale rate of one per cent below the retail price, instead of the traditional 2 or 3 per cent underwriting commission.

Price-cutting! Horror of horrors! Not since the 1930s had Bay Street witnessed so much hand-wringing. Some of the underwriting clients, the people who were benefiting from this unaccustomed competition, took a ghoulish delight in the spectacle. "Things will never be the same on Bay Street," one of them told me. "Those guys are finally going to have to go to work."

But where? By mid-1984, it seemed apparent that Bay Street was ripe for a massive shakeout. The largest firms would almost certainly survive, although they might become multinational corporations in the process, doing as much business in London and New York as they once did in Canada. And there would always be a place for smaller, highly specialized "boutiques." It was the middle-of-the-pack firms, dozens of them, which seemed to be threatened with extinction.

Perhaps the industry deserves to undergo the shakeout it appears to be facing. But my main criticism of stockbrokers is not that they churn and burn their clients, or that they're preposterously overpaid, or that they're amiably inefficient, although all those criticisms are at least occasionally valid. No, the main problem with the industry, it seems to me, is that they've done a remarkably poor job selling their product.

It's a matter of statistical fact that the stock market, if it's approached in a patient and conservative manner, is an excellent place to put your money – a better place than a bank account in all but the most inflationary periods, and a far better place than a life-insurance policy almost any time. The fact that Canadians are one of the most heavily-insured populations on the planet, and that our rate of participation in the stock market is about half that of Americans, suggests to me that the securities industry simply hasn't got its act together.

So what? Who needs stockbrokers, anyway? Well, I'm prepared to argue that the survival of a healthy securities industry should be a matter of genuine public concern. The argument over the "four pillars" isn't merely a squabble between competing sectors of the financial industry; it's an issue that affects almost every Canadian with a few dollars to spare. The more choices you have in investing those spare dollars, the more genuine freedom you have – and the healthier is our financial system.

But whether or not the banks are allowed to muscle their way onto the nation's trading floors, a major restructuring of the securities industry seems inevitable. Sooner or later, whether by the banks, the brokers or by new, hybrid institutions, Canadians will be offered one-stop service by so-called "financial supermarkets." A single firm will be able to handle all your financial needs: sell you insurance, loan you money, pay you interest on your savings, buy and sell your stocks and bonds and manage your investment portfolio. It's already happening in the United States, where financial supermarkets are becoming increasingly familiar. American Express now owns a major brokerage house, and so does Sears Roebuck; and both firms now offer one-stop financial service. Canada won't be far behind. And when that happens, the chances are that the Bay Street Village will be more professional and more profitable. It will consist of fewer, larger firms. It will also be less diverse, less individualistic and, I fear, far less interesting.

Reorganizations and Resignations of Member Firms 1960-1981

The traders themselves are as dedicated to change as any of the most active companies on the stock market. During the period 1960 to 1981, over 300 changes have taken place within the brokerage industry. Although there will undoubtedly be change in the future as the industry responds to new realities of the marketplace, the traders themselves and the role they play will remain constant.

NAME OF THE FIRM	YEAR	CHANGE	NEW FIRM	MERGED WITH / TAKEN OVER BY
A.E. Ames & Co. Limited	81	CO	Dominion Securities Ames Limited	Dominion Securities Limited
Adam & Co. Ltd.	74	CO	Carlisle Douglas Adam & Co. Ltd.	Carlisle Douglas & Co. Ltd.
Adams, Reid Limited	61	OB		
Anderson & Company Limited	65	CO		Burns Bros. and Denton Limited
Andras, Bartlett, Cayley Ltd.	79	RE	Andras, Hatch & Hetherington Ltd.	
Andras, Hatch & McCarthy	63	RE	Andras, Hatch & Hetherington Limited	
Andrews and Belanger Co. Ltd.	71	OB		
Anglin, Bell & Company Limited	67	OB		
Angus & Company	71	OB		
Annett Mackay Limited	74	CO		McDermid, Miller & McDermid Limited
Annett Partners Ltd.	71	OB		
O.E. Armstrong & Co.	61	OB		
Asta Securities Corporation Limited	72	SE		

Category of Change OB – Out of Business   CO – Corporate Combinations   RE – Corporate Reorganizations   SE – Suspended/Expelled

NAME OF THE FIRM	YEAR	CHANGE	NEW FIRM	MERGED WITH / TAKEN OVER BY
Astaire, Taylor International Limited	73	RE	D.W. Taylor & Company Limited	
Atlantic Securities Limited	75	CO		Walwyn, Stodgell & Gairdner Ltd.
Atlantic Securities Limited	81	SE		
G.A. Auger & Company Limited	62	OB		
Bache & Co. Canada Limited	76	CO	Bache Halsey Stuart Canada Ltd.	
Bache & Co. Incorporated	74	RE	Bache & Co. Canada Limited	
Baker, Weeks & Co. of Canada Ltd.	77	CO	Reynolds Securities (Canada) Ltd.	Reynolds Securities International Inc.
Bankers Securities of Canada Limited	74	OB		
Barclay & Crawford	65	RE		
Barclay & Crawford Limited	71	OB		
Barnett & Company	67	CO		MacDougall, MacDougall & MacTier Ltd.
Barrett, Goodfellow & Company Limited	66	OB		
Barry & McManamy	75	CO		MacDougal, MacDougall & MacTier Ltd.
Bawlf Securities Ltd.	81	OB		
Beatty Webster & Company Limited	72	OB		
L.G. Beaubien & Co. Limited	63	CO	J.L. Levesque & L.G. Beaubien Ltd.	Credit Interprovincial
Belanger Inc.	70	RE	Molson, Rousseau & Co. Limited	
Belanger, Garneau, Joron Inc.	68	RE	Garneau, Joron Inc.	
Belshaw & Company Limited	75	OB		
Bennett, Jennings & Co. Limited	60	OB		
Blanchard, O'Connor & Co. Ltd.	73	SE		
Blyth Canada Ltd.	70	OB		
Blyth Canada Ltd.	72	RE	Blyth Eastman Dillon & Co. Ltd.	
Blyth Eastman Dillon & Co. Ltd.	80	RE	Paine Webber Jackson & Curtis Limited	

Category of Change OB – Out of Business CO – Corporate Combinations RE – Corporate Reorganizations SE – Suspended/Expelled

NAME OF THE FIRM	YEAR	CHANGE	NEW FIRM	MERGED WITH / TAKEN OVER BY
Bongard and Company Limited	65	CO	Bongard, Leslie & Co. Ltd.	G.E. Leslie & Co.
Bongard, Leslie & Co. Ltd.	77	CO	Nesbitt Thomson Bongard Inc.	Nesbitt, Thomson and Company Limited
Bontrad Inc.	81	CO		F.H. Deacon Hodgson Inc.
T.J. Boswick & Company	78	OB		
Bouchard & Co. Ltd.	75	OB		
J.C. Boulet Inc.	69	CO		Pitfield, Mackay, Ross & Co. Limited
Brault, Guy, Chaput Inc.	74	CO	Brault, Guy, O'Brien Inc.	O'Brien & Williams
Breckenridge, McDonald & Co	70	OB		
F.J. Brennan & Company (N.S.) Limited	62	RE		
F.J. Brennan and Co. Ltd.	63	OB		
S.J. Brooks & Co.	67	OB		
Brown, Baldwin & Co. Ltd.	65	RE	Brown, Baldwin, Nisker Limited	
Bulman, Evans & Co. Limited	70	OB		
C.H. Burgess and Company Limited	70	CO	Burgess Graham Securities Limited	J.L. Graham & Company Limited
Burleigh & Partners Ltd.	71	RE	Crumb Beamer Ltd.	
Burnett Co.	67	OB		
Burns Bros. and Denton Limited	76	CO	Burns Fry Limited	Fry Mills Spence Limited
A. Campbell Investments	67	RE	Carlisle Douglas & Co. Ltd.	
J.P. Cannon & Co. Ltd	74	CO	Yorkton Securities Inc.	Yorkton Securities Limited
Carlisle Douglas & Co. Ltd.	74	CO	Carlisle Douglas Adam & Co. Ltd.	Adam & Co. Ltd.
Carlisle Douglas Adam & Co. Ltd.	76	CO	Continental Carlisle Douglas Ltd.	Continental Securities Corp. (1971) Ltd.
Marc Carriere Limitee	62	OB		
Castle Securities Limited	71	OB		
V.S. Castledine & Company Limited	69	OB		

Category of Change OB – Out of Business   CO – Corporate Combinations   RE – Corporate Reorganizations   SE – Suspended/Expelled

253

NAME OF THE FIRM	YEAR	CHANGE	NEW FIRM	MERGED WITH / TAKEN OVER BY
Charbonneau, Allart, Pelletier & Forey Inc.	71	OB		
Chartrand, Lemay, Quinn, Senecal & Co. Ltd.	72	RE	Chartrand, Quinn, Senecal & Co. Ltd.	
Chartrand, Quinn, Senecal & Co. Ltd.	73	SE		
Citymont Investments Inc.	67	OB		
T.G. Clark Limited	62	OB		
Clement, Guimont Inc.	68	SE		
Cliche et Associes Ltee.	76	OB		
Cochran Murray & Wisner Limited	77	CO	Walwyn Stodgell Cochran Murray Ltd.	Walwyn, Stodgell & Gairdner Ltd.
Cochran Murray Limited	74	CO	Cochran Murray & Wisener Limited	Wisener & Partners Company Limited
Collier, Norris & Quinlan Limited	75	CO	A.E. Osler, Norris, Gendron Ltd.	A.E. Osler, Gendron Ltd.
Continental Securities Corp. (1971) Ltd.	76	CO	Continental Carlisle Douglas Ltd.	Carlisle Douglas Adam & Co. Ltd.
W.J. Corcoran Company Ltd.	81	OB		
Cornell, MacGillivray Limited	76	CO		A.E. Ames & Co.
La Corporation des Prets de Quebec	73	OB		
Craig, Ballantyne & Co. Ltd.	61	RE	Craig, Forget & Co. Ltd.	
Craig, Forget & Co. Limited	66	OB		
Craig, Forget & Co. Ltd.	65	RE	Craig, Forget & Co. Limited	
J.B. Crane and Company Limited	62	OB		
J.H. Crang & Co. Limited	72	CO	Crang & Ostiguy Inc.	Morgan Ostiguy & Hudon Inc.
Crang & Ostiguy Inc.	77	CO		Greenshields Inc.
F.J. Crawford & Co. Limited	63	CO	Ross, Knowles & Company Ltd.	Ross, Knowles & Co.
Credit Anglo-Francais Limitee	60	OB		
Credit Interprovincial	64	CO	J.L. Levesque and L.G. Beaubien Ltd.	L.G. Beaubien Ltd.
D.D. Creighton & Co. Incorporated	68	CO		Collier, Norris, Quinlan Limited
Crumb, Beamer & Co. Ltd.	74	SE		

Category of Change OB – Out of Business   CO – Corporate Combinations   RE – Corporate Reorganizations   SE – Suspended/Expelled

254

NAME OF THE FIRM	YEAR	CHANGE	NEW FIRM	MERGED WITH / TAKEN OVER BY
Peter D. Curry & Co. Ltd.	74	RE	Edward Glasgow & Co. Ltd.	
Dattels & Company Limited	70	OB		
Davidson & Co. Ltd.	78	SE		
Dawson, Hannaford Limited	61	CO	Greenshields Incorporated	Greenshields & Co. Inc.
F.H. Deacon & Company Limited	77	CO	F.H. Deacon, Hodgson Inc.	C.J. Hodgson, Richardson Inc.
Deacon Findlay Coyne Limited	67	RE		
Desjardins, Couture Inc.	79	CO		Grenier, Ruel & Cie Inc.
Desrosiers & Co.	60	OB		
Draper Dobie & Company Limited	77	CO		Dominion Securities Ltd.
Doherty McCuaig Limited	74	CO	Midland Doherty Limited	Midland-Osler Securities Limited
Doherty Roadhouse & Co.	62	CO	Doherty Roadhouse & McCuaig Bros.	McCuaig Bros. & Co.
Doherty Roadhouse & McCuaig	71	RE	Doherty McCuaig Limited	
Dominion Securities Corporation Limited	73	CO	Dominion Secs. Corp. Harris & Ptnrs. Ltd.	Harris & Partners Limited
Dominion Securities Limited	81	CO	Dominion Securities Ames Limited	A.E. Ames & Co. Limited
Donaldson Securities Ltd.	77	SE		
Dorchester Securities Limited	74	OB		
Dreman & Co. Ltd.	77	OB		
D.M. Duggan Investments Limited	64	SE		
duPont Glore Forgan Canada Limited	74	OB		
Eastern Securities Company Limited	69	OB		
Easton, Fisher & Company Limited	75	CO		A.E. Ames
Elphick Securities Limited	72	CO	Rademaker, MacDougall & Company	MacDougall and Granger Limited
Equitable Securities Limited	81	CO		Levesque, Beaubien Inc.
Jenkin Evans & Co. Limited	71	OB		
H.M.E. Evans & Company Limited	68	OB		
Fairclough Co. Limited	69	OB		
Ralph K. Farris	64	OB		

Category of Change OB – Out of Business CO – Corporate Combinations RE – Corporate Reorganizations SE – Suspended/Expelled

NAME OF THE FIRM	YEAR	CHANGE	NEW FIRM	MERGED WITH / TAKEN OVER BY
Gingras, Reid, Gaudreau, Inc.	72	OB		
Edward Glasgow & Co. Ltd.	77	OB		
J.L. Goad & Co. Limited	71	RE	St. Lawrence Securities Limited	
Gordon-Daly Grenadier Ltd.	74	OB		
Gordon, Eberts & Company Limited	71	RE	Gordon Securities Limited	
Goss and Company Limited	62	OB		
Goulding, Rose & Company Limited	69	RE		
Graham & Co.	63	CO	Oswald Drinkwater & Graham Ltd.	Oswald & Drinkwater
J.L. Graham & Company Limited	70	CO	Burgess Graham Securities Limited	C.H. Burgess and Company Limited
Graham, Armstrong Securities Ltd.	74	CO		Levesque, Beaubien Inc.
Grant Johnston Limited	72	CO		C.J. Hodgson & Company Inc.
J.E. Grasett & Co.	71	OB	C.J. Hodgson Securities Ltd.	
Gray, Tapp, Turney & Company Ltd.	67	OB		
Hagar Investments Ltd.	70	CO		Pitfield Mackay Ross
D.J. Hall & Company Ltd.	72	OB		
Hall Securities Limited	63	OB		
Hamel, Fugere & Cie. Limitee	71	OB		
Goodwin Harris & Co. Ltd.	74	CO	Kingwest Securities Limited	McEwen Securities Limited
Harris & Partners Limited	73	CO	Dominion Secs. Corp. Harris & Ptnrs. Ltd.	Dominion Securities Corporation Limited
H.H. Hemsworth	68	RE	Hemsworth, Turton & Co. Ltd.	
Hemsworth, Turton & Co. Ltd.	72	RE	Canarim Investment Corporation	
Heritage Securities Limited	81	CO		Burns Fry Limited
Herrndorf Securities Ltd.	69	OB		
Hevenor & Co. Limited	72	OB		
Hickey, Dow & Muir	73	OB		
C.J. Hodgson & Co. Inc.	72	CO	C.J. Hodgson Securities Ltd.	Grant Johnston Limited

Category of Change OB – Out of Business   CO – Corporate Combinations   RE – Corporate Reorganizations   SE – Suspended/Expelled

NAME OF THE FIRM	YEAR	CHANGE	NEW FIRM	MERGED WITH / TAKEN OVER BY
C.J. Hodgson Securities Ltd.	74	CO	C.J. Hodgson, Richardson Inc.	T.A. Richardson & Co. Limited
C.J. Hodgson, Richardson Inc.	76	CO	F.H. Deacon, Hodgson Inc.	F.H. Deacon & Company Limited
Holland, Andrews Investments Ltd.	65	RE	Holland, Andrews, Perrier & Co. Ltd.	
Holland, Andrews, Perrier & Co. Ltd.	72	OB		
Institutional Securities Corp. Limited	79	CO		Goulding, Rose, Turner Limited
Intercity Securities	69	OB		
Isard, Robertson & Co. Limited	67	RE	Isard, Robertson, Easson Co. Limited	
Isard, Robertson, Easson Co. Limited	74	RE	McEwen Easson Limited	
Jackson, McFadyen Securities Limited	68	OB		
Jenkin, Evans & Co. Ltd.	71	OB		
Jennings, Petrie & Co. Limited	71	OB		
Kamm, Garland & Co. Limited	77	CO		Pope & Company
C.A. Kee & Company	73	OB		
F.W. Kerr & Co.	61	OB		
H.C. Ketcheson Investments Ltd.	65	OB		
A.M. Kidder & Co. Inc.	63	RE	Francis I. duPont & Co.	
Charles King & Co.	73	OB		
Kingstone & MacKenzie	70	CO		MacDougall, MacDougall & MacTier Ltd.
Kingwest Securities Limited	75	CO		Yorkton Securities Inc.
Kippen & Company Inc.	74	CO		Bongard, Leslie & Co. Ltd.
J.E. Laflamme Limitee	73	OB		
Lagueux & Desrochers Limitee	70	OB		
Lagueux & Desrochers Ltee	66	SE		
T.K. Laidlaw & Co. Ltd.	74	RE	Fisher Securities Ltd.	

Category of Change OB – Out of Business   CO – Corporate Combinations   RE – Corporate Reorganizations   SE – Suspended/Expelled

NAME OF THE FIRM	YEAR	CHANGE	NEW FIRM	MERGED WITH / TAKEN OVER BY
Laidlaw Securities Canada Limited	74	CO		Nesbitt, Thomson & Company Limited
Lajoie, Robitaille & Cie, Limitee	61	OB		
Lamont and Company Limited	74	OB		
Lampman, Laidlaw Securities Limited	62	RE	T.K. Laidlaw & Co. Ltd.	
T.M. Lanthier & Company Ltd.	70	OB		
A.D. Lauder & Company Limited	61	OB		
Rene T. Leclerc Inc.	79	CO	Geoffrion, Leclerc Inc.	Geoffrion, Robert & Gelinas Ltd.
Leeburn Securities Limited	81	CO		Yorkton Securities Inc.
Legatt, Bell, Gouinlock Ltd.	71	RE	Bell Gouinlock & Company Limited	
G.E. Leslie & Co.	65	CO	Bongard, Leslie & Co. Ltd.	Bongard and Company Limited
Frank S. Leslie & Co. Limited	75	CO		Hector M. Chisholm & Co. Limited
William E. Lewis Company Ltd.	68	SE		
Locke, Gray & Company	62	CO	Gray, Trap, Turney & Company Ltd.	
E.T. Lynch & Co. Limited	70	CO	Malone Lynch Securities Ltd.	Robertson Malone & Co. Ltd.
MacDougall & MacDougall	60	CO	MacDougall, MacDougall & MacTier Ltd.	MacTier & Co.
MacDougall and Granger Limited	75	CO	Rademaker, MacDougall & Company	Elphick Securities Ltd.
Thomas Mackay & Co. Ltd.	66	RE	Annett Mackay Limited	
Hugh Mackay & Company Ltd.	66	CO	Pitfield, Mackay & Company Limited	W.C. Pitfield & Company Limited
D.F. Mackenzie Ltd.	62	CO		Norman R. Whittal
Macleod, Riddell & Co.	60	OB		
N.L. MacNames & Company Limited	66	SE		
Macrae & Company	62	OB		
Macrae & Company	69	OB		

Category of Change OB – Out of Business   CO – Corporate Combinations   RE – Corporate Reorganizations   SE – Suspended/Expelled

NAME OF THE FIRM	YEAR	CHANGE	NEW FIRM	MERGED WITH / TAKEN OVER BY
MacTier & Co.	60	CO	MacDougall, MacDougall & MacTier Ltd.	MacDougall & MacDougall
La Maison Bienvenu Limitee	67	RE		
Malone Lynch Securities Ltd.	71	SE		
Markdale Securities Ltd.	72	OB		
J.L. Marler & Co. Ltd.	68	OB		
Martens, Ball, Albrecht Securities Ltd.	75	RE	MBA Securities Ltd.	
Martonmere Securities Limited	79	CO		Loewen, Ondaatje, McCutcheon & Co. Ltd.
Mason & Crysdale Limited	68	OB		
Massey, Lavoie & Associates Inc.	73	SE		
Matthews & Company Limited	76	CO		A.E. Ames & Co.
May, Mikkila and Co. Limited	77	CO		Goulding, Rose & Turner Limited
MBA Securities Limited	77	OB		
McCuaig Bros. & Co.	62	CO	Doherty Roadhouse & McCuaig Bros.	Doherty Roadhouse & Co.
McDonnell, Adams & Co. Limited	72	OB		
McDougall & Christmas Ltd.	70	RE	Gordon, Eberts & Company Limited	
McEwen Securities Limited	75	CO	Kingwest Securities Limited	Goodwin Harris & Co. Ltd.
McFetrick & Company	64	OB		
George J. McKiee & Son	78	OB		
McLeod, Young, Weir & Ratcliffe	72	RE	McLeod, Young, Weir & Company Limited	
Mead & Co. Limited	80	CO	Gestion M.C.I. Inc.	
Mead & Co. Limited	81	RE		Walwyn, Stodgell Cochran Murray Ltd.
Meggeson, Goss & Co. Limited	67	SE		
Meighen Wood Limited	81	OB		

Category of Change OB – Out of Business CO – Corporate Combinations RE – Corporate Reorganizations SE – Suspended/Expelled

NAME OF THE FIRM	YEAR	CHANGE	NEW FIRM	MERGED WITH / TAKEN OVER BY
Merrill Lynch, Pierce, Fenner & Smith Inc.	72	CO	Merrill Lynch Royal Securities Limited	Royal Securities Limited
Michelin Forey Inc.	74	OB		
Midland Securities Corpn. Limited	63	CO	Midland-Osler Securities Limited	Osler, Hammond & Nanton Limited
Midland-Osler Securities Limited	73	CO	Midland Doherty Limited	Doherty McCuaig Limited
Mills, Spence & Co. Limited	71	CO	Fry Mills Spence Securities Limited	Fry Securities Limited
Milner, Spence & Co. Limited	68	RE	Mills, Spence & Co. Limited	
W.G. Mitchell, & Co.	66	OB		
R. Moat & Co.	67	OB		
Molson & Company Limited	69	RE	Molson, Rousseau & Co. Ltd.	
J.R. Mooney, & Co. Limited	68	OB		
Morgan & Co. Ltd.	65	RE	Morgan, Ostiguy & Hudon Inc.	
Morgan Ostiguy & Hudon Inc.	72	CO	Crang & Ostiguy Inc.	J.H. Crang & Co. Limited
Nesbitt, Thomson and Company Limited	77	CO	Nesbitt Thomson Bongard Inc.	Bongard, Leslie & Co. Ltd.
G.W. Nicholson & Company Limited	70	OB		
A.H. Nicol & Company	65	OB		
O'Brien & Williams	74	CO	Brault, Guy, O'Brien Inc.	Brault, Guy, Chaput Inc.
Odlum Brown Investments Ltd.	65	CO	Odlum Brown & T.B. Read Ltd.	Thomas B. Read Company Ltd.
Okanagan Investments Limited	69	OB		
Oldfield, Kirby & Gardner Securities Ltd.	67	OB		
Oscar Dube & Cie Inc.	72	OB		
A.E. Osler Company Limited	73	CO	A.E. Osler, Gendron Ltd.	J.T. Gendron Inc.
A.E. Osler, Gendron Ltd.	74	CO	A.E. Osler, Norris, Gendron Ltd.	Collier, Norris & Quinlan Limited
Osler, Hammond & Nanton Limited	63	CO	Midland-Osler Securities Limited	Midland Securities Corpn. Limited
A.E. Osler, Norris, Gendron Limited	77	CO	A.E. Osler, Wills, Bickle Limited	Wills, Bickle & Company Limited

Category of Change OB – Out of Business CO – Corporate Combinations RE – Corporate Reorganizations SE – Suspended/Expelled

NAME OF THE FIRM	YEAR	CHANGE	NEW FIRM	MERGED WITH / TAKEN OVER BY
Oswald & Drinkwater	63	CO	Oswald Drinkwater & Graham Ltd.	Graham & Co.
Oswald Drinkwater & Graham Ltd.	74	CO		Levesque, Beaubien Inc.
Pacific Western Securities Limited	74	OB		
Parsons & Landrigan Limited	75	OB		
Peters Hugo & Company Limited	75	RE	Peters & Co. Limited	
W.C. Pitfield & Company Limited	66	CO	Pitfield, Mackay & Company Limited	Hugh Mackay & Company Ltd.
Pitfield, Mackay & Company Limited	67	RE	Pitfield, Mackay, Ross & Company Limited	
Playfair & Co. Limited	70	CO	Fry Securities Limited	
E.H. Pooler & Co. Limited	70	RE	Yorkton Securities Limited	
A.A. Pritchard Investments Ltd.	62	RE	A. Campbell Investments Ltd.	
Pyne, May and Co. Limited	71	RE	May, Mikkila and Company Limited	
J.R. Pyper Ltd.	61	OB		
Rainville & Co.	67	OB		
Ramsay Securities Co. Limited	66	OB		
Read Bros. & Co. Limited	67	OB		
Thomas B. Read Company Ltd.	65	CO	Odlum Brown & T.B. Read Ltd.	Odlum Brown Investments Ltd.
A.D.G. Reid Corporation Limited	77	OB		
G.H. Rennie & Co. Limited	62	SE		
Reynolds Securities (Canada) Ltd.	80	RE	Dean Witter Reynolds Sec. (Canada) Ltd.	
Reynolds Securities International Inc.	77	CO	Reynolds Securities (Canada) Ltd.	Baker, Weeks of Canada Ltd.
T.A. Richardson & Co. Limited	74	CO	C.J. Hodgson, Richardson Inc.	C.J. Hodgson Securities Ltd.
James Richardson & Sons	67	RE	Richardson Securities of Canada	
G.B. Richardson and Company	64	OB		
Ringland, Meredith & Company Limited	64	RE		
Ringland, Meredith & Hunt Limited	66	OB		

261

Category of Change OB – Out of Business   CO – Corporate Combinations   RE – Corporate Reorganizations   SE – Suspended/Expelled

NAME OF THE FIRM	YEAR	CHANGE	NEW FIRM	MERGED WITH / TAKEN OVER BY
Robertson, Malone & Co. Ltd.	70	CO	Malone Lynch Securities Ltd.	E.T. Lynch & Co. Limited
C.S. Robinson Investments Ltd.	67	CO		Sydie, Sutherland & Ritchie Ltd.
Rosmar Corporation Limited	74	OB		
Ross, Knowles & Co. Ltd.	63	CO	Ross, Knowles & Company Ltd.	F.J. Crawford & Co.
Ross, Knowles & Company Limited	67	OB		
L.F. Rothschild & Co.	77	RE		
L.F. Rothschild, Unterberg, Towbin	77	OB		
Royal Securities Corporation Limited	71	CO	Merrill Lynch, Royal Securities Limited	Merrill Lynch, Pierce, Fenner & Smith
Royden Morris & Co. Ltd.	69	CO		Wolverton & Co. Ltd.
Ryan Investments Limited	74	CO		Pemberton Securities Limited
Samis & Co. Ltd.	71	OB		
N.L. Sandler & Co. Limited	78	RE	Merit Investment Corporation	
Saunders Cameron Limited	64	RE	E.M. Saunders Limited	
E.M. Saunders Limited	76	RE	Saunders Hatt Limited	
Savard & Hart Inc.	64	OB		
R.H. Scarlett, & Co. Limited	62	OB		
Scottish Securities Corporation Limited	68	OB		
Senate Securities Ltd.	67	RE	Cochran, Murray & Hay Western Ltd.	
H Shapiro & Co.	67	RE	Shapiro, Brown & Co. Ltd.	
Shapiro, Brown & Co. Ltd.	70	RE	Castle Securities Limited	
Shearson Hayden Stone (Canada) Inc.	80	RE	Shearson, Loeb, Rhoades (Canada) Inc.	
Shearson, Hammill & Co. Incorporated	75	RE	Shearson, Hayden Stone Inc.	
J.F. Simard Company Limited	70	OB		
Hart Smith & Co.	65	OB		
Ralph M. Smith Investments Limited	60	OB		

Category of Change OB – Out of Business   CO – Corporate Combinations   RE – Corporate Reorganizations   SE – Suspended/Expelled

NAME OF THE FIRM	YEAR	CHANGE	NEW FIRM	MERGED WITH / TAKEN OVER BY
Societe de Placements et Cie. Ltee.	72	CO		
Societe Generale de Finance Inc.	70	SE		
Stanbury & Company Limited	68	SE		
Standard Securities Ltd.	77	OB		
R.D. Steers & Company Ltd.	69	OB		
Sterling-Atkins Limited	74	OB		
G.H. Stevenson & Company Limited	73	RE	MacDougall and Granger Ltd.	
Stevenson-Donegani Securities Ltd.	61	RE	Stevenson and Ryan Limited	
J. Bradley Streit & Company Limited	75	OB		
Sydie, Sutherland & Ritchie Ltd.	67	RE	Senate Securities Ltd.	
Tanner Bros. Limited	81	OB		
Templehurst Securities Limited	79	OB		
Thomson & McKinnon Inc.	70	RE	Thomson & McKinnon Auchincloss Inc.	
Thomson & McKinnon Auchincloss Inc.	71	OB		Burns Bros. and Denton Ltd.
J.R. Timmins & Co. Incorporated	72	CO		
Toole, Peet Investments Limited	64	OB		
Trimont Securities Ltd.	77	OB		
Turcot Wood Power & Cundill Ltd.	76	CO		A.E. Osler, Norris, Gendron Ltd.
Union Securities Ltd.	75	OB		
Waite, Reid and Company Limited	65	OB		
Walker, Hardaker & Company Limited	68	OB		
Walters Securities Ltd.	74	SE		
Walwyn, Stodgell & Co. Limited	73	CO	Walwyn Stodgell & Gairdner Limited	Gairdner & Company Limited
Walwyn, Stodgell & Gairdner Ltd.	77	CO	Walwyn, Stodgell Cochran Murray Ltd.	Cochran, Murray & Wisener Ltd.

Category of Change OB – Out of Business   CO – Corporate Combinations   RE – Corporate Reorganizations   SE – Suspended/Expelled

NAME OF THE FIRM	YEAR	CHANGE	NEW FIRM	MERGED WITH / TAKEN OVER BY
Waterloo Bond Corporation Limited	71	OB		
Watt & Watt	62	RE	Watt & Watt Limited	
Watt & Watt Limited	64	SE		
Donald R. Watt Securities Limited	72	RE	Watt, Carmichael Securities Limited	
L.J. West & Co. Ltd.	63	SE		
The Western City Company Limited	60	OB		
J.B. White & Company Limited	77	OB		
White Weld & Co. of Canada Ltd.	75	OB		
Norman R. Whittall Limited	67	CO		Richardson Securities of Canada
J.H. Whittome & Co. Limited	70	OB		
The M.G. Wilkinson Investment Service	61	CO	Doherty Roadhouse & Co.	
Willrich Securities Limited	76	OB		
Wills, Bickle & Company Limited	77	CO	A.E. Osler, Wills, Bickle Limited	A.E. Osler, Norris, Gendron Limited
Winslow & Winslow Limited	74	OB		
Wisener & Partners Company Limited	74	CO	Cochran Murray & Wisener Limited	Cochran, Murray Limited
Wisener, Mackellar and Company Limited	73	SE		
Yorkshire Securities (1968) Limited	77	OB		
Yorkshire Securities Limited	69	OB		
Yorkton Securities Limited	74	CO	Yorkton Securities Inc.	J.P. Cannon & Co. Ltd.

Category of Change OB – Out of Business   CO – Corporate Combinations   RE – Corporate Reorganizations   SE – Suspended/Expelled

264

Index

267